THE ALL-NEW

FRESH FOOD
fast

= THE ALL-NEW =

FRESH FOOD *fast*

200+ incredibly flavorful
5-ingredient, 15-minute recipes

FROM THE EDITORS OF CookingLight

Oxmoor
House

Published by Oxmoor House, an imprint of Time Inc. Books
225 Liberty Street, New York, NY 10281

Senior Editor: Rachel Quinlivan West, R.D.
Project Editor: Lacie Pinyan
Design Director: Melissa Clark
Photo Director: Paden Reich
Designer: AnnaMaria Jacob
Photographers: Daniel Agee, Caitlin Bensel, Jennifer Causey, Greg DuPree, Alison Miksch,
 Victor Protasio
Prop Stylists: Mary Clayton Carl, Kay E. Clarke, Thom Driver, Lindsey Lower, Claire Spollen
Food Stylists: Torie Cox, Margaret Monroe Dickey, Emily Nabors Hall, Anna Hampton,
 Karen Shroeder-Rankin
Prop Coordinator: Audrey Davis
Recipe Developers and Testers: Allene Arnold, Robin Bashinsky, Mary Claire Britton,
 Adam Dolge, Paige Grandjean, Emily Nabors Hall, Adam Hickman, Julia G. Levy,
 Pam Lolley, Robby Melvin, Ivy Odom, Karen Rankin, Marianne Williams, Deb Wise,
 Loren Wood
Senior Production Manager: Greg A. Amason
Associate Manager for Project Management and Production: Anna Muñiz
Copy Editors: Adrienne Davis, Jacqueline Giovanelli
Indexer: Mary Ann Laurens
Fellows: Kaitlyn Pacheco, Holly Ravazzolo, Hanna Yokeley

ISBN-13: 978-0-8487-5379-5

Library of Congress Control Number: 2017962703

First Edition 2018

Printed in the United States of America

10 9 8 7 6 5 4 3 2 1

Time Inc. Books products may be purchased for business or promotional use.
For information on bulk purchases, please contact Christi Crowley in the
Special Sales Department at (845) 895-9858.

We welcome your comments and suggestions about Time Inc. Books.
Please write to us at:
Time Inc. Books
Attention: Book Editors
P.O. Box 62310
Tampa, Florida 33662-2310

CONTENTS

WELCOME

When creating this book, our goal was always to make your life a little easier, particularly on those harried nights when cooking is the last thing you feel like doing. (We can relate.) We've also noticed that days like those are often when a homemade meal is the most comforting and the most appreciated—a situation that presents somewhat of a conundrum. We hope *The All-New Fresh Food Fast* is your solution.

This book is ideal for when you want something satisfying that doesn't take all day to make. Every recipe requires only five ingredients or less (excluding water, cooking spray, salt, black pepper, and optional ingredients) *or* it's ready in 15 minutes or less—many deliver on both.

The more than 200 recipes artfully combine fresh ingredients, smart store-bought products, and time-saving techniques to bring boldly flavored meals to your table without sacrificing your health. You'll find a wide range of easy-to-make recipes, from breakfasts that are worth waking up for; to soups, sandwiches, and salads ideal for lunch or dinner; to entrées that quench an array of cravings; as well as quick sides and desserts to finish off your meal.

We hope this book helps you make a home-cooked meal a reality, even on the busiest of days.

—the editors of *Cooking Light*

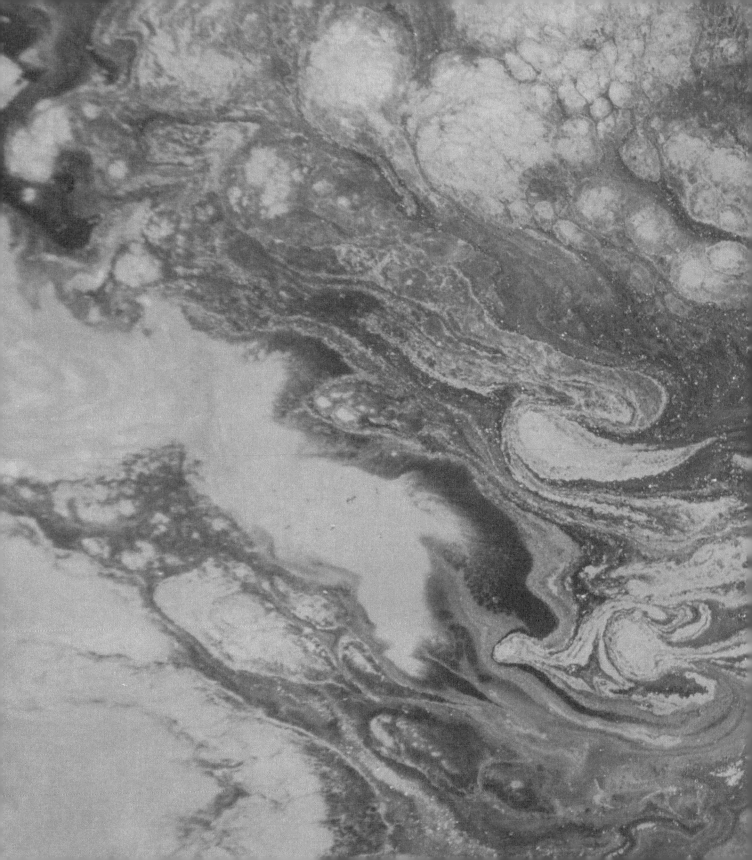

CHAPTER 1

BREAKFAST & BRUNCH

CARDAMOM OATMEAL *with* HONEY-LIME YOGURT *and* PISTACHIOS

Cashew milk has a rich, creamy flavor and subtle nuttiness. It's worth seeking out for recipes like this. You can stir it into other breakfast whole grains or add it to smoothies.

HANDS-ON: 10 MIN. • TOTAL: 10 MIN. • SERVES 4

3   cups water
2   cups uncooked regular rolled oats
¾   teaspoon ground cardamom
½   teaspoon kosher salt
¼   teaspoon black pepper
1   cup cashew milk or 2% reduced-fat milk

1   cup plain yogurt
3   tablespoons honey, divided
1   teaspoon lime zest (from 1 lime)
½   cup chopped roasted salted pistachios (about 2½ ounces)

1. Combine the water, oats, cardamom, salt, and pepper in a medium saucepan; bring to a boil over medium-high, stirring occasionally. Reduce the heat to medium-low to maintain a simmer; cook, stirring occasionally, until the oats are tender, about 3 minutes. Remove from the heat, and stir in the cashew milk.

2. Whisk together the yogurt, 2 tablespoons of the honey, and zest. Divide the oatmeal among 4 bowls; top with the yogurt mixture, sprinkle with the pistachios and drizzle with the remaining 1 tablespoon honey.

(**SERVING SIZE:** 1 cup oatmeal, ¼ cup yogurt mixture, and 2 tablespoons pistachios): **CALORIES** 330; **FAT** 12g (sat 3g, unsat 9g); **PROTEIN** 11g; **CARB** 48g; **FIBER** 6g; **SUGARS** 18g (added sugars 13g); **SODIUM** 375mg; **CALC** 21% DV; **POTASSIUM** 8% DV

NUT MILKS

Nut milks, including cashew, are lower in calories than all other milks. They also have negligible sat fat and are usually fortified with calcium and vitamins A and D. However, most nut milks offer no significant protein and very little vitamin E (unless they're fortified) despite the fact that nuts themselves are rich in protein and vitamin E.

PUMPKIN SPICE OATMEAL ▸

When you stir in the oats, be sure to whisk as you pour them so they don't clump together. Top with chopped red pear for a fresh finish.

HANDS-ON: 10 MIN. • **TOTAL: 10 MIN.** • **SERVES 6**

3   cups almond milk
1½ cups water
⅓   cup pure maple syrup, divided
1½ teaspoons pumpkin pie spice

¼   teaspoon kosher salt
1½ cups uncooked quick-cooking steel-cut oats
½   cup canned pumpkin

Whisk together the almond milk, water, 4 tablespoons syrup, pumpkin pie spice, and salt in a medium saucepan. Bring to a boil over medium-high, whisking occasionally. Reduce the heat to medium-low, and whisk in the oats. Cook, stirring often, until the oats are tender, about 6 minutes. Remove from the heat; stir in the pumpkin and drizzle with the remaining syrup.

(**SERVING SIZE:** about ⅔ cup): **CALORIES** 220; **FAT** 4g (sat 1g, unsat 3g); **PROTEIN** 6g; **CARB** 41g; **FIBER** 5g; **SUGARS** 12g (added sugars 11g); **SODIUM** 168mg; **CALC** 25% DV; **POTASSIUM** 3% DV

MAPLE-BACON OATMEAL

Baking bacon not only creates less mess—no grease all over your stovetop— it also cooks bacon evenly with crispy results. Brushing the bacon with maple syrup gives it a sticky, delicious glaze. Adding a bit of butter to the cinnamon oats at the end gives them a velvety richness.

HANDS-ON: 15 MIN. • **TOTAL: 30 MIN.** • **SERVES 4**

3   center-cut bacon slices
¼   cup pure maple syrup
6   cups water
¾   teaspoon kosher salt

3   cups uncooked regular rolled oats
¼   teaspoon ground cinnamon
1   tablespooon unsalted butter

1. Preheat the oven to 400°F. Place the bacon on a wire rack on a sheet pan; bake in the preheated oven for 10 minutes. Remove from the oven, and brush the bacon with the maple syrup. Return to the oven, and bake until crisp, about 10 minutes. Crumble the bacon.
2. While the bacon cooks, bring the water and salt to a boil in a large saucepan over high. Stir in the oats and cinnamon. Reduce the heat to medium; cook, stirring often, until tender, 5 to 6 minutes. Remove from the heat, and stir in the butter. Spoon into 4 bowls. Top evenly with the crumbled bacon, and serve immediately.

(**SERVING SIZE:** 1½ cups): **CALORIES** 332; **FAT** 8g (sat 2g, unsat 1g); **PROTEIN** 12g; **CARB** 54g; **FIBER** 6g; **SUGARS** 14g (added sugars 12g); **SODIUM** 428mg; **CALC** 5% DV; **POTASSIUM** 1% DV

COCONUT, MANGO, *and* BLUEBERRY SMOOTHIE BOWL

Smoothie bowls are a bit more relaxed than their to-go cup counterparts. The sit-down versions allow for incorporating toppings that add an array of texture and flavor variations, like the granola and coconut in this recipe.

HANDS-ON: 5 MIN. • TOTAL 5 MIN. • SERVES 4

1½ cups frozen mango chunks (about 6½ ounces)

1 cup coconut water

2 tablespoons fresh lime juice (from 1 lime)

¼ teaspoon kosher salt

1 cup fresh blueberries (about 5 ounces)

½ cup oats-and-honey granola

2 tablespoons unsweetened flaked coconut, toasted

2 tablespoons chia seeds

Process the mango, coconut water, lime juice, and salt in a blender until smooth and pourable, 1 to 2 minutes. Pour into 4 bowls; top with the blueberries, granola, toasted coconut, and chia seeds.

(**SERVING SIZE:** ½ cup smoothie mixture, ¼ cup blueberries, 2 tablespoons granola, ½ tablespoon coconut, and ½ tablespoon chia seeds): **CALORIES** 177; **FAT** 6g (sat 2g, unsat 1g); **PROTEIN** 3g; **CARB** 32g; **FIBER** 6g; **SUGARS** 19g (added sugars 2g); **SODIUM** 168mg; **CALC** 7% DV; **POTASSIUM** 5% DV

STRAW VS. SPOON SMOOTHIES

One difference between straw vs. spoon smoothies is the thickness. Smoothie bowls are supposed to be thicker than your average smoothie because you don't want all the topping sinking to the bottom of the bowl. In smoothie bowl versions, the liquid in the recipe is often there to aid in blending, so if you want to convert your favorite smoothie to a bowl, start by reducing the liquid.

BLUEBERRY-PECAN BREAKFAST BAR

Sweet and crunchy, this breakfast bar is an ideal on-the-go breakfast or snack.

HANDS-ON: 10 MIN. • TOTAL: 40 MIN. • SERVES 12

Cooking spray

1½ cups unsweetened crisp brown rice cereal (about 2 ounces)

½ cup chopped pecans, toasted

½ cup sweetened dried blueberries

3 tablespoons chia seeds

⅔ cup brown rice syrup or pure maple syrup

½ teaspoon kosher salt

1. Line a 2-quart baking dish with parchment paper, allowing 1 inch of parchment to extend over the 2 long sides. Coat the parchment with cooking spray; set aside.
2. Toss together the cereal, pecans, blueberries, and chia seeds in a large heatproof bowl.
3. Combine the syrup and salt in a small saucepan. Bring to a boil over medium, stirring occasionally. Reduce the heat to low to maintain a simmer; cook, stirring occasionally, until slightly thickened, about 4 minutes. Pour the syrup over the cereal mixture; gently stir to coat.
4. Pour the mixture into the prepared baking dish, and smooth the top. Cool to room temperature, about 30 minutes, pressing down on the mixture with a spatula to flatten after 15 minutes. Cut into 12 bars.

(**SERVING SIZE:** 1 bar): **CALORIES** 157; **FAT** 5g (sat 0g, unsat 4g); **PROTEIN** 2g; **CARB** 29g; **FIBER** 2g; **SUGARS** 21g (added sugars 16g); **SODIUM** 121mg; **CALC** 3% DV; **POTASSIUM** 3% DV

MELON BOWL *with* PROSCIUTTO *and* YOGURT

This bowl combines the always-enjoyable combination of sweet cantaloupe and salty prosciutto. It gets an additional boost of flavor and crunch from the granola and almonds and a wonderful tang from the yogurt.

HANDS-ON: 10 MIN. · **TOTAL: 10 MIN.** · **SERVES 2**

4   cups chopped cantaloupe (from 1 cantaloupe)
½   cup plain low-fat yogurt
⅓   cup sliced almonds, toasted
¼   cup granola
2   ounces thinly sliced prosciutto
2   tablespoons thinly sliced fresh mint
⅛   teaspoon black pepper

Divide the cantaloupe between 2 bowls. Top with the yogurt, almonds, granola, prosciutto, mint, and pepper.

(**SERVING SIZE:** 2 cups cantaloupe, ¼ cup yogurt, 8 teaspoons almonds, 2 tablespoons granola, and 1 ounce prosciutto): **CALORIES** 337; **FAT** 13g (sat 2g, mono 10g); **PROTEIN** 17g; **CARB** 44g; **FIBER** 6g; **SUGARS** 32g (added sugars 2g); **SODIUM** 553mg; **CALC** 20% DV; **POTASSIUM** 33% DV

BUYING CANTALOUPES

If ripe, cantaloupes will smell noticeably fruity where the stem was attached, and the other end will give slightly when pressed. Cantaloupes will continue to ripen if kept at room temperature. Place ripe ones in the refrigerator for up to a week.

BREAKFAST SALAD *with* QUINOA, GRAPEFRUIT, *and* BLUEBERRIES

Made in a jar, this make-ahead breakfast salad is easily portable for a filling breakfast or lunch on the go. You can easily change the fruit with the seasons (dried fruit also works nicely), and vary the nuts to suit your tastes.

HANDS-ON: 10 MIN. • **TOTAL: 15 MIN.** • **SERVES 4**

- 2 (8-ounce) packages precooked microwavable quinoa (such as Simply Balanced)
- ¼ cup olive oil
- 2 tablespoons white balsamic vinegar
- 1 teaspoon honey
- ½ teaspoon Dijon mustard
- 1 teaspoon kosher salt
- ¼ teaspoon cracked black pepper
- 1 cup fresh blueberries (about 5 ounces)
- ¼ cup sliced almonds, toasted
- 1 medium grapefruit, peeled and sectioned
- 4 ounces baby spinach

1. Microwave the quinoa according to the package directions. Transfer to a bowl; cool slightly.
2. Whisk together the oil, vinegar, honey, mustard, salt, and pepper in a small bowl. Pour the dressing evenly into 4 clean 1-pint jars with lids. Layer ¼ cup blueberries, 1 tablespoon almonds, ¼ cup grapefruit, 1 cup quinoa, and 1 cup spinach in each jar. Cover the jars, and chill overnight, if desired. Shake the jars to coat the salads with the dressing, and serve.

(**SERVING SIZE:** 1 jar): **CALORIES** 353; **FAT** 19g (sat 2g, unsat 16g); **PROTEIN** 8g; **CARB** 41g; **FIBER** 6g; **SUGARS** 12g (added sugars 1g); **SODIUM** 525mg; **CALC** 9% DV; **POTASSIUM** 10% DV

SALAD FOR BREAKFAST

Salads are light, fresh, and balanced, making them a superb way to start your day. To get them breakfast-friendly, forgo strong-flavored elements (think raw garlic), which can be overpowering first thing in the a.m. To make sure they keep you full until lunch, incorporate fat and protein, such as an egg, cheese, bacon, nuts, or canned beans for protein and olive and nut oils, avocado, or nuts for healthy fats.

LEMONY KALE *and* SMOKED TROUT *on* TOAST

The lightness from the fresh kale is the perfect balance to the rich, smoky trout. If you'd like a deeper, more caramelized flavor from the onions, you can cook them longer before adding the kale to the pan.

HANDS-ON: 15 MIN. • TOTAL: 15 MIN. • SERVES 4

6   cups water
2   tablespoons apple cider vinegar
4   large eggs
2   tablespoons olive oil
1   cup chopped yellow onion
5   cups chopped kale

2   tablespoons fresh lemon juice (from 1 lemon)
½   teaspoon black pepper
4   (1-ounce) whole-grain bread slices, toasted
4   ounces smoked trout fillet, flaked

1. Bring the water and vinegar to a simmer in a large saucepan over high. Reduce the heat to medium-low to maintain a gentle simmer. Using a spoon, swirl the water in a circular motion. Break the eggs into each of 4 small cups. With the water swirling, gently slip 1 egg into the center of the vortex. Cook, continuing to swirl the water, until the whites are just set, 3½ minutes to 4 minutes. Using a slotted spoon, transfer the egg to a plate lined with paper towels. Repeat procedure with remaining eggs.
2. Heat the oil in a large skillet or Dutch oven over high. Add the onion; cook, stirring occasionally, until lightly caramelized, 3 to 4 minutes. Add the kale; cook, stirring occasionally, until wilted, 5 to 6 minutes. Stir in the lemon juice and pepper.
3. Place the toast slices on each of 4 plates. Top with the kale mixture, flaked trout, and poached eggs.

(SERVING SIZE: 1 toast slice, ¾ cup kale mixture, 1 ounce trout, and 1 egg): **CALORIES** 278; **FAT** 15g (sat 3g, unsat 10g); **PROTEIN** 17g; **CARB** 20g; **FIBER** 3g; **SUGARS** 4g (added sugars 0g); **SODIUM** 569mg; **CALC** 11% DV; **POTASSIUM** 9% DV

SMOKED SALMON, CUCUMBER, *and* LABNEH TOASTS ▶

HANDS-ON: 10 MIN. • TOTAL: 10 MIN. • SERVES 4

½   cup cultured labneh (Middle Eastern yogurt cheese)
8   sprouted-grain bread slices, toasted
½   teaspoon cracked black pepper

1   small English cucumber, cut in half crosswise and thinly sliced lengthwise
8   ounces thinly sliced smoked salmon
1   tablespoon chopped fresh dill

Spread 1 tablespoon labneh on each bread slice; sprinkle evenly with the pepper. Top evenly with the cucumber and salmon; sprinkle evenly with the dill.

(SERVING SIZE: 2 toast slices): **CALORIES** 315; **FAT** 9g (sat 4g, unsat 2g); **PROTEIN** 21g; **CARB** 34g; **FIBER** 7g; **SUGARS** 3g (added sugars 0g); **SODIUM** 566mg; **CALC** 8% DV; **POTASSIUM** 6% DV

POACHING EGGS

Poaching an egg may seem intimidating, but it really isn't difficult. Here are a few tips to help: Crack each egg into a ramekin or measuring cup. This not only allows you to easily add them to the simmering water but also helps prevent adding an egg that has a broken yolk—broken yolks won't poach. Adding vinegar to the water helps the whites set more quickly, and swirling the water helps keep the white circulating around the yolk so they don't separate.

This hearty toast has some tang. The labneh lends the salmon a little acidity, while the fresh dill adds brightness. Sprouted-grain bread has a nice crunchy texture—feel free to use your favorite seeded bread. Look for labneh in specialty stores or Middle Eastern markets. If you can't find it, use cream cheese.

GRILLED CINNAMON TOAST
with ZESTY STRAWBERRIES

The addition of cardamom to this grilled toast adds a faint smokiness that's a wonderful complement to the classic cinnamon flavor. Macerating the berries gives them a syrupy consistency that's the ideal topping. Feel free to use whatever berries you like. Sprinkle with powdered sugar and fresh mint leaves for a pretty finish.

HANDS-ON: 15 MIN. · TOTAL: 15 MIN. · SERVES 4

- 2 cups fresh strawberries, hulled and quartered
- ½ teaspoon lime zest plus 2 teaspoons fresh juice (from 1 lime)
- 2 tablespoons sugar, divided
- 1 teaspoon ground cinnamon
- ¼ teaspoon ground cardamom
- 8 (¾-ounce) French bread slices
- Cooking spray

1. Stir together the strawberries, zest, juice, and 2 teaspoons of the sugar in a bowl. Set aside.
2. Stir together the cinnamon, cardamom, and remaining 1 tablespoon plus 1 teaspoon sugar in a small bowl. Generously coat both sides of the bread slices with the cooking spray. Sprinkle 1 side of the bread slices evenly with half of the cardamom mixture.
3. Heat a grill pan coated with cooking spray over medium-high. Place the bread, spice sides down, on the pan. Sprinkle evenly with the remaining cardamom mixture. Grill until charred, about 1 minute per side. (Be careful; these will burn quickly.)
4. Place toast slices on each of 4 plates. Top with the strawberry mixture.

(**SERVING SIZE:** 2 toast slices and ½ cup strawberry mixture): **CALORIES** 169; **FAT** 1g (sat 0g, unsat 1g); **PROTEIN** 5g; **CARB** 35g; **FIBER** 3g; **SUGARS** 12g (added sugars 6g); **SODIUM** 257mg; **CALC** 4% DV; **POTASSIUM** 5% DV

JOHNNY CAKES *with* BACON SYRUP

Perfect on these rustic johnny cakes, the salty-sweet syrup is also tasty on pretty much anything—classic pancakes, biscuits, waffles, or a breakfast sandwich. The boiling water helps soften the cornmeal to create the right texture. If you're serving a crowd, keep the prepared johnny cakes warm on a baking sheet lined with a wire rack in a 200°F oven while you finish preparing the rest.

HANDS-ON: 15 MIN. • **TOTAL 15 MIN.** • **SERVES 4**

3   center-cut bacon slices, chopped
⅓   cup pure maple syrup
¼   teaspoon black pepper
1½ cups (about 8⅝ ounces) plain yellow cornmeal
¾   cup 2% reduced-fat milk

1   large egg
1½ tablespoons boiling water
½   teaspoon baking powder
¼   teaspoon kosher salt
1   tablespoon canola oil, divided

1. Cook the bacon in a small saucepan over medium-high, stirring often, until crispy, about 5 minutes. Remove from the heat. Stir in the syrup and pepper.
2. Whisk together the cornmeal, milk, egg, boiling water, baking powder, and salt in a medium bowl until smooth. Heat ½ tablespoon of the oil in a large cast-iron skillet over medium-high. Spoon about 3 tablespoons batter for each johnny cake into the hot oil to make 4 cakes. Cook until golden brown around the edges and bubbly on the top, 2 to 3 minutes. Turn and cook until done, 1 to 2 minutes. Repeat the procedure with the remaining ½ tablespoon oil and batter. Serve the johnny cakes with the bacon syrup.

(**SERVING SIZE:** 2 johnny cakes and 2 tablespoons syrup): **CALORIES** 326; **FAT** 9g (sat 2g, unsat 5g); **PROTEIN** 8g; **CARB** 55g; **FIBER** 3g; **SUGARS** 19g (added sugars 16g); **SODIUM** 330mg; **CALC** 12% DV; **POTASSIUM** 8% DV

WAFFLES *with* ARUGULA, FRIED EGG, *and* GOAT CHEESE BUTTER

This dish takes waffles to the savory side, pairing them with rich goat cheese butter and peppery arugula; the eggs are the ideal semi-runny yolk consistency. Covering the pan with a lid while the eggs cook helps ensure the yolks get there.

HANDS-ON: 15 MIN. • **TOTAL 15 MIN.** • **SERVES 4**

COMPOUND BUTTER

Making compound butters is an easy but elegant way to amp up an everyday meal. To prepare, allow the butter to soften to room temperature to make it easy to work with. Then choose your additions, which can range from savory combinations (like the one used in this recipe) such as fresh herbs, garlic, cheese, and citrus to sweet varieties like cinnamon, honey, or maple syrup.

8   frozen whole-grain waffles (such as Kashi 7 Grain)
1   ounce goat cheese, softened (about ¼ cup)
½   teaspoon lemon zest (from 1 lemon)
¼   teaspoon black pepper, plus more for garnish
1½ tablespoons unsalted butter, softened and divided
3   ounces arugula
4   large eggs
1   tablespoon water
¼   teaspoon kosher salt

1. Toast the waffles according to the package directions.
2. Stir together the goat cheese, zest, pepper, and 1 tablespoon of the butter in a small bowl. Set aside.
3. Melt ½ teaspoon of the butter in a large nonstick skillet over medium; add the arugula, and cook, stirring often, about 2 minutes. Transfer the arugula to a bowl.
4. Melt the remaining 1 teaspoon butter in the same skillet over medium. Add the eggs, and cook just until set on the bottom, about 1 minute. Add the water; cover and cook just until the whites are set and the yolks are still runny, about 3 minutes.
5. Place waffles on each of 4 plates. Top with the goat cheese butter; top with the arugula and eggs. Sprinkle with the salt and black pepper, and serve immediately.

(**SERVING SIZE:** 2 waffles, 1½ teaspoons goat cheese butter, ½ cup arugula, and 1 egg): **CALORIES** 304; **FAT** 14g (sat 5g, unsat 5g); **PROTEIN** 16g; **CARB** 34g; **FIBER** 6g; **SUGARS** 5g (added sugars 1g); **SODIUM** 560mg; **CALC** 13% DV; **POTASSIUM** 8% DV

SMASHED EGG *and* AVOCADO ENGLISH MUFFIN SANDWICHES

This hearty breakfast sandwich offers a wonderful mix of textures with a creamy avocado spread and crunch from the fresh sprouts and radishes. Sprinkle with additional freshly ground black pepper.

HANDS-ON: 10 MIN. • **TOTAL: 10 MIN.** • **SERVES 4**

4   large hard-cooked eggs, peeled
1   medium-sized ripe avocado, chopped
1   tablespoon fresh lemon juice (from 1 lemon)
1   teaspoon hot sauce (such as Cholula)
½   teaspoon kosher salt
½   teaspoon black pepper
4   whole-grain English muffins, split and toasted
1   large heirloom tomato, thinly sliced
1   cup kale or alfalfa sprouts (about 1 ounce)
¼   cup thinly sliced radishes

Combine the eggs, avocado, lemon juice, hot sauce, salt, and pepper in a bowl; roughly mash with a fork until combined, but slightly chunky. Spread the mixture evenly on the bottom halves of the muffins. Top evenly with the tomato slices, sprouts, and radishes. Cover with the top halves of the muffins, and serve immediately.

(SERVING SIZE: 1 sandwich): CALORIES 288; FAT 13g (sat 3g, unsat 9g); PROTEIN 12g; CARB 32g; FIBER 6g; SUGARS 2g (added sugars 0g); SODIUM 570mg; CALC 12% DV; POTASSIUM 11% DV

HARD-COOKED EGGS

Here's the secret to perfectly cooked hard-boiled eggs: Place the eggs in a single layer in a saucepan and fill the pan with water up to about two inches over the eggs. Bring to a boil over high heat, and then remove the pan from the heat, cover, and let stand for 12 minutes. This method gradually increases the eggs' temperature during the cooking process, yielding perfectly cooked yolks.

This spin on chicken and waffles pairs the classic ingredients with a maple-Dijon mayonnaise–based spread that makes this breakfast taste decadent. You can top this with additional maple syrup if you like.

CHICKEN *and* WAFFLES

HANDS-ON: 15 MIN. • **TOTAL: 15 MIN.** • **SERVES 2**

Cooking spray
½ pound chicken breast cutlets
½ teaspoon black pepper
¼ teaspoon kosher salt
1 tablespoon pure maple syrup
2 teaspoons Dijon mustard
2 teaspoons canola mayonnaise

2 whole-grain frozen waffles (such as Kashi 7 Grain)
2 (½-ounce) reduced-fat sharp Cheddar cheese slices
¼ teaspoon hot sauce (optional)
Chopped fresh chives (optional)

1. Preheat the broiler with the oven rack 6 to 8 inches from the heat. Heat a grill pan coated with cooking spray over high. Sprinkle the chicken evenly with pepper and salt. Grill the chicken until done, 2 to 3 minutes per side.
2. Whisk together the maple syrup, Dijon, and mayonnaise in a small bowl. Set aside.
3. Toast the waffles according to the package directions. Spread 2 teaspoons of the syrup mixture on each waffle. Top the waffles evenly with the chicken; top each with 1 cheese slice. Place on a baking sheet, and broil until the cheese is melted, about 2 minutes. If desired, top evenly with the hot sauce and sprinkle with chives.

(SERVING SIZE: 1 open-faced sandwich): CALORIES 311; **FAT** 9g (sat 3g, unsat 4g); **PROTEIN** 33g; **CARB** 25g; **FIBER** 3g; **SUGARS** 8g (added sugars 6g); **SODIUM** 734mg; **CALC** 15% DV; **POTASSIUM** 14% DV

EGG *and* SAUSAGE BURRITOS

If you can't find reduced-fat sausage, use turkey or chicken sausage instead.

HANDS-ON: 15 MIN. • **TOTAL: 15 MIN.** • **SERVES 2**

2 large egg whites
1 large egg
2 ounces reduced-fat breakfast sausage
¼ teaspoon black pepper
⅔ cup no-salt-added black beans, drained and rinsed

⅔ cup cooked brown rice (from 1 [8.8-ounce] pouch microwavable rice)
2 (8-inch) whole-wheat flour tortillas
2 teaspoons Mexican hot sauce
1 tablespoon chopped fresh cilantro

1. Lightly beat the egg whites and egg in a small bowl; set aside.
2. Cook the sausage in a nonstick skillet over medium-high, stirring to crumble, until browned. Add the eggs and pepper; cook, stirring often, until the eggs are just set, 2 to 3 minutes. Remove from the heat.
3. Combine the beans and rice in a microwave-safe bowl; cover tightly with plastic wrap. Microwave on HIGH until hot, about 1 minute and 30 seconds.
4. Heat the tortillas according to the package directions. Place on a work surface. Divide the rice mixture evenly between the tortillas. Top evenly with the sausage mixture, hot sauce, and cilantro. Roll up the burritos, and serve immediately.

(SERVING SIZE: 1 burrito): CALORIES 348; **FAT** 9g (sat 3g, unsat 1g); **PROTEIN** 21g; **CARB** 44g; **FIBER** 6g; **SUGARS** 0g (added sugars 0g); **SODIUM** 530mg; **CALC** 11% DV; **POTASSIUM** 8% DV

CAULIFLOWER *and* SAUSAGE SCRAMBLE

This is a tasty—and fast—way to get some vegetables in at breakfast. Cauliflower and red bell pepper add texture and color while the sausage kicks in some spice.

HANDS-ON: 20 MIN. • **TOTAL: 20 MIN.** • **SERVES 4**

2   tablespoons olive oil
8   ounces reduced-fat turkey breakfast sausage, chopped
8   ounces cauliflower, roughly chopped (about 3 cups)
1   red bell pepper, chopped (about ¾ cup)

5   large eggs, lightly beaten
2   tablespoons chopped fresh flat-leaf parsley
¼   teaspoon kosher salt

Heat the oil in a large nonstick skillet over high. Add the sausage; cook, stirring often, until browned, 4 to 5 minutes. Add the cauliflower and bell pepper; cook, stirring occasionally, until tender, 5 to 6 minutes. Reduce the heat to medium-low. Add the eggs; cook, stirring constantly, just until set, 2 to 3 minutes. Stir in the parsley and salt; serve immediately.

(**SERVING SIZE:** 1 cup): **CALORIES** 262; **FAT** 18g (sat 5g, unsat 11g); **PROTEIN** 19g; **CARB** 6g; **FIBER** 2g; **SUGARS** 2g (added sugars 0g); **SODIUM** 576mg; **CALC** 7% DV; **POTASSIUM** 9% DV

FRITTATA *with* GREENS, TOMATO, *and* FETA ▶

This colorful frittata gets richness and a lovely salty punch of flavor from the feta. You can also serve it with a simple salad for lunch or brunch. Sprinkle with fresh parsley and basil leaves, if you'd like.

HANDS-ON: 10 MIN. • **TOTAL: 20 MIN.** • **SERVES 2**

4   large eggs
½   (10-ounce) package frozen chopped spinach, thawed and squeezed dry
1   tablespoon 1% low-fat milk
¼   teaspoon kosher salt

¼   teaspoon black pepper
1   teaspoon olive oil
1   plum tomato, thinly sliced
2   tablespoons crumbled feta cheese

1. Preheat the oven to 400°F. Whisk together the eggs, spinach, milk, salt, and pepper in a medium bowl. Set aside.
2. Heat the oil in a medium-sized nonstick ovenproof skillet over medium. Add the egg mixture, and cook, stirring constantly, until the eggs begin to set, about 2 minutes. Top evenly with the tomato slices and feta. Bake in the preheated oven until set and the top is golden brown, about 10 minutes. Serve immediately.

(**SERVING SIZE:** ½ frittata): **CALORIES** 209; **FAT** 13g (sat 5g, unsat 8g); **PROTEIN** 16g; **CARB** 5g; **FIBER** 1g; **SUGARS** 3g (added sugars 0g); **SODIUM** 594mg; **CALC** 15% DV; **POTASSIUM** 7% DV

QUICK HUEVOS RANCHEROS

Pico de gallo adds a fresh-tasting element to this satisfying—and convenient—breakfast. You'll usually find it in the refrigerated cases in the produce section of most grocery stores. Sprinkle with black pepper and chopped fresh cilantro, if you like.

HANDS-ON: 10 MIN. • **TOTAL: 10 MIN.** • **SERVES 4**

1   tablespoon olive oil
4   large eggs
1   (15½-ounce) can unsalted black beans, drained and rinsed

1   cup pico de gallo, divided
4   ounces baked tortilla chips
⅛   teaspoon kosher salt
¼   cup reduced-fat sour cream

1. Heat the oil in a large nonstick skillet over medium-high. Break the eggs into the pan. Cook until the whites are set, 2 to 3 minutes. Carefully turn. (Do not break the yolks.) Cook to desired degree of doneness, 1 to 2 minutes for over medium.
2. Combine the beans and ½ cup of the pico de gallo in a saucepan. Cook over high, stirring occasionally, until the liquid has almost evaporated, about 5 minutes.
3. Divide the tortilla chips among 4 plates. Top with the bean mixture, salt, eggs, sour cream, and remaining ½ cup pico de gallo.

(**SERVING SIZE:** 1 ounce chips, ⅓ cup black bean mixture, 1 egg, 1 tablespoon sour cream, and 2 tablespoons pico de gallo): **CALORIES** 355; **FAT** 14g (sat 4g, unsat 9g); **PROTEIN** 17g; **CARB** 40g; **FIBER** 8g; **SUGARS** 1g (added sugars 0g); **SODIUM** 597mg; **CALC** 15% DV; **POTASSIUM** 12% DV

HUEVOS RANCHEROS

This classic Mexican breakfast dish traditionally features eggs with deliciously runny yolks, plenty of fiery salsa, and fresh corn tortillas that are fried to soften them. Here, we made it fast using tortilla chips instead of fried tortillas both for ease and added crunch. Some recipes call for refried beans, but we opted for black beans for their creamy texture.

GREEN SHAKSHUKA

While the eggs cook, the bottom of the greens mixture gets a wonderful slightly browned crust, adding some umami depth to this dish. You can find a bag mix of kale, spinach, and chard that works nicely in this recipe—and there's thankfully no need to chop the greens before wilting them.

HANDS-ON: 15 MIN. • TOTAL: 15 MIN. • SERVES 2

1   tablespoon olive oil
1   cup chopped yellow onion (from 1 medium onion)
2   teaspoons minced garlic (from 2 garlic cloves)
4   cups chopped greens (such as kale, Swiss chard, or spinach; about 5 ounces)

2   teaspoons chopped fresh dill, plus more for serving
½   teaspoon chopped fresh oregano
½   teaspoon black pepper
⅜   teaspoon kosher salt
4   large eggs
2   tablespoons crumbled feta cheese

1. Heat the oil in a large skillet over medium; add the onion, and cook, stirring occasionally, until translucent, about 5 minutes. Add the garlic; cook, stirring constantly, until fragrant, about 1 minute. Stir in the greens, dill, oregano, pepper, and salt; cook, stirring often, until the greens are wilted and tender, about 2 minutes.

2. Using the back of a spoon, make 4 indentations in the greens mixture. Gently break 1 egg into each indentation. Cover and cook until the whites are set and the yolks are still runny, 5 to 6 minutes. Remove from the heat, and sprinkle with the feta and the desired amount of dill.

(SERVING SIZE: 2 eggs and ¾ cup greens): **CALORIES** 275; **FAT** 18g (sat 5g, unsat 12g); **PROTEIN** 16g; **CARB** 13g; **FIBER** 3g; **SUGARS** 5g (added sugars 0g); **SODIUM** 583mg; **CALC** 17% DV; **POTASSIUM** 13% DV

BREAKFAST POLENTA *with* MUSHROOMS *and* SUN-DRIED TOMATO PESTO

Make sure your pan and oil are hot before adding the mushrooms—you want a nice sear on them, and mushrooms have a tendency to go soggy if they're cooked at a temperature that's too low. Make the pesto the night before to save time during time-crunched mornings—and so the food processor doesn't wake up the rest of the house!

HANDS-ON: 15 MIN. • TOTAL: 15 MIN. • SERVES 4

3   tablespoons olive oil, divided
8   ounces sliced mixed mushrooms (such as cremini, oyster, and shiitake)
¾   cup boiling water
¼   cup sun-dried tomatoes
¼   cup packed fresh basil leaves
2   tablespoons toasted pine nuts
½   teaspoon black pepper
2   tablespoons grated fresh Parmesan cheese
1   teaspoon kosher salt, divided
3   cups water
¾   cup uncooked instant polenta
Fresh basil leaves (optional)

STORING PESTO

With the help of a food processor, it takes only minutes to make a batch of homemade pesto. It will keep for up to 2 weeks in the refrigerator in a sealed container or up to 3 months in the freezer.

1. Heat 1 tablespoon of the oil in a large nonstick skillet over medium-high. Add the mushrooms, and cook, stirring occasionally, until browned and tender, about 8 minutes. Remove from the heat, and set aside.
2. Combine the boiling water and tomatoes in a heatproof bowl; let stand until softened and rehydrated, about 4 minutes. Drain and chop the tomatoes.
3. Process the tomatoes, basil, pine nuts, pepper, Parmesan, ¼ teaspoon of the salt, and the remaining 2 tablespoons oil in a food processor until finely chopped, stopping to scrape down the sides of the bowl as necessary.
4. Bring 3 cups water to a boil in a medium saucepan over high. Add the polenta, and cook, whisking constantly, until the water is absorbed, about 5 minutes. Remove from the heat; stir in the remaining ¾ teaspoon salt. Swirl in the tomato pesto. Spoon the polenta mixture into 4 bowls. Top with the mushrooms, and sprinkle with basil leaves, if desired.

(**SERVING SIZE:** ½ cup polenta and ¼ cup mushrooms): **CALORIES** 259; **FAT** 14g (sat 2g, unsat 11g); **PROTEIN** 5g; **CARB** 23g; **FIBER** 4g; **SUGARS** 3g (added sugars 0g); **SODIUM** 539mg; **CALC** 4% DV; **POTASSIUM** 8% DV

SHRIMP *and* GRITS

A lighter take on a classic, this warm and satisfying dish is a welcome meal for breakfast, brunch, or dinner. Use the freshest shrimp you can find and have the fishmonger peel and devein them for you.

HANDS-ON: 15 MIN. • **TOTAL: 15 MIN.** • **SERVES 4**

4   cups unsalted chicken stock (such as Swanson)
1   cup uncooked yellow grits or polenta
2   ounces fresh Parmesan cheese, grated (about ½ cup)
½   teaspoon black pepper
2   center-cut bacon slices, chopped
8   ounces sliced cremini mushrooms
1   pound peeled and deveined raw large shrimp
1   cup chopped tomato (about 6 ounces)
¼   teaspoon cayenne pepper
Sliced scallions (optional)

1. Bring the stock to a boil in a large saucepan over high. Whisk in the grits; reduce the heat to medium, and cook, whisking often, until thickened but not stiff, about 5 minutes. Remove from the heat, and stir in the Parmesan and black pepper.
2. While the grits cook, cook the bacon in a large skillet over high, stirring occasionally, until crispy, 4 to 5 minutes. Add the mushrooms, and cook, stirring occasionally, until the mushrooms release their liquid, about 6 minutes. Stir in the shrimp; cook 2 minutes. Add the tomato and cayenne; cook, stirring occasionally, until the shrimp are opaque, about 2 minutes.
3. Divide the grits among 4 shallow bowls; top with the shrimp mixture. If desired, sprinkle with the scallions. Serve immediately.

(SERVING SIZE: 1 cup grits and ¾ cup shrimp mixture): CALORIES 322; FAT 6g (sat 3g, unsat 2g); PROTEIN 29g; CARB 35g; FIBER 3g; SUGARS 3g (added sugars 0g); SODIUM 603mg; CALC 20% DV; POTASSIUM 15% DV

This dish is simple but impressive. It showcases fresh summer produce that is simply seasoned for a wonderfully colorful and fresh meal you can serve for breakfast or as a light dinner. If you want the bacon to stay super crispy, remove it and sprinkle it in at the end after sautéing the vegetables.

GARDEN SUCCO-HASH

HANDS-ON: 15 MIN. • **TOTAL: 15 MIN.** • **SERVES 4**

4   center-cut bacon slices, chopped
3   cups chopped zucchini
1½ cups fresh corn kernels (about 3 ears)
2   cups cherry tomatoes, halved
½   teaspoon kosher salt
½   teaspoon black pepper
1   tablespoon olive oil
4   large eggs

1. Cook the bacon in a large skillet over medium-high, stirring often, until crispy, 4 to 5 minutes. Add the zucchini and corn; cook, stirring often, just until tender, 4 to 5 minutes. Add the tomatoes; cook, stirring occasionally, until the tomatoes burst and the juice starts to thicken, 4 to 5 minutes. Stir in the salt and pepper.
2. Heat the oil in a large nonstick skillet over medium-high. Break the eggs into the pan. Cook until the whites are set, 2 to 3 minutes. Carefully turn. (Do not break the yolks.) Cook to the desired degree of doneness, 1 to 2 minutes for over medium.
3. Divide the succo-hash among 4 plates. Top with the eggs.

(**SERVING SIZE:** 1½ cups succo-hash and 1 egg): **CALORIES** 222; **FAT** 12g (sat 3g, unsat 7g); **PROTEIN** 13g; **CARB** 21g; **FIBER** 3g; **SUGARS** 9g (added sugars 0g); **SODIUM** 469mg; **CALC** 5% DV; **POTASSIUM** 20% DV

SWEET POTATO BREAKFAST HASH

If you'd rather, serve the eggs over easy or sunny side up instead of poached.

HANDS-ON: 10 MIN. • **TOTAL: 20 MIN.** • **SERVES 4**

1   pound sweet potatoes, peeled and cut into ½-inch pieces
1½ cups water
2   tablespoons olive oil
1   cup chopped red bell pepper
1   teaspoon ground cumin
¾   teaspoon kosher salt
2   tablespoons apple cider vinegar, divided
8   large eggs
Fresh cilantro leaves (optional)

1. Combine the sweet potatoes and water in a microwave-safe bowl. Cover with plastic wrap, and microwave on HIGH until the potatoes are tender, 8 to 9 minutes. Drain.
2. Heat a large cast-iron skillet over medium-high; add the oil and bell pepper. Cook, stirring often, until slightly softened and browned, about 2 minutes. Stir in the sweet potatoes and cumin; cook, pressing to flatten in an even layer, until browned on the bottom, about 7 minutes. Stir in the salt and 1 tablespoon of the vinegar. Remove from the heat.
3. Bring a medium saucepan filled with water to a boil. Add the remaining 1 tablespoon vinegar; reduce the heat to maintain a simmer. Gently break the eggs, 1 at a time, into the simmering water. Cook until the whites are set, about 1½ minutes. Using a slotted spoon, transfer the poached eggs to a plate lined with paper towels.
4. Divide the hash among 4 bowls; top each with the eggs. If desired, sprinkle with cilantro.

(**SERVING SIZE:** ½ cup potato mixture and 2 eggs): **CALORIES** 315; **FAT** 17g (sat 4g, unsat 7g); **PROTEIN** 15g; **CARB** 26g; **FIBER** 4g; **SUGARS** 7g (added sugars 0g); **SODIUM** 567mg; **CALC** 10% DV; **POTASSIUM** 17% DV

DE-KERNELING CORN

Removing the kernels from fresh corn can be a messy affair. The traditional method—standing an ear of corn on it's end and cutting downward—can send kernels flying all over your kitchen. Instead, place a whole ear on its side on a cutting board and cut downwards, rotating the ear until all the kernels have been removed. Or, if you prefer the traditional method, cut the ear in half, and then stand each piece on its flat end in a large bowl when cutting it to limit the corn projectiles.

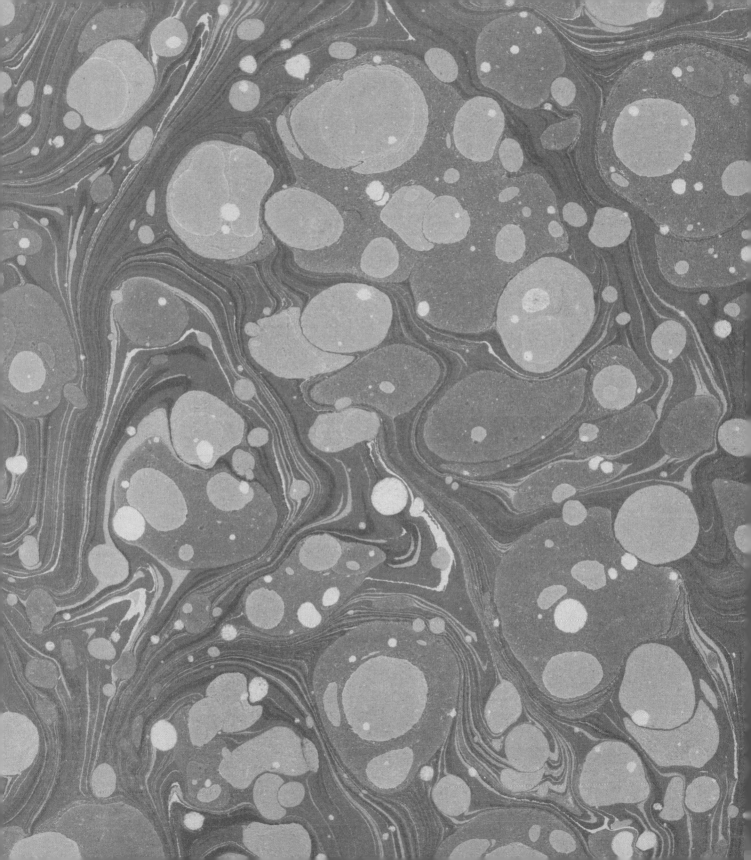

CHAPTER 2

SOUPS & SANDWICHES

QUICK BEEF CHILI

Let everyone customize their bowls at the table with the desired toppings. Pair with cornbread or tortilla chips to round out the meal.

HANDS-ON: 15 MIN. • **TOTAL: 15 MIN.** • **SERVES 8**

1 pound 90/10 lean ground beef
½ pound hot Italian ground turkey sausage
1 (6-ounce) package prechopped yellow onion
1 (1.25-ounce) packet chili seasoning (such as McCormick)
2 teaspoons dark brown sugar
2 (15-ounce) cans no-salt-added red kidney beans, drained and rinsed
1 (15-ounce) can no-salt-added crushed tomatoes
1 (10-ounce) can diced tomatoes and green chiles (such as Rotel)
1 cup water
⅞ teaspoon kosher salt
Toppings: shredded reduced-fat Cheddar cheese, reduced-fat sour cream, sliced scallions, lime wedges (optional)

Cook the beef and turkey sausage in a large skillet over medium-high, stirring until crumbled and brown, about 4 minutes. Place the cooked meat mixture in a colander, and drain the excess fat from the meat. Return the meat mixture to the pan. Add the onion, chili seasoning, and brown sugar, and cook, stirring often, until the onion is translucent, about 2 minutes. Add the beans, tomatoes, water, and salt; cover and cook, stirring occasionally, until heated through, 6 to 8 minutes. Divide the chili among 8 bowls. Serve with your choice of toppings, if desired.

(SERVING SIZE: 1 cup): **CALORIES** 283; **FAT** 9g (sat 2g, unsat 3g); **PROTEIN** 25g; **CARB** 26g; **FIBER** 10g; **SUGARS** 5g (added sugars 1g); **SODIUM** 629mg; **CALC** 6% DV; **POTASSIUM** 16% DV

COCONUT-TOFU SOUP

The tofu readily absorbs all the bold-flavored spices found in this dish as they sauté together. Covering the pot allows for the liquid to boil faster, helping this meal get on the table in 15 minutes.

HANDS-ON: 15 MIN. • **TOTAL: 15 MIN.** • **SERVES 4**

PRESSING TOFU

To get a crispy brown crust on tofu, the water that tofu usually comes packaged in needs to be pressed out—the more, the better. Slice the tofu and place it between several layers of paper towels, and then top it with a cast-iron skillet or another heavy pan. Let it stand for at least 15 minutes, pressing down occasionally.

1 tablespoon canola oil
12 ounces extra-firm tofu, drained, pressed, and cut into ½-inch cubes
1 tablespoon grated peeled fresh ginger
1 teaspoon curry powder
2 teaspoons sambal oelek (ground fresh chili paste)
2 (15-ounce) cans light coconut milk, well shaken

1 cup lower-sodium vegetable broth
1 tablespoon fresh lime juice (from 1 large lime)
¾ cup matchstick carrots (about 2 ounces)
½ teaspoon kosher salt
Fresh cilantro leaves (optional)
Thinly sliced scallions (optional)

Heat the oil in a large Dutch oven over medium-high. Add the tofu, and cook, stirring occasionally, until golden brown, about 4 minutes. Add the ginger, curry powder, and sambal oelek, and cook, stirring constantly, until fragrant, about 30 seconds. Stir in the coconut milk, broth, and lime juice. Cover and bring the mixture to a boil, about 7 minutes; uncover and reduce the heat to medium. Stir in the carrots and salt; simmer until the carrots are tender-crisp, about 3 minutes. Divide the soup among 4 bowls; top with the cilantro leaves and sliced scallions, if desired.

(**SERVING SIZE:** 1½ cups): **CALORIES** 274; **FAT** 19g (sat 9g, unsat 7g); **PROTEIN** 9g; **CARB** 18g; **FIBER** 3g; **SUGARS** 7g (added sugars 0g); **SODIUM** 527mg; **CALC** 8% DV; **POTASSIUM** 2% DV

UDON NOODLE *and* MUSHROOM SOUP

This inviting Asian-inspired soup is on your table in minutes. Sautéing the mushrooms first keeps them from getting soft and spongy in the broth.

HANDS-ON: 15 MIN. • **TOTAL: 15 MIN.** • **SERVES 8**

2   tablespoons toasted sesame oil
8   ounces fresh shiitake mushrooms, sliced (about 4 cups)
2   garlic cloves, minced
1   tablespoon grated peeled fresh ginger
8   cups unsalted vegetable stock

2   (7.1-ounce) pouches fresh udon noodles
8   ounces extra-firm tofu, drained, pressed, and cut into ½-inch cubes
¼   cup lower-sodium soy sauce
⅛   teaspoon kosher salt
½   cup thinly sliced scallions (optional)

Heat the oil in a large pot or Dutch oven over medium-high. Add the mushrooms, garlic, and ginger, and cook, stirring often, until fragrant and the mushrooms are lightly browned, about 5 minutes. Increase the heat to high; stir in the stock, and bring to a boil. Reduce the heat to medium. Stir in the noodles, tofu, soy sauce, and salt, and cook until heated through, 3 to 4 minutes. Divide the soup among 8 bowls. Top with the scallions, if desired.

(**SERVING SIZE:** 1¼ cups): **CALORIES** 277; **FAT** 7g (sat 1g, unsat 4g); **PROTEIN** 14g; **CARB** 42g; **FIBER** 4g; **SUGARS** 2g (added sugars 0g); **SODIUM** 635mg; **CALC** 4% DV; **POTASSIUM** 7% DV

LEMON-CHICKEN-ORZO SOUP

If you can find it, use whole-wheat orzo for an extra dose of whole grains. Serve with a lemon wedge and a hunk of bread for dipping up the brothy goodness.

HANDS-ON: 10 MIN. • **TOTAL: 25 MIN.** • **SERVES 4**

1   tablespoon olive oil
12 ounces boneless, skinless chicken breasts, cut into ¾-inch pieces
1½ cups (about 6 ounces) frozen chopped onion, celery, and carrot blend, thawed
4   cups unsalted chicken stock

½   cup (about 4 ounces) uncooked orzo
1   lemon
⅞   teaspoon kosher salt
¼   teaspoon black pepper
Chopped fresh dill (optional)

1. Heat the oil in a Dutch oven over medium-high. Add the chicken; cook, stirring occasionally, until browned and cooked through, 5 to 7 minutes. Remove to a plate. Add the vegetable blend to the Dutch oven; cook, stirring often, until the vegetables are almost tender, about 4 minutes. Increase heat to high; stir in the stock, and bring mixture to a boil. Reduce heat to medium; add the orzo, and cook until the orzo is tender, about 8 minutes. Return the chicken to the Dutch oven; remove from the heat.
2. Grate the lemon zest to equal 1 teaspoon; squeeze the juice to equal 2 tablespoons. Stir the zest, juice, salt, and pepper into the soup. Sprinkle with fresh dill, if desired.

(**SERVING SIZE:** 1¼ cups): **CALORIES** 271; **FAT** 6g (sat 1g, unsat 4g); **PROTEIN** 27g; **CARB** 26g; **FIBER** 2g; **SUGARS** 4g (added sugars 0g); **SODIUM** 610mg; **CALC** 2% DV; **POTASSIUM** 10% DV

UDON NOODLES

Udon are thick, chewy wheat flour-based noodles that are a key component of many beloved Japanese dishes. Their neutral flavor makes them chameleon-like, absorbing the flavors of whatever they're paired with. Fresh udon noodles can usually be found at large grocery stores with the refrigerated fresh pastas or in the international aisle, and they're also available at Asian markets. If you can't find fresh udon, you can purchase dried and prepare them according to the package directions.

SPINACH *and* MEATBALL SOUP

If you like, substitute tofu for the meatballs. Use ¾ of a pound of tofu, pressed (see page 48), and cut into ½-inch cubes.

HANDS-ON: 15 MIN. • **TOTAL: 15 MIN.** • **SERVES 4**

PREPARED FRESH MEATBALLS

Prepared fresh meatballs are not only big timesavers, but they also add richness and depth to soups, sandwiches, and pastas. You can find these fresh meatballs near the deli meats in the refrigerated meats section of most grocery stores.

1   tablespoon olive oil
1   cup matchstick carrots
1   (8-ounce) package caramelized onion chicken meatballs (such as Aidells)
4   cups unsalted chicken stock (such as Swanson)
1   (8.8-ounce) package precooked microwavable brown rice (such as Uncle Ben's)
4   cups loosely packed fresh baby spinach
¼   teaspoon black pepper
⅛   teaspoon kosher salt
2   tablespoons shredded pecorino romano cheese (optional)

Heat the oil in a Dutch oven over medium-high. Add the carrots, and cook, stirring often, until almost tender, about 4 minutes. Add the meatballs, and cook, stirring occasionally, until lightly browned, about 5 minutes. Stir in the chicken stock; bring to a boil over high. Reduce the heat to medium. Stir in the rice, spinach, pepper, and salt, and cook, stirring until the spinach is wilted and the rice is hot, about 3 minutes. Sprinkle with the cheese, if desired.

(**SERVING SIZE:** 1½ cups): **CALORIES** 285, **FAT** 13g (sat 3g, unsat 3g); **PROTEIN** 16g; **CARB** 24g; **FIBER** 2g; **SUGARS** 3g (added sugars 0g); **SODIUM** 654mg; **CALC** 7% DV; **POTASSIUM** 1% DV

Feel free to use your favorite salsa in this recipe so you can customize the flavor and heat level to your liking. Many large supermarkets also sell fresh salsa at the deli counter, which would be nice in this soup.

SOUTHWESTERN CHICKEN SOUP

HANDS-ON: 10 MIN. • **TOTAL: 15 MIN.** • **SERVES 6**

1   tablespoon olive oil
1½ cups prechopped yellow onion
4   cups unsalted chicken stock (such as Swanson)
1   (15-ounce) can no-salt-added black beans, drained and rinsed
1   (10-ounce) can diced tomatoes with green chiles, undrained

2   cups shredded rotisserie chicken breast
½   cup loosely packed fresh cilantro leaves, plus more for topping
⅜   teaspoon kosher salt
Toppings: tortilla chips, diced ripe avocado, sour cream, lime wedges (optional)

Heat the oil in a large pot or Dutch oven over medium-high. Add the onion, and cook, stirring often, until tender, 3 to 4 minutes. Increase the heat to high; stir in the stock, beans, and diced tomatoes, and bring to a boil. Reduce heat to medium, and cook 5 minutes. Stir in chicken, cilantro, and salt; cook 1 minute. Serve with desired toppings.

(**SERVING SIZE:** about 1⅓ cups): **CALORIES** 189; **FAT** 4g (sat 1g, unsat 3g); **PROTEIN** 21g; **CARB** 16g; **FIBER** 5g; **SUGARS** 4g (added sugars 0g); **SODIUM** 523mg; **CALC** 4% DV; **POTASSIUM** 11% DV

MUSHROOM, WILD RICE, *and* CHICKEN SOUP

While the vegetables are cooking, heat the chicken stock and water. This step helps speed prep because adding hot liquid to the pan means it only takes a minute or so to bring to a boil. Serve this soup with crusty bread.

HANDS-ON: 15 MIN. • **TOTAL: 15 MIN.** • **SERVES 6**

2   tablespoons olive oil
4   ounces sliced cremini mushrooms
6   ounces prechopped yellow onion, carrot, and celery blend (about 1¼ cups)
1   garlic clove, minced
3   cups unsalted chicken stock
1   cup water

1   tablespoon white wine vinegar
1   (8.8-ounce) package precooked microwavable long-grain and wild rice (such as Uncle Ben's)
2½ cups coarsely shredded rotisserie chicken breast
Chopped fresh rosemary (optional)

1. Heat the oil in a large saucepan over medium-high. Add the mushrooms, and cook, stirring occasionally, until golden brown, about 3 minutes. Add the prechopped onion mixture and garlic; cook, stirring often, until tender, about 3 minutes.

2. Stir together the chicken stock and water in a large microwave-safe measuring cup; microwave on HIGH until steaming, about 3 minutes. Stir the chicken stock mixture and vinegar into the mushroom mixture in the saucepan; cover and bring to a boil over high. Stir in the rice and chicken; reduce the heat to medium-high, and cook until heated through, about 3 minutes. Divide the soup among 6 bowls; Sprinkle evenly with the chopped rosemary, if desired.

(**SERVING SIZE:** 1 cup): **CALORIES** 249; **FAT** 9g (sat 1g, unsat 6g); **PROTEIN** 26g; **CARB** 18g; **FIBER** 2g; **SUGARS** 2g (added sugars 0g); **SODIUM** 623mg; **CALC** 5% DV; **POTASSIUM** 11% DV

Quick-cooking grains are a boon to weeknight cooks, but make sure the brand of farro you purchase is a whole grain. A lot of the farro you find at the supermarket is pearled, a process that strips away most of the fiber- and nutrient-rich bran. Quick-cooking whole-grain farro has simply been par-boiled, and then dried, making it shelf stable. Then, all you have to do is reconstitute it in the microwave.

TURKEY SAUSAGE, FARRO, *and* CHARD SOUP

This warming soup is an ideal weeknight meal in the fall. Pair it with a grilled cheese sandwich to amp up the comfort factor.

HANDS-ON: 10 MIN. • **TOTAL: 25 MIN.** • **SERVES 6**

1 tablespoon olive oil
12 ounces mild Italian ground turkey sausage
4 cups unsalted chicken stock (such as Swanson)
8 ounces prechopped fresh butternut squash

1 (8-ounce) package precooked microwavable farro (such as Simply Balanced)
4 ounces chopped Swiss chard, stems removed
3/8 teaspoon kosher salt
Shaved ricotta salata (optional)

Heat the oil in a Dutch oven over medium-high. Add the turkey sausage, and cook, stirring until browned and crumbled, about 4 minutes. Add the stock; cover and bring to a boil, about 8 minutes. Reduce the heat to medium; add the squash, and cook, stirring occasionally, until tender, about 8 minutes. Add the farro, chard, and salt, and cook, stirring often, until the chard is wilted, about 2 minutes. Divide the soup among 6 bowls. Top with the shaved ricotta salata, if desired.

(**SERVING SIZE:** 1 cup) **CALORIES** 181; **FAT** 9g (sat 2g, unsat 5g); **PROTEIN** 14g; **CARB** 14g; **FIBER** 2g; **SUGARS** 2g (added sugars 0g); **SODIUM** 613mg; **CALC** 3% DV; **POTASSIUM** 6% DV

COLD *and* CREAMY CUCUMBER SOUP

While cucumbers are easily available year-round, this refreshing soup is even better in the summer when fresh cucumbers are at their peak. Serve it with toast or a baguette for dunking.

HANDS-ON: 5 MIN. • **TOTAL: 10 MIN.** • **SERVES 4**

3 English cucumbers (about 2 pounds), peeled and roughly chopped
1 cup plain low-fat Greek yogurt
⅔ cup whole buttermilk
1 cup loosely packed fresh cilantro leaves
½ cup unsalted chicken stock (such as Swanson)

2 tablespoons fresh lemon juice (from 1 lemon)
2 teaspoons granulated sugar
1 teaspoon kosher salt
½ teaspoon black pepper

Process all the ingredients in a blender on high speed until creamy, 1 to 2 minutes. (If the mixture is too thick, add water, ¼ cup at a time, until desired consistency.) Chill until ready to serve.

(**SERVING SIZE:** 1½ cups): **CALORIES** 99; **FAT** 3g (sat 2g, unsat 1g); **PROTEIN** 9g; **CARB** 12g; **FIBER** 2g; **SUGARS** 9g (added sugars 2g); **SODIUM** 560mg; **CALC** 13% DV; **POTASSIUM** 12% DV

ENGLISH CUCUMBERS

With a thinner, less waxy skin and smaller, edible seeds, English cucumbers can help speed prep on busy weeknights—no peeling or deseeding required! The flavor is also a bit milder than regular cucumbers.

◄ ARUGULA STRACCIATELLA

This Italian soup is reminiscent of egg drop soup. It's deeply comforting without being heavy. You can substitute spinach, kale, or Swiss chard for the arugula or do a combination of greens, if you like.

HANDS-ON: 5 MIN. • **TOTAL: 15 MIN.** • **SERVES 4**

5 cups unsalted chicken stock (such as Swanson)
½ teaspoon kosher salt
½ teaspoon black pepper
3 large eggs
¾ ounce Parmesan cheese, grated (about 2½ tablespoons)

1½ cups loosely packed arugula leaves (about 1½ ounces)
¼ cup coarsely chopped fresh flat-leaf parsley

1. Bring the chicken stock, salt, and pepper to a boil in a Dutch oven over high, about 8 minutes.
2. Whisk together the eggs and Parmesan in a small bowl until well blended.
3. Reduce the heat to medium-low, and bring the stock mixture to a gentle simmer. While stirring in a circular motion, gradually stir the egg mixture into the stock mixture. Using a fork, stir gently until thin strands form, about 1 minute. Stir in the arugula; sprinkle the top with the parsley, and serve immediately.

(**SERVING SIZE:** 1½ cups): **CALORIES** 106; **FAT** 5g (sat 2g, unsat 3g); **PROTEIN** 12g; **CARB** 3g; **FIBER** 0g; **SUGARS** 2g (added sugars 0g); **SODIUM** 557mg; **CALC** 9% DV; **POTASSIUM** 4% DV

CREAMY BACON-CORN CHOWDER

This chowder is comfort food at its finest, offering a sweet and savory contrast thanks respectively to the corn and bacon. Frozen and canned corn allow you to make this soup year-round, but you can also use fresh corn when it's in season. Char the corn in a skillet or on the grill if you have time to add another layer of flavor.

HANDS-ON: 15 MIN. • TOTAL: 15 MIN. • SERVES 4

CENTER-CUT BACON

This type of bacon is cut from the same section as traditional bacon, but it has a higher meat-to-fat ratio, meaning it also has about 20 percent less saturated fat. You can find it in regular and thick-cut varieties.

4   center-cut bacon slices
¾   cup prechopped yellow onion
1½ teaspoons minced garlic (about 2 garlic cloves)
3   cups whole milk
2   tablespoons all-purpose flour
1½ cups frozen whole kernel corn, thawed

1½ cups frozen shredded hash browns, thawed
1   (14.5-ounce) can cream-style corn
½   teaspoon black pepper
⅛   teaspoon kosher salt
Chopped fresh thyme or flat-leaf parsley (optional)

1. Cook the bacon in a Dutch oven over medium-high until crisp, about 5 minutes. Drain the bacon on a plate lined with paper towels, reserving the drippings in the Dutch oven. Add the onion and garlic to the Dutch oven, and cook, stirring often, until slightly softened, about 3 minutes.

2. Whisk together the milk and flour; add to the mixture in the Dutch oven, and bring to a boil over high, stirring constantly. Reduce the heat to medium. Stir in the corn kernels, hash browns, cream-style corn, pepper, and salt, and cook until the vegetables are tender and the soup is thickened, about 3 minutes. Crumble the bacon, and sprinkle over the soup. Sprinkle with the parsley, if desired.

(**SERVING SIZE:** 1¼ cups): **CALORIES** 320; **FAT** 9g (sat 5g, unsat 2g); **PROTEIN** 13g; **CARB** 50g; **FIBER** 4g; **SUGARS** 18g (added sugars 0g); **SODIUM** 608mg; **CALC** 22% DV; **POTASSIUM** 16% DV

WHITE BEAN SOUP

This soup is super creamy without the cream. Instead, it gets its texture from including the bean liquid from the can and pureeing the soup. Sprinkle with additional fresh rosemary, if you like.

HANDS-ON: 15 MIN. • **TOTAL: 20 MIN.** • **SERVES 4**

3 tablespoons olive oil, divided
3 cups (about 12 ounces) frozen chopped onion, carrot, and celery blend, thawed
3 garlic cloves, minced
2 (15-ounce) cans no-salt-added cannellini beans, undrained
1 tablespoon chopped fresh rosemary, divided
1 cup unsalted vegetable stock (such as Swanson)
1 teaspoon kosher salt
1 teaspoon black pepper

1. Heat 1 tablespoon of the oil in a large pot or Dutch oven over medium-high. Add the vegetable blend and garlic, and cook, stirring often, until tender and browned, 8 to 10 minutes. Add the undrained beans and 2 teaspoons of the rosemary, and bring to a boil. Reduce the heat to medium-low, and simmer 5 minutes.

2. Carefully transfer the mixture to a blender. Remove the center piece of the blender lid (to allow steam to escape); secure the lid on the blender, and place a clean towel over the opening in the lid. Process on high speed until smooth, about 30 seconds.

3. Return the mixture to the pot; stir in the stock, salt, and pepper, and cook over low, stirring occasionally, until heated through. Drizzle with the remaining 2 tablespoons olive oil, and sprinkle with the remaining 1 teaspoon rosemary.

(**SERVING SIZE:** 1 cup): **CALORIES** 274; **FAT** 12g (sat 1g, unsat 9g); **PROTEIN** 11g; **CARB** 33g; **FIBER** 10g; **SUGARS** 4g (added sugars 0g); **SODIUM** 643mg; **CALC** 9% DV; **POTASSIUM** 11% DV

CREAMY CAULIFLOWER SOUP

If you have one, you can use an immersion blender to blend the mixture right in the pan, saving you the step of transferring the soup to your blender. Riced fresh cauliflower is available in the produce section of most large grocery stores.

HANDS-ON: 15 MIN. • TOTAL: 15 MIN. • SERVES 4

RICED CAULIFLOWER

If your grocery store doesn't sell riced fresh cauliflower, you can make your own. Grate a head of fresh cauliflower using the medium-sized holes of a box grater or pulse it into rice-sized pieces in a food processor using the grater blade.

2 teaspoons olive oil
2 garlic cloves, minced
2 teaspoons minced fresh thyme, plus leaves for garnish
1 (16-ounce) package riced fresh cauliflower
2 cups unsalted vegetable stock (such as Swanson)
1 (15-ounce) can no-salt-added white beans, drained and rinsed
½ cup half-and-half
1 teaspoon kosher salt
½ teaspoon black pepper
1½ ounces Parmesan cheese, grated (about 5 tablespoons), divided
3½ tablespoons chopped toasted pecans

1. Heat the oil in a large saucepan over medium-high. Add the garlic and minced thyme, and cook, stirring constantly, until fragrant, about 30 seconds. Stir in the cauliflower, and cook, stirring often, until lightly toasted, about 3 minutes. Increase the heat to high. Stir in the stock and beans; cover and bring to a boil. Reduce the heat to medium, and cook, stirring occasionally, until the cauliflower is tender, about 3 minutes.

2. Working in 2 batches, carefully place the soup in a blender. Remove the center piece of the blender lid (to allow steam to escape); secure the lid on the blender, and place a clean towel over the opening in the lid. Process until smooth. Return the soup to the Dutch oven; stir in the half-and-half, salt, pepper, and 3 tablespoons of the Parmesan cheese, and cook over medium-low until combined and heated through.

3. Divide the soup among 4 bowls. Top with the pecans and the remaining 2 tablespoons Parmesan cheese. Garnish with the thyme leaves.

(**SERVING SIZE:** 1½ cups soup, about 1 tablespoon pecans, and ½ tablespoon cheese): **CALORIES** 241; **FAT** 13g (sat 4g, unsat 6g); **PROTEIN** 10g; **CARB** 24g; **FIBER** 7g; **SUGARS** 3g (added sugars 0g); **SODIUM** 702mg; **CALC** 16% DV; **POTASSIUM** 16% DV

PORTOBELLO MUSHROOM PITAS

Brushing the mushrooms with the oil and vinegar mixture before and during the broiling process quickly infuses them. Fresh arugula gives this sandwich a peppery bite, while the balsamic dressing adds some brightness.

HANDS-ON: 15 MIN. • TOTAL: 15 MIN. • SERVES 4

2 tablespoons olive oil
2 tablespoons balsamic vinegar
⅞ teaspoon kosher salt
¼ teaspoon black pepper
4 large portobello mushroom caps (about 12 ounces), gills removed
4 (¾-ounce) Swiss cheese slices
¼ cup canola mayonnaise (such as Hellmann's)

1 teaspoon refrigerated garlic paste (from tube)
1 teaspoon chopped fresh oregano
2 (2-ounce) whole-wheat pita rounds, halved (such as Thomas' Sahara)
1 cup loosely packed arugula (about 1 ounce)

1. Preheat the broiler with the oven rack 4 to 6 inches from the heat. Whisk together the olive oil, vinegar, salt, and pepper until well combined.
2. Place the mushroom caps, top sides down, on a rimmed baking sheet; brush with 1½ tablespoons of the balsamic mixture. Broil until browned, about 5 minutes. Turn the caps, and brush with 1½ tablespoons of the balsamic mixture. Broil 2 minutes. Place 1 Swiss cheese slice on each mushroom cap; broil until the cheese is melted, about 1 minute. Brush the mushrooms with the remaining balsamic mixture.
3. Whisk together the mayonnaise, garlic paste, and oregano in a small bowl. Spread 1 tablespoon mayonnaise mixture in each pita half, and add 1 mushroom and about ¼ cup arugula. Serve immediately.

(**SERVING SIZE:** ½ pita): **CALORIES** 345; **FAT** 25g (sat 6g, unsat 17g); **PROTEIN** 11g; **CARB** 20g; **FIBER** 3g; **SUGARS** 5g (added sugars 0g); **SODIUM** 714mg; **CALC** 22% DV; **POTASSIUM** 10% DV

EGGPLANT SOUVLAKI PITA

The cool, creamy yogurt-cucumber sauce is a nice contrast to the meaty, flash-broiled eggplant. You can warm the pitas if you like to make them more pliable and easy to stuff.

HANDS-ON: 15 MIN. • **TOTAL: 15 MIN.** • **SERVES 4**

1 medium eggplant (about ¾ pound), cut into ¼-inch slices

3 (¼-inch-thick) red onion slices (from 1 onion)

2 tablespoons olive oil

½ teaspoon kosher salt, divided

½ teaspoon black pepper, divided

¼ cup plain fat-free Greek yogurt

¼ cup grated cucumber (from 1 cucumber)

1½ teaspoons fresh lemon juice (from 1 lemon)

2 (2-ounce) whole-wheat pita rounds, halved (such as Thomas' Sahara)

4 ounces feta cheese, crumbled (about 1 cup)

¼ cup loosely packed fresh mint leaves, torn

1. Preheat the broiler with the oven rack 4 to 6 inches from the heat. Place the eggplant and onion slices on an aluminum foil-lined baking sheet; brush with the oil. Sprinkle with ¼ teaspoon each of the salt and pepper. Broil until browned, about 4 minutes; turn the eggplant, and broil until slightly browned, about 4 minutes.

2. Whisk together the yogurt, grated cucumber, lemon juice, and remaining ¼ teaspoon each salt and pepper. Spread 2 tablespoons yogurt mixture in each pita half. Divide the eggplant and red onion evenly among the pita halves; sprinkle evenly with the feta and mint. Serve immediately.

(**SERVING SIZE:** ½ pita): **CALORIES** 250; **FAT** 14g (sat 5g, unsat 8g); **PROTEIN** 10g; **CARB** 24g; **FIBER** 5g; **SUGARS** 7g (added sugars 0g); **SODIUM** 625mg; **CALC** 21% DV; **POTASSIUM** 9% DV

ROASTED BEET *and* GOAT CHEESE SANDWICH

A pleasingly hefty serving of goat cheese on these sandwiches adds lots of rich texture, while the pecans provide just the right amount of crunch. You'll find the beets in a vacuum-sealed package already peeled, roasted, and ready to slice.

HANDS-ON: 15 MIN. • **TOTAL: 15 MIN.** • **SERVES 4**

5   ounces goat cheese, softened
3   tablespoons chopped pecans, toasted
2   teaspoons chopped fresh thyme
1   teaspoon sherry vinegar
¼   teaspoon black pepper
8   (1-ounce) whole-grain sourdough
    sandwich bread slices, toasted

1   pound preroasted unsalted refrigerated
    red beets, cut into ¼-inch-thick slices
¼   teaspoon kosher salt
1   ounce baby arugula (about 1 cup)

Stir together the goat cheese, pecans, thyme, vinegar, and pepper until combined. Spread the mixture evenly over 4 bread slices. Top evenly with the beet slices. Sprinkle evenly with the salt; top evenly with the arugula. Cover with the remaining bread slices. Cut in half, and serve immediately.

(SERVING SIZE: 1 sandwich): **CALORIES** 332; **FAT** 13g (sat 6g, unsat 5g); **PROTEIN** 14g; **CARB** 38g; **FIBER** 6g; **SUGARS** 13g (added sugars 0g); **SODIUM** 622mg; **CALC** 13% DV; **POTASSIUM** 12% DV

ROASTING BEETS

If you can't find the preroasted beets, here's how to cook them yourself: Wrap each beet in foil, and then bake at 375°F for 1 hour and 30 minutes or until tender. Let them cool enough that you can handle them, and then peel them. Since they take some time, albeit hands-off, prepare them on the weekend when you have a bit more time or the night before you plan to use them.

SUPER GREEN SANDWICH

This sandwich may be on the monochromatic side, but it offers a range of flavors and textures that are sure to please: velvety cheese, crispy vegetables, and creamy avocado.

HANDS-ON: 10 MIN. • **TOTAL: 10 MIN.** • **SERVES 4**

8 (1-ounce) whole-grain bread slices with seeds (such as Dave's Killer Bread)
1 ripe avocado, sliced
½ teaspoon kosher salt, divided
¼ teaspoon black pepper, divided
1 cup loosely packed baby spinach (about 1 ounce)

1 cup thinly sliced English cucumber (from 1 cucumber)
¾ cup alfalfa sprouts
2½ ounces Havarti cheese, cut into 4 slices

Layer 4 bread slices evenly with the avocado slices; sprinkle with ¼ teaspoon of the salt and ⅛ teaspoon of the pepper. Top evenly with the spinach and cucumber; sprinkle with the remaining ¼ teaspoon salt and ⅛ teaspoon pepper. Top evenly with the alfalfa sprouts and cheese slices. Cover with the remaining bread slices, and cut in half to serve.

(SERVING SIZE: 1 sandwich): **CALORIES** 282; **FAT** 14g (sat 5g, unsat 6g); **PROTEIN** 13g; **CARB** 29g; **FIBER** 7g; **SUGARS** 4g (added sugars 0g); **SODIUM** 579mg; **CALC** 20% DV; **POTASSIUM** 10% DV

HAM *and* PEAR SANDWICH ▶

This dressed-up ham sandwich gets a nice crunch from fresh pear and a bit of bite from the lemon aioli.

HANDS-ON: 10 MIN. • **TOTAL: 10 MIN.** • **SERVES 4**

¼ cup canola mayonnaise (such as Hellmann's)
1 teaspoon lemon zest plus 1 tablespoon fresh juice (from 1 lemon)
8 (1-ounce) whole-grain bread slices with seeds, lightly toasted (such as Dave's Killer Bread)

4 ounces lower-sodium deli ham slices
1 medium-sized ripe pear, thinly sliced
1 cup watercress, arugula, or spinach (about 2 ounces)
2 tablespoons whole-grain mustard

Whisk together the mayonnaise, lemon zest, and lemon juice. Spread about 1 tablespoon of the mayonnaise mixture on each of 4 bread slices. Layer evenly with the ham slices, pear slices, and watercress. Spread the mustard evenly on the remaining 4 bread slices, and place on the top. Cut the sandwiches in half to serve.

(SERVING SIZE: 1 sandwich): **CALORIES** 318; **FAT** 14g (sat 1g, unsat 10g); **PROTEIN** 11g; **CARB** 37g; **FIBER** 5g; **SUGARS** 10g (added sugars 0g); **SODIUM** 692mg; **CALC** 15% DV; **POTASSIUM** 4% DV

TURKEY REUBEN

A healthy upgrade turns this once-in-awhile treat into an option for any day of the week. Turkey replaces traditional pastrami or corned beef, saving you some saturated fat and sodium, without sacrificing the classic flavors.

HANDS-ON: 10 MIN. • TOTAL: 10 MIN. • SERVES 2

2 tablespoons light Thousand Island dressing
4 (1-ounce) rye bread slices
2 (1-ounce) Swiss cheese slices
2 ounces thinly sliced lower-sodium deli turkey breast
¼ cup drained refrigerated sauerkraut (such as Bubbies)
Cooking spray

Heat a griddle or large nonstick skillet over medium. Spread the Thousand Island dressing on 2 bread slices; top evenly with the cheese, turkey, and sauerkraut. Cover with the remaining bread slices; coat both sides of the sandwiches with the cooking spray. Cook on the hot griddle until the bread is lightly toasted and the cheese is melted, about 3 minutes per side.

(SERVING SIZE: 1 sandwich): **CALORIES** 321; **FAT** 12g (sat 6g, unsat 5g); **PROTEIN** 19g; **CARB** 33g; **FIBER** 4g; **SUGARS** 5g (added sugars 2g); **SODIUM** 735mg; **CALC** 28% DV; **POTASSIUM** 6% DV

◄ PROSCIUTTO *and* MOZZARELLA SANDWICH

This sandwich proves simple, fresh ingredients can still deliver big flavor. The salty prosciutto and creamy fresh mozzarella are the perfect complement to the fresh tomato and basil. The balsamic vinegar adds a lovely hit of acidity.

HANDS-ON: 15 MIN. • TOTAL: 15 MIN. • SERVES 4

2 teaspoons olive oil
2 teaspoons balsamic vinegar
¼ teaspoon kosher salt
¼ teaspoon black pepper
2½ ounces sliced prosciutto
4 ounces fresh mozzarella cheese, torn
2 plum tomatoes, thinly sliced
1 tablespoon torn fresh basil
4 (3½-ounce) ciabatta rolls, halved crosswise and centers hollowed out
Cooking spray

1. Stir together the olive oil, balsamic vinegar, salt, and pepper in a bowl; set aside.
2. Layer the prosciutto, mozzarella, tomato slices, and basil evenly on the bottom halves of the ciabatta rolls. Drizzle each with 1 teaspoon of the olive oil mixture. Cover with the top halves of the rolls.
3. Heat a large cast-iron skillet coated with cooking spray over medium; place the sandwiches in the skillet. Place another heavy-bottomed skillet on top of the sandwiches; cook until browned and heated through, about 3 minutes on each side.

(SERVING SIZE: 1 sandwich): **CALORIES** 288; **FAT** 11g (sat 5g, unsat 3g); **PROTEIN** 14g; **CARB** 32g; **FIBER** 2g; **SUGARS** 1g (added sugars 0g); **SODIUM** 716mg; **CALC** 1% DV; **POTASSIUM** 3% DV

SAUERKRAUT

Gut-healthy, probiotic-rich sauerkraut is an easy entry point to the glories of fermentation. In its most basic form, sauerkraut is just cabbage and salt. Millions of good-for-you bacteria (the same found in yogurt) live on the surface of cabbage. When sealed airtight, they convert the natural plant sugars to lactic acid, which aids in digestion, increases vitamin availability, and gives sauerkraut that pleasantly sour edge. Choose refrigerated varieties instead of canned; the latter have been pasteurized, which kills all the probiotics.

OPEN-FACED CUBAN SANDWICH

You can find capicola, a spiced and smoked pork shoulder cold cut, at the deli counter in both hot and sweet varieties.

HANDS-ON: 15 MIN. • **TOTAL: 15 MIN.** • **SERVES 4**

1 tablespoon yellow mustard
1 (4-ounce) baguette, cut in half lengthwise
2 ounces thinly sliced Swiss cheese, divided
3 ounces lower-sodium deli ham, thinly sliced

2 ounces spicy deli capicola, thinly sliced
¼ cup thinly sliced red onion
4 dill pickle sandwich slices

1. Preheat the oven to 425°F. Spread the mustard on the cut sides of the baguette halves. Layer each half with ¼ ounce of the Swiss cheese. Divide the ham, capicola, red onion, pickle slices, and remaining Swiss cheese evenly between the halves; place on a baking sheet.
2. Bake the baguette halves in the preheated oven until the cheese is melted and the bread is crisp, about 10 minutes. Cut each in half to make 4 pieces.

(**SERVING SIZE:** 1 piece): **CALORIES** 199; **FAT** 6g (sat 3g, unsat 2g); **PROTEIN** 14g; **CARB** 22g; **FIBER** 1g; **SUGARS** 1g (added sugars 0g); **SODIUM** 812mg; **CALC** 12% DV; **POTASSIUM** 2% DV

ROASTED PORK *and* BROCCOLI RABE SANDWICH ▶

HANDS-ON: 10 MIN. • **TOTAL: 15 MIN.** • **SERVES 4**

1 tablespoon olive oil
2 cups trimmed and chopped fresh broccoli rabe (about 4 ounces)
¼ teaspoon crushed red pepper
¼ teaspoon kosher salt
1 (8-ounce) whole-wheat baguette

8 ounces sliced deli roasted pork
4 (1-ounce) Swiss cheese slices
2 tablespoons canola mayonnaise (such as Hellmann's)
2 teaspoons stone-ground mustard

1. Preheat the broiler with the oven rack 6 inches from the heat.
2. Heat the olive oil in a large skillet over medium-high. Add the broccoli rabe, and cook, stirring occasionally, until tender, about 7 minutes. Stir in the crushed red pepper and salt; set aside.
3. Cut the baguette in half horizontally; hollow out the centers of the halves, and place, cut sides up, on a baking sheet. Layer the sliced pork and Swiss cheese on the baguette bottom. Broil both halves until the cheese is melted and the bread is toasted, about 2 minutes. Top the melted cheese with the broccoli rabe mixture.
4. Stir together the mayonnaise and mustard; spread on the cut side of the top half, and cover the bottom. Cut into 4 pieces, and serve immediately.

(**SERVING SIZE:** 1 piece): **CALORIES** 382; **FAT** 17g (sat 6g, unsat 5g); **PROTEIN** 30g; **CARB** 26g; **FIBER** 2g; **SUGARS** 0g (added sugars 0g); **SODIUM** 619mg; **CALC** 34% DV; **POTASSIUM** 1% DV

Broccoli rabe is an underutilized vegetable, but its spicy, earthy flavor shines in this sandwich, pairing perfectly with the cheese and pork. A little crushed red pepper lends just enough heat.

PHO WRAP

The beloved Vietnamese soup is made over in sandwich form. You can customize these wraps by including extra Sriracha, lime, and hoisin or adding in soy sauce, nuts, or extra herbs.

HANDS-ON: 10 MIN. • TOTAL: 10 MIN. • SERVES 2

1   tablespoon hoisin sauce
2   teaspoons fresh lime juice (from 1 lime)
1   teaspoon Sriracha chili sauce
4   (8-inch) rice paper sheets

4   ounces deli roast beef slices
½   cup bean sprouts (about 1 ounce)
¼   cup loosely packed fresh cilantro leaves
2   scallions, thinly sliced

1. Stir together the hoisin, lime juice, and Sriracha in a small bowl.
2. Pour very hot water into a shallow dish or pie plate to a depth of ½ inch. Soak the rice paper sheets, 1 at a time, in hot water until softened, about 30 seconds. Arrange the sheets on a clean, flat work surface; place about 1 ounce beef just below the center of each. Top evenly with the sprouts, cilantro, and scallions. Fold the opposite sides of the sheet over the filling, and roll up. Serve with the hoisin mixture.

(**SERVING SIZE:** 2 wraps): **CALORIES** 158; **FAT** 2g (sat 1g, unsat 0g); **PROTEIN** 14g; **CARB** 22g; **FIBER** 1g; **SUGARS** 4g (added sugars 1g); **SODIUM** 623mg; **CALC** 1% DV; **POTASSIUM** 2% DV

PHO

This fragrant broth-based rice noodle soup, traditionally made with savory beef or chicken (you'll also see adaptations with seafood or pork), is a national dish of Vietnam. It's usually served with an assortment of fresh, crunchy toppings like bean sprouts, fresh herbs, and slices of hot chiles.

AVOCADO PESTO–TURKEY WRAP ▶

The avocado spread is a creamy, cooling contrast to the crunch from the sprouts and red onion.

HANDS-ON: 15 MIN. • TOTAL: 15 MIN. • SERVES 4

1 ripe avocado	4 (7- to 8-inch) whole-wheat flour tortillas
¼ cup loosely packed fresh basil leaves	7 ounces thinly sliced lower-sodium turkey breast
3 tablespoons blanched almonds, chopped	
1 tablespoon extra-virgin olive oil	6 ounces alfalfa sprouts
2 teaspoons fresh lemon juice (from 1 lemon)	¼ cup thinly sliced red onion (from 1 small onion)
¼ teaspoon black pepper	

1. Process the avocado, basil, almonds, olive oil, lemon juice, and pepper in a blender until almost smooth, about 1 minute.
2. Place the tortillas on a clean, flat surface. Spread the avocado mixture down the center of each tortilla. Top evenly with the turkey, sprouts, and red onion. Roll up each tortilla tightly to make a wrap.

(SERVING SIZE: 1 wrap): **CALORIES** 352; **FAT** 17g (sat 2g, unsat 14g); **PROTEIN** 19g; **CARB** 34g; **FIBER** 8g; **SUGARS** 6g (added sugars 0g); **SODIUM** 731mg; **CALC** 5% DV; **POTASSIUM** 13% DV

THAI CHICKEN SALAD LETTUCE WRAP

The yogurt adds a smoothness to the peanut butter, creating a flavorful dressing that more easily and thoroughly coats the chicken and cabbage.

HANDS-ON: 15 MIN. • TOTAL: 15 MIN. • SERVES 4

½ cup plain fat-free Greek yogurt	1 cup shredded angel hair cabbage (from a 10-ounce package)
2 tablespoons crunchy peanut butter	
1 tablespoon lower-sodium soy sauce	4 large butter lettuce leaves
2 teaspoons Sriracha chili sauce	Sesame seeds (optional)
2 teaspoons fresh lime juice (from 1 lime)	Sliced radishes (optional)
½ teaspoon kosher salt	Matchstick carrots (optional)
2 cups shredded rotisserie chicken breast (about 8½ ounces)	

Stir together the yogurt, peanut butter, soy sauce, Sriracha, lime juice, and salt until well combined. Fold in the chicken and cabbage until thoroughly coated. Place the lettuce leaves on a clean, flat surface; spoon ½ cup chicken mixture just below the center of each. If desired, top with the sesame seeds, radishes, and carrots. Fold the opposite sides of the lettuce leaf over the filling, and roll up.

(SERVING SIZE: 1 wrap): **CALORIES** 188; **FAT** 7g (sat 1g, unsat 4g); **PROTEIN** 27g; **CARB** 5g; **FIBER** 1g; **SUGARS** 2g (added sugars 0g); **SODIUM** 539mg; **CALC** 4% DV; **POTASSIUM** 9% DV

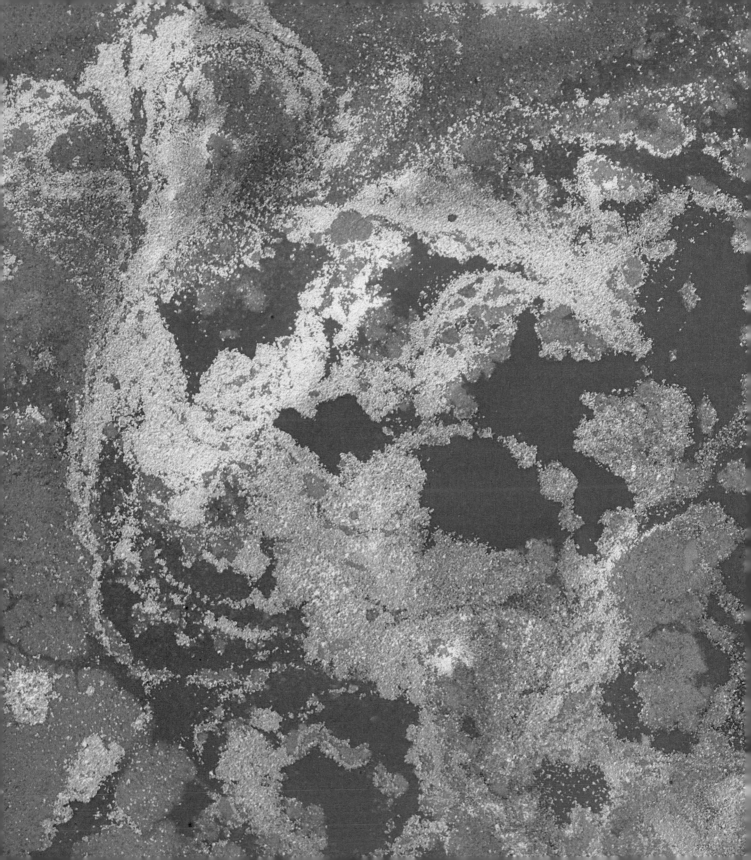

CHAPTER 3

MAIN-DISH SALADS

QUINOA SALAD *with* CRANBERRIES *and* WALNUTS

This is a filling salad on its own, but feel free to add sliced grilled chicken breast or rotisserie chicken if you want more heft. If you can find goat cheese that is not precrumbled, opt for that, as it's creamier.

HANDS-ON: 15 MIN. • TOTAL: 15 MIN. • SERVES 4

- 2 (8-ounce) packages precooked microwavable quinoa (such as Simply Balanced)
- 3 tablespoons olive oil
- 2 tablespoons white wine vinegar
- ¾ teaspoon kosher salt
- ½ teaspoon black pepper
- 1 (5-ounce) package baby kale
- ½ cup chopped walnuts, toasted
- ¼ cup thinly sliced shallots (from 1 medium shallot)
- ¼ cup dried sweetened cranberries
- 3 ounces goat cheese, crumbled (about ¾ cup)

1. Prepare the quinoa according to the package directions. While the quinoa cooks, whisk together the oil, vinegar, salt, and pepper in a small bowl.
2. Transfer the quinoa to a large bowl, and fluff with a fork to loosen and cool. Add the kale, walnuts, shallots, cranberries, and goat cheese; toss gently. Drizzle with the dressing, and toss to coat.

(**SERVING SIZE: 2 cups**): **CALORIES** 419; **FAT** 27g (sat 6g, unsat 20g); **PROTEIN** 13g; **CARB** 36g; **FIBER** 6g; **SUGARS** 7g (added sugars 3g); **SODIUM** 488mg; **CALC** 19% DV; **POTASSIUM** 14% DV

QUINOA

A tiny beige, red, or black seed about the size of couscous, quinoa is a time-saving whole grain for weeknight cooks. Even if you can't find the precooked variety, regular quinoa is ready in 10 to 20 minutes. You'll need to rinse it before cooking to remove its bitter-flavored natural coating.

ARUGULA SALAD *with* LENTILS *and* PINE NUTS

This recipe is a wonderful pairing of smart convenience products (precooked lentils) with fresh ingredients for a quick, good-for-you salad.

HANDS-ON: 10 MIN. • TOTAL: 10 MIN. • SERVES 4

- 3 tablespoons olive oil
- 1½ tablespoons sherry vinegar
- 1 teaspoon kosher salt
- ¼ teaspoon black pepper
- 1 (1-pound) package precooked lentils
- 1 (5-ounce) package baby arugula
- 3 ounces crumbled goat cheese (about ½ cup)
- 3 tablespoons toasted pine nuts

Whisk together the oil, vinegar, salt, and pepper in a large bowl. Add the lentils and arugula, and toss to combine. Top with goat cheese and pine nuts.

(**SERVING SIZE: 1¼ cups**): **CALORIES** 331; **FAT** 20g (sat 5g, unsat 13g); **PROTEIN** 16g; **CARB** 25g; **FIBER** 10g; **SUGARS** 3g (added sugars 0g); **SODIUM** 590mg; **CALC** 11% DV; **POTASSIUM** 17% DV

SPICY THAI EDAMAME SALAD

This is not your average chopped salad. All those good-for-you green components get rich flavor from the peanut dressing and a kick of spice from the red chile pepper.

HANDS-ON: 15 MIN. • **TOTAL: 15 MIN.** • **SERVES 4**

2   cups frozen shelled edamame (about 10 ounces)
3   tablespoons creamy peanut butter
2   tablespoons water
2   tablespoons lower-sodium soy sauce
2   tablespoons rice vinegar

5   cups chopped romaine (about 10 ounces)
½   cup sliced English cucumber
1   red chile, seeds removed, thinly sliced
¼   cup chopped roasted unsalted peanuts
2   tablespoons sliced scallions (from 2 scallions; optional)

1. Prepare the edamame according to the package directions. Drain well, and run under cold water to cool.
2. While the edamame cooks, whisk together the peanut butter, water, soy sauce, and vinegar in a large bowl. Add the romaine, edamame, cucumber, and chile pepper; toss to coat. Divide among 4 bowls, and sprinkle evenly with the peanuts and, if desired, the scallions.

(**SERVING SIZE:** 1¾ cups): **CALORIES** 257; **FAT** 14g (sat 2g, unsat 11g); **PROTEIN** 14g; **CARB** 20g; **FIBER** 7g; **SUGARS** 7g (added sugars 0g); **SODIUM** 495mg; **CALC** 8% DV; **POTASSIUM** 9% DV

SOUTHWESTERN "FATTOUSH" SALAD
with BLACK BEANS ▶

In this salad, tortilla chips take the place of the bread that's traditionally used. Bulk it up even more by adding spicy grilled chicken breast or rotisserie chicken.

HANDS-ON: 15 MIN. • **TOTAL: 15 MIN.** • **SERVES 6**

5   cups coarsely chopped romaine lettuce hearts (about 8 ounces)
1   (15-ounce) can unsalted black beans, drained and rinsed
1   cup cherry tomatoes, halved (about 6 ounces)
2   ounces baked corn tortilla chips, coarsely broken (about 2 cups whole chips)

2   ounces Cotija cheese, crumbled (about ½ cup)
3   tablespoons olive oil
1½ tablespoons fresh lime juice (from 1 lime)
¼   teaspoon kosher salt
1   medium-sized ripe avocado, chopped
3   tablespoons roasted pepitas (shelled pumpkin seeds)

1. Combine the romaine, beans, tomatoes, tortilla chips, and cheese in a large bowl.
2. Whisk together the oil, lime juice, and salt in a small bowl. Drizzle over the salad, and toss. Top with the avocado and pepitas. Serve immediately.

(**SERVING SIZE:** about 1⅓ cups): **CALORIES** 273; **FAT** 17g (sat 4g, unsat 10g); **PROTEIN** 9g; **CARB** 24g; **FIBER** 8g; **SUGARS** 1g (added sugars 0g); **SODIUM** 295mg; **CALC** 14% DV; **POTASSIUM** 15% DV

EGG and POTATO SALAD

Boiling the potatoes and eggs in the same pot is a time-saver, keeping you from having to clean another pot. Just remove the eggs first and continue cooking the potatoes. If you can't find fingerlings, use baby gold potatoes instead.

HANDS-ON: 25 MIN. • TOTAL: 25 MIN. • SERVES 4

6 large eggs
1 pound small fingerling potatoes, halved
1 lemon
2 tablespoons whole-grain mustard
2 tablespoons olive oil
¾ teaspoon kosher salt
½ teaspoon black pepper
1 (5-ounce) package baby arugula (about 5 cups)
1 tablespoon chopped fresh dill (optional)

1. Fill a large saucepan with water; cover and bring to a boil over high. Add the eggs and potatoes, and cook, uncovered, 10 minutes. Using tongs, transfer the eggs to an ice bath to cool. Allow the potatoes to continue cooking until tender, about 4 more minutes. Drain well.
2. While the potatoes and eggs cook, grate the zest from the lemon to measure 1 teaspoon, and squeeze the juice to measure 1 tablespoon. Whisk together the mustard, oil, lemon zest, lemon juice, salt, and pepper in a large bowl; remove and reserve 1 tablespoon dressing.
3. Peel the cooled eggs, and chop. Add the chopped eggs and potatoes to the mustard mixture; fold gently. Toss the arugula with the reserved 1 tablespoon dressing. Divide the arugula among 4 plates; top with the egg and potato mixture. Sprinkle with dill, if desired.

(SERVING SIZE: 1¼ cups arugula and 1 cup egg and potato mixture): **CALORIES** 282; **FAT** 15g (sat 3g, unsat 11g); **PROTEIN** 13g; **CARB** 22g; **FIBER** 3g; **SUGARS** 2g (added sugars 0g); **SODIUM** 677mg; **CALC** 13% DV; **POTASSIUM** 8% DV

CITRUS ZEST

When zesting lemons, limes, or any citrus, make sure you grate just the colorful surface. If you grate the white part, you'll end up with bitter zest.

BEET, WHITE BEAN, *and* SPINACH SALAD ▶

Beets and white beans complement each other beautifully, while the white balsamic pairs perfectly with the citrusy flavors from the orange zest.

HANDS-ON: 10 MIN. • TOTAL: 10 MIN. • SERVES 4

2 tablespoons white balsamic vinegar
¾ teaspoon kosher salt
½ teaspoon orange zest (from 1 small orange)
¼ teaspoon black pepper
¼ cup olive oil
1 (5-ounce) package baby spinach

2 cups no-salt-added cannellini beans, drained and rinsed (from 2 [15-ounce] cans)
2 (8.8-ounce) packages precooked beets (such as Love Beets), quartered
½ cup chopped walnuts, toasted

1. Whisk together the vinegar, salt, zest, and black pepper in a small bowl. Slowly drizzle in the olive oil, whisking constantly until emulsified.
2. Combine the spinach, beans, beets, and walnuts in a large bowl. Drizzle with the dressing and toss. Serve immediately.

(**SERVING SIZE:** 1¼ cups): **CALORIES** 372; **FAT** 23g (sat 3g, unsat 18g); **PROTEIN** 11g; **CARB** 34g; **FIBER** 9g; **SUGARS** 12g (added sugars 0g); **SODIUM** 526mg; **CALC** 11% DV; **POTASSIUM** 20% DV

SPICY SEARED TOFU *and* CABBAGE SALAD

To ensure the tofu becomes golden, make sure you've patted it dry—the drier the better—and you add it to the pan after the oil is hot.

HANDS-ON: 15 MIN. • TOTAL: 15 MIN. • SERVES 4

14 ounces extra-firm tofu, drained and patted dry
¼ teaspoon kosher salt
2 tablespoons olive oil
3 tablespoons canola mayonnaise (such as Hellmann's)

2 tablespoons water
1 tablespoon Sriracha chili sauce
1 tablespoon lower-sodium soy sauce
1 (14-ounce) package coleslaw mix
¼ cup chopped dry-roasted unsalted peanuts (optional)

1. Cut the tofu into 2 (1-inch-thick) steaks. Sprinkle evenly with the salt. Heat the oil in a medium nonstick skillet over medium-high. Add the tofu, and cook until golden, about 3 minutes per side. Transfer to a cutting board; cool completely, about 10 minutes.
2. While the tofu sears, whisk together the mayonnaise, water, Sriracha, and soy sauce in a large bowl. Add the coleslaw mix, and toss to coat.
3. Cut the tofu into bite-sized cubes, and add to the salad; toss to coat. Top with chopped peanuts, if desired.

(**SERVING SIZE:** 1½ cups): **CALORIES** 262; **FAT** 20g (sat 2g, unsat 17g); **PROTEIN** 11g; **CARB** 9g; **FIBER** 4g; **SUGARS** 4g (added sugars 0g); **SODIUM** 441mg; **CALC** 12% DV; **POTASSIUM** 0% DV

SALMON *and* KALE SALAD *with* LEMON-ANCHOVY DRESSING

The dressing is a versatile all-purpose dressing you can use with other salads. It's not fishy at all, but has a nice bite from the Parmesan. Massaging the kale with the dressing wilts it slightly and mellows some of its bitter edge.

HANDS-ON: 15 MIN. • **TOTAL: 15 MIN.** • **SERVES 4**

1   (1-pound) skinless salmon fillet
½   teaspoon kosher salt, divided
½   teaspoon black pepper, divided
5   tablespoons olive oil, divided
½   teaspoon lemon zest plus 2 tablespoons fresh juice (from 1 medium lemon)
1   teaspoon Dijon mustard

½   teaspoon anchovy paste
1   ounce Parmesan cheese, finely grated (using a Microplane grater; about ⅔ cup)
5   cups chopped curly kale (from 1 bunch; about 4 ounces)
1   cup cherry tomatoes, halved

1. Sprinkle the salmon with ¼ teaspoon of the salt and ⅛ teaspoon of the pepper. Heat 1½ teaspoons of the oil in a large nonstick skillet over medium; add the salmon, and cook until the desired degree of doneness, 4 to 5 minutes per side for medium. Remove from the pan, and flake into large pieces with a fork.
2. Whisk together the lemon zest, lemon juice, mustard, anchovy paste, and remaining ¼ teaspoon salt and ⅜ teaspoon pepper in a large bowl. Slowly add the Parmesan and remaining 4½ tablespoons oil while whisking. Toss the kale in the dressing; massage the dressing into the leaves until softened, about 1 minute. Add the cherry tomatoes, and toss to combine. Serve the salad topped with salmon pieces.

(**SERVING SIZE:** 1½ cups): **CALORIES** 366; **FAT** 27g (sat 5g, unsat 20g); **PROTEIN** 26g; **CARB** 6g; **FIBER** 2g; **SUGARS** 2g (added sugars 0g); **SODIUM** 505mg; **CALC** 12% DV; **POTASSIUM** 23% DV

ANCHOVY PASTE

Made from ground anchovies, salt, and oil, this concentrated fish paste adds deep savoriness when used in small doses without imbuing the dish with an overly fishy flavor. Stir it into dressings (not just Caesar) and sauces (tomato-based sauces certainly benefit) to amp up the flavor. It's widely available in large supermarkets in easy-to-use tubes.

SALMON TZATZIKI SALAD

The garlicky dressing pairs perfectly with the salmon. Serve it with naan or pita.

HANDS-ON: 15 MIN. • TOTAL: 15 MIN. • SERVES 4

4   (6-ounce) salmon fillets (about 1-inch thick)
¾   teaspoon kosher salt, divided
¾   teaspoon black pepper, divided
1   tablespoon olive oil
1   lemon

¼   cup plain low-fat Greek yogurt
1   garlic clove, grated
1   medium English cucumber
5   cups chopped romaine lettuce
½   cup roasted red bell peppers, cut into strips

1. Sprinkle the salmon with ½ teaspoon each of the salt and pepper. Heat the oil in a large nonstick skillet over medium-high. Add the salmon to the pan, and cook to the desired degree of doneness, 3 minutes per side for medium-well. Transfer to a plate.
2. Zest the lemon to measure 1 teaspoon lemon zest. Cut the lemon in half; squeeze the juice to measure 1 tablespoon. Whisk together the yogurt, garlic, 1 tablespoon water, lemon zest, lemon juice, and the remaining ¼ teaspoon each salt and pepper.
3. Slice the cucumber in half lengthwise; set 1 half aside. Grate the remaining half using the large holes of a box grater. Stir ¼ cup of the grated cucumber into the dressing, discard the remaining grated cucumber. Thinly slice other the half of the cucumber.
4. Divide the greens among 4 plates, and top evenly with the cucumber slices, roasted red pepper strips, and salmon. Drizzle with the yogurt dressing.

(**SERVING SIZE:** 1½ cups salad, 1 salmon fillet, and 2 tablespoons dressing): **CALORIES** 306; **FAT** 15g (sat 2g, unsat 11g); **PROTEIN** 37g; **CARB** 6g; **FIBER** 2g; **SUGARS** 3g (added sugars 0g); **SODIUM** 505mg; **CALC** 7% DV; **POTASSIUM** 31% DV

SEARED TUNA SALAD *with* HARICOTS VERTS ▸

HANDS-ON: 15 MIN. • TOTAL: 15 MIN. • SERVES 4

1   (1-pound) albacore tuna steak
1   teaspoon black pepper
¾   teaspoon kosher salt, divided
¼   cup olive oil, divided
1   (8-ounce) package microwave-in-bag haricots verts (French green beans)

1   (5-ounce) package mixed baby greens
1   cup cherry tomatoes, halved
4   hard-cooked eggs, peeled and halved
2   tablespoons Champagne vinegar
1   tablespoon minced shallots
1   teaspoon Dijon mustard

1. Sprinkle the tuna with the pepper and ½ teaspoon of the salt. Heat 1 tablespoon of the oil in a large skillet over high. Add the tuna, and sear until browned on both sides, about 2 minutes per side. Transfer to a cutting board; thinly slice.
2. Prepare haricots verts according to package directions. Remove from bag; transfer to an ice bath. Toss together beans, greens, and tomatoes in a bowl; divide among 4 plates. Top each with 2 egg halves. Whisk together vinegar, shallots, mustard, and remaining ¼ teaspoon salt and 3 tablespoons oil. Drizzle over salad; top with tuna.

(**SERVING SIZE:** 1¾ cups greens mixture, 2 egg halves, 1 tablespoon dressing, and 4 ounces tuna): **CALORIES** 351; **FAT** 19g (sat 4g, unsat 15g); **PROTEIN** 36g; **CARB** 9g; **FIBER** 3g; **SUGARS** 3g (added sugars 0g); **SODIUM** 547mg; **CALC** 9% DV; **POTASSIUM** 23% DV

Make sure the pan is nice and hot before you add the tuna. That's key to ensuring the fish gets a lovely browned crust while the interior remains rare.

AVOCADO *and* SHRIMP SALAD

If you're preparing this salad ahead or packing it for lunch, toss the avocado in a bit of lemon juice to prevent it from browning.

HANDS-ON: 15 MIN. • **TOTAL: 15 MIN.** • **SERVES 4**

RADISHES

1½ pounds raw large shrimp, peeled and deveined
½ teaspoon kosher salt, divided
½ teaspoon black pepper, divided
3 tablespoons olive oil, divided
2 tablespoons fresh lemon juice (from 1 lemon)

1 (5-ounce) package baby arugula
½ cup thinly sliced red onion (from 1 medium onion)
1 medium-sized avocado, sliced
¼ cup sliced radish (about 1 ounce)

1. Toss the shrimp with ¼ teaspoon each of the salt and pepper. Heat 1 tablespoon of the oil in a large nonstick skillet over medium-high. Add the shrimp, and cook until cooked through and opaque, about 2 minutes per side. Transfer to a plate.
2. Whisk together the lemon juice and the remaining 2 tablespoons oil and ¼ teaspoon each salt and pepper in a large bowl. Add the arugula and onion, and toss to coat. Divide among 4 plates; top with the shrimp, avocado, and radish.

(**SERVING SIZE:** ½ cup salad, 4 ounces shrimp, ¼ avocado, and 1 tablespoon radish): **CALORIES** 309; **FAT** 19g (sat 3g, unsat 15g); **PROTEIN** 25g; **CARB** 9g; **FIBER** 4g; **SUGARS** 2g (added sugars 0g); **SODIUM** 509mg; **CALC** 16% DV; **POTASSIUM** 18% DV

While radishes are available year-round, you'll get the best peppery bites when they're at their peak in the spring. When purchasing, look for plump, firm roots, preferably with the leaves still attached— wilted leaves are a sure sign of mealy radishes below. But, be sure to chop off the greens if they remain attached once you get home, as they'll pull moisture from the crisp root. You can serve the mild, aromatic greens raw or cooked. If the radishes have become spongy, crisp them by placing them in a bowl of ice water for up to an hour.

CHICKEN, BERRIES, *and* GREENS *with* ZESTY LIME DRESSING

Use any berries—or combination of berries—that you prefer. Blackberries and raspberries would also be delicious. Substitute sliced toasted almonds for the walnuts, if you like.

HANDS-ON: 15 MIN. • **TOTAL: 15 MIN.** • **SERVES 4**

Cooking spray
4 (4-ounce) chicken cutlets
1 teaspoon kosher salt, divided
½ teaspoon black pepper, divided
2 tablespoons olive oil
1 teaspoon lime zest plus 1 tablespoon fresh juice (from 1 lime)

2 teaspoons honey
1 (5-ounce) package mixed salad greens
1 cup sliced fresh strawberries
1 cup fresh blueberries
2 tablespoons chopped walnuts, toasted

1. Heat a grill pan coated with cooking spray over medium-high. Sprinkle the chicken evenly with ½ teaspoon of the salt and ¼ teaspoon of the pepper. Cook the chicken in the hot grill pan until cooked through, 2 to 3 minutes per side. Transfer to a cutting board.
2. Whisk together the oil, lime zest, lime juice, honey, and the remaining ½ teaspoon salt and ¼ teaspoon pepper in a large bowl. Add the greens, and toss to coat.
3. Slice the chicken into thin strips. Divide the greens among 4 plates; top evenly with the chicken, strawberries, blueberries, and walnuts.

(**SERVING SIZE:** 2½ cups): **CALORIES** 273; **FAT** 12g (sat 2g, unsat 9g); **PROTEIN** 28g; **CARB** 14g; **FIBER** 3g; **SUGARS** 9g (added sugars 3g); **SODIUM** 561mg; **CALC** 5% DV; **POTASSIUM** 14% DV

RANCH VEGGIE *and* CHICKEN SALAD

If you have trouble finding baby kale, substitute regular and remove the stems and chop the greens.

HANDS-ON: 15 MIN. • **TOTAL: 15 MIN.** • **SERVES 4**

1 (5-ounce) package baby kale
2 cups shaved carrots (from 1 large carrot)
1 cup fresh corn kernels (from about 2 ears)
1 cup sliced cucumber (from 1 medium cucumber)
12 ounces chopped skinless rotisserie chicken breast (about 2½ cups)
2 tablespoons canola mayonnaise (such as Hellmann's)

1½ tablespoons buttermilk
1 tablespoon apple cider vinegar
½ teaspoon kosher salt
½ teaspoon black pepper
2 tablespoons chopped fresh chives (optional)

Arrange the kale, carrots, corn, cucumber, and chicken on a large platter. Whisk together the mayonnaise, buttermilk, vinegar, salt, and pepper in a small bowl. Drizzle over the salad, and toss to coat. Sprinkle with the chives, if desired.

(SERVING SIZE: 2 cups): CALORIES 245; FAT 9g (sat 2g, unsat 6g); PROTEIN 27g; CARB 16g; FIBER 4g; SUGARS 6g (added sugars 0g); SODIUM 633mg; CALC 17% DV; POTASSIUM 22% DV

CHICKEN, RICE, *and* FETA SALAD *with* LEMONY DRESSING

The textures in this salad play perfectly with one another: crunch from the greens and almonds, creaminess from the feta, chew from the rice and chicken, all finished with a lemon dressing for a nice hit of bright citrusy flavor.

HANDS-ON: 10 MIN. • **TOTAL: 10 MIN.** • **SERVES 4**

1 (8.8-ounce) package precooked microwaveable brown rice (such as Uncle Ben's)
2 tablespoons fresh lemon juice
2 tablespoons olive oil
2 teaspoons honey
½ teaspoon kosher salt

½ teaspoon black pepper
8 ounces shredded skinless rotisserie chicken breast (about 1⅔ cups), warmed
1 (5-ounce) package mixed salad greens
2 ounces crumbled feta cheese (about ½ cup)
2 tablespoons sliced almonds, toasted

1. Prepare the rice according to the package directions; set aside.
2. Whisk together the lemon juice, oil, honey, salt, and pepper in a large bowl. Add the chicken, and toss to combine. Add the rice and greens, and toss gently. Sprinkle with the feta and almonds.

(SERVING SIZE: 1½ cups): CALORIES 296; FAT 14g (sat 4g, unsat 9g); PROTEIN 22g; CARB 24g; FIBER 3g; SUGARS 4g (added sugars 3g); SODIUM 584mg; CALC 11% DV; POTASSIUM 6% DV

ASIAN VEGETABLE and CHICKEN SALAD

There are many different brands and versions of Asian salad mix. Just pick the one that looks best to you. Substitute sautéed shrimp for the chicken, if you like.

HANDS-ON: 10 MIN. • TOTAL: 10 MIN. • SERVES 4

3 tablespoons toasted sesame oil
3 tablespoons unseasoned rice vinegar
1½ tablespoons honey
1½ teaspoons grated fresh ginger
¾ teaspoon kosher salt
¾ teaspoon black pepper
1 (12-ounce) package Asian chopped salad mix (such as Dole Asian Blend), omitting packaged dressing (about 6½ cups)

8 ounces chopped skinless rotisserie chicken breast (about 1⅔ cups)
1 cup frozen shelled edamame, thawed (about 6 ounces)
⅓ cup chopped unsalted cashews, toasted

1. Whisk together the oil, vinegar, honey, ginger, salt, and black pepper in a small bowl.
2. Combine the salad mix, chicken breast, edamame, and cashews in a large bowl. Drizzle the dressing over the salad, and toss.

(**SERVING SIZE:** about 2 cups): **CALORIES** 334; **FAT** 19g (sat 3g, unsat 14g); **PROTEIN** 23g; **CARB** 21g; **FIBER** 4g; **SUGARS** 11g (added sugars 6g); **SODIUM** 575mg; **CALC** 8% DV; **POTASSIUM** 7% DV

GARLIC-COATED PORK TENDERLOIN over ESCAROLE-FENNEL-APPLE SALAD

Pork tenderloins (often available in packs of two) range in size. Opt for smaller ones to keep the total time on this recipe to 15 minutes. Slicing the pork before broiling it helps shorten the time it spends under the broiler.

HANDS-ON: 15 MIN. • TOTAL: 15 MIN. • SERVES 4

- 1 small fennel bulb with fronds (about 6 ounces)
- 1 tablespoon minced garlic (about 3 garlic cloves)
- ¼ cup olive oil, divided
- 2 teaspoons Dijon mustard, divided
- ¾ teaspoon kosher salt, divided
- ¾ teaspoon black pepper, divided
- 1 (1-pound) pork tenderloin, trimmed and cut into 12 slices
- 1½ tablespoons apple cider vinegar
- 5 cups chopped escarole (about 5 ounces)
- 2 cups thinly sliced Gala apple (from 2 small apples)

1. Preheat the broiler with the oven rack 6 inches from the heat. Finely chop the fennel fronds to measure 1 tablespoon. Thinly slice the fennel bulb to measure 1 cup.
2. Combine the garlic, 1 tablespoon of the oil, 1 teaspoon of the mustard, and ½ teaspoon each of the salt and pepper on a baking sheet lined with aluminum foil. Add the pork; toss to coat. Broil in the preheated oven until a thermometer inserted in the pork registers 145°F, about 7 minutes.
3. While the pork broils, whisk together the vinegar, the remaining 3 tablespoons oil, 1 teaspoon mustard, and ¼ teaspoon each of salt and pepper in a large bowl. Add the escarole, apple, fennel slices, and reserved 1 tablespoon fronds; toss to coat in the dressing. Top the salad with the pork.

(**SERVING SIZE:** about 2 cups salad and 3 slices pork): **CALORIES** 301; **FAT** 16g (sat 3g, unsat 13g); **PROTEIN** 25g; **CARB** 13g; **FIBER** 4g; **SUGARS** 7g (added sugars 0g); **SODIUM** 512mg; **CALC** 6% DV; **POTASSIUM** 23% DV

SHAVED BRUSSELS SPROUTS
with BACON *and* WHITE BEANS

While the bacon is cooking, you have time to slice the Brussels sprouts by hand, but you could also shred them in a food processor using the slicing blade.

HANDS-ON: 15 MIN. • **TOTAL: 15 MIN.** • **SERVES 4**

3 bacon slices
1 tablespoon olive oil
1 tablespoon apple cider vinegar
2 teaspoons honey
½ teaspoon kosher salt
½ teaspoon black pepper

1 pound Brussels sprouts, trimmed and thinly sliced (about 4½ cups)
1 medium-sized red apple (such as Gala), thinly sliced (about 2 cups)
1 (15-ounce) can lower-sodium cannellini beans, drained and rinsed

Cook the bacon in a nonstick skillet over medium until crisp and cooked through, 4 to 5 minutes per side. Remove the skillet from the heat; transfer the bacon to a plate lined with paper towels, reserving the bacon drippings in a large bowl. Whisk in the olive oil, vinegar, honey, salt, and pepper. Add the Brussels sprouts, apples, and beans; toss to coat. Divide among 4 plates. Chop or crumble the bacon; sprinkle over servings.

(**SERVING SIZE:** 1¾ cups): **CALORIES** 299; **FAT** 12g (sat 3g, unsat 8g); **PROTEIN** 13g; **CARB** 37g; **FIBER** 11g; **SUGARS** 13g (added sugars 3g); **SODIUM** 686mg; **CALC** 10% DV; **POTASSIUM** 16% DV

BRUSSELS SPROUTS

While Brussels sprouts are available year-round, their peak season is from September to mid-February. Look for bright-green sprouts that are small and firm—the smaller they are, the sweeter. Avoid those that look soft, wilted, or dull in color.

The deep, earthy flavors of the steak and blue cheese are a perfect match for the classic balsamic vinaigrette and sweet sliced pear.

◀ STEAK *and* PEAR SALAD *with* BLUE CHEESE

HANDS-ON: 10 MIN. • TOTAL: 15 MIN. • SERVES 4

1   (1-pound) boneless sirloin steak
¾   teaspoon kosher salt, divided
¾   teaspoon black pepper, divided
Cooking spray
1½ tablespoons balsamic vinegar
3   tablespoons olive oil

1   (5-ounce) package baby romaine lettuce, roughly chopped
1   red Anjou pear, thinly sliced lengthwise (about 6 ounces)
1   ounce crumbled blue cheese (about ¼ cup)

1. Sprinkle the steak with ½ teaspoon each of the salt and pepper. Coat the steak with cooking spray. Heat a nonstick grill pan over medium-high; add the steak, and cook to the desired degree of doneness, 4 minutes per side for medium-rare. Remove and let rest 5 minutes. Cut the steak diagonally across the grain into thin slices.
2. Whisk together the balsamic vinegar and remaining ¼ teaspoon each salt and pepper in a large bowl. Slowly drizzle in the oil, whisking constantly until emulsified. Add the romaine, pear, and steak; toss with the dressing. Top with the blue cheese.

(**SERVING SIZE:** 1¼ cups salad and 3 ounces steak): **CALORIES** 313; **FAT** 21g (sat 6g, unsat 13g); **PROTEIN** 22g; **CARB** 9g; **FIBER** 2g; **SUGARS** 6g (added sugars 0g); **SODIUM** 506mg; **CALC** 6% DV; **POTASSIUM** 5% DV

WARM BEEF *and* CABBAGE SALAD

Cutting the steak into thin strips helps it cook quickly and brown nicely. The lime juice mixture softens and tenderizes the cabbage, resulting in a texture similar to a slaw.

HANDS-ON: 10 MIN. • TOTAL: 15 MIN. • SERVES 4

6   cups shredded napa cabbage
1   (1-pound) sirloin steak, trimmed
5   tablespoons fresh lime juice (from 2 limes)
1½ tablespoons lower-sodium soy sauce
1½ tablespoons sugar

1   teaspoon black pepper
2   tablespoons olive oil, divided
½   cup thinly sliced red onion (from 1 large)
2   garlic cloves, minced
¼   teaspoon kosher salt

1. Arrange the cabbage on a serving platter. Cut the steak into ⅛-inch-thick slices about 3 inches long; set aside.
2. Whisk together the lime juice, soy sauce, sugar, and pepper in a bowl; set aside.
3. Heat 1 tablespoon of the oil in a 10-inch cast-iron skillet over medium-high; add the onion to the hot oil; cook, stirring constantly, 2 minutes. Spoon onion over cabbage.
4. Return the pan to the heat; heat the remaining 1 tablespoon oil in the pan. Add the beef and garlic to the hot oil. Cook, stirring constantly, until the beef is browned and tender, about 3 minutes. Transfer to the lime juice mixture, and toss to coat. Top the cabbage and onion with the beef mixture. Sprinkle with the salt, and gently mix. Serve immediately.

(**SERVING SIZE:** 1½ cups): **CALORIES** 346; **FAT** 21g (sat 7g, unsat 12g); **PROTEIN** 25g; **CARB** 12g; **FIBER** 2g; **SUGARS** 7g (added sugars 5g); **SODIUM** 411mg; **CALC** 10% DV; **POTASSIUM** 12% DV

FIGS

Although fresh figs are used interchangeably in most recipes, each variety—Black Mission, Kadota, Brown Turkey, Calimyrna—has a subtle but distinctive flavor. Whichever variety you choose, select figs that are plump and heavy for their size and yield slightly with gentle pressure. The skin should be smooth and the fruit fragrant. Purchase ripe figs—the fruit doesn't always ripen well once harvested.

PEPPER-CRUSTED STEAK *and* FIG SALAD

Fresh figs are wonderful in this salad, but if you can't find them, use fresh sliced peaches instead.

HANDS-ON: 15 MIN. • TOTAL: 15 MIN. • SERVES 4

1   (12-ounce) beef strip steak, trimmed
1   teaspoon black pepper, divided
¾   teaspoon kosher salt, divided
2   tablespoons olive oil, divided
1   tablespoon Champagne vinegar

1   tablespoon honey
1   shallot, thinly sliced (about ⅓ cup)
1   (5-ounce) package baby arugula
6   fresh figs, quartered

1. Sprinkle the steak evenly with ¾ teaspoon of the pepper and ¼ teaspoon of the salt. Heat ½ tablespoon of the oil in a medium skillet over high. Add the steak to the pan, and cook until the desired degree of doneness, 2 to 3 minutes per side for medium. Transfer to a cutting board.
2. While the steak cooks, whisk together the vinegar, honey, and the remaining 1½ tablespoons oil, ½ teaspoon salt, and ¼ teaspoon pepper in a large bowl. Stir in the shallots.
3. Thinly slice the steak across the grain. Add the arugula to the shallot mixture, and toss to coat. Divide the salad among 4 plates. Top evenly with the figs and steak.

(**SERVING SIZE:** 1½ cups): **CALORIES** 342; **FAT** 17g (sat 5g, unsat 11g); **PROTEIN** 26g; **CARB** 23g; **FIBER** 3g; **SUGARS** 18g (added sugars 4g); **SODIUM** 423mg; **CALC** 10% DV; **POTASSIUM** 19% DV

FLANK STEAK PANZANELLA

This salad shines when made with fresh, in-season tomatoes. Use the freshest ones you can find (they don't have to be heirlooms), preferably locally grown for unrivaled flavor.

HANDS-ON: 25 MIN. • **TOTAL: 25 MIN.** • **SERVES 4**

1 (1-pound) flank steak, trimmed
½ teaspoon kosher salt, divided
½ teaspoon black pepper, divided
8 ounces whole-wheat baguette (or other crusty bread), torn into bite-sized pieces (about 4½ cups)

1 large heirloom tomato, chopped and juices reserved, divided (about 8 ounces)
2 tablespoons canola mayonnaise (such as Hellmann's)
4 cups baby spinach-and-arugula mix (about 4 ounces)

1. Preheat the oven to 400°F. While the oven preheats, heat a grill pan over medium-high. Sprinkle the steak with ¼ teaspoon each of the salt and pepper. Cook the steak in the grill pan to the degree of doneness, about 5 minutes per side for medium. Transfer to a cutting board.
2. Place the bread on a baking sheet, and bake in the preheated oven until toasted, about 10 minutes.
3. While the bread toasts, whisk together the reserved tomato juices, mayonnaise, and remaining ¼ teaspoon each salt and pepper in a large bowl. Stir in the spinach-and-arugula mix, chopped tomato, and bread; toss to coat. Divide among 4 plates. Slice the steak across the grain into thin strips, and divide among the servings.

(**SERVING SIZE:** 1¼ cups salad and 4 ounces steak): **CALORIES** 349; **FAT** 13g (sat 3g, unsat 7g); **PROTEIN** 30g; **CARB** 28g; **FIBER** 2g; **SUGARS** 2g (added sugars 0g); **SODIUM** 616mg; **CALC** 6% DV; **POTASSIUM** 11% DV

RAS EL HANOUT

Some versions of this North African spice blend featured heavily in Moroccan cooking can contain dozens of spices. It isn't a heat-heavy blend, but rather adds a warm, pungent flavor to dishes. An excellent rub on beef, chicken, or salmon, it can also perk up roasted vegetables or rice.

MOROCCAN COUSCOUS SALAD ▶

HANDS-ON: 10 MIN. • **TOTAL: 30 MIN.** • **SERVES 4**

1 (15-ounce) can no-salt-added chickpeas (garbanzo beans), drained, rinsed, and patted dry
1 cup thinly sliced red onion (from 1 onion)
1 teaspoon ras el hanout
2 tablespoons olive oil, divided

1½ cups uncooked whole-wheat Israeli (pearl) couscous
¼ cup pitted and halved Castelvetrano or picholine olives (about 9 olives)
½ teaspoon kosher salt
½ teaspoon black pepper
Chopped fresh cilantro (optional)

1. Preheat the oven to 425°F. Toss the chickpeas, onion, ras el hanout, and 1 tablespoon of the oil in a large bowl. Spread in an even layer on a rimmed baking sheet. Bake in the preheated oven until the chickpeas are crisp and the onion is tender, about 15 minutes, stirring after 10 minutes.
2. Prepare the couscous according to the package directions, omitting salt and fat. Drain. Transfer to a large bowl. Toss the couscous with the chickpea mixture, olives, salt, pepper, and the remaining 1 tablespoon oil. Sprinkle with the cilantro, if desired.

(**SERVING SIZE:** 1 cup): **CALORIES** 416; **FAT** 9g (sat 1g, unsat 6g); **PROTEIN** 14g; **CARB** 71g; **FIBER** 9g; **SUGARS** 2g (added sugars 0g); **SODIUM** 513mg; **CALC** 5% DV; **POTASSIUM** 7% DV

STEAK *and* MUSHROOM PASTA SALAD

Substitute top sirloin or thick flat iron steak if you can't find flank steak.

HANDS-ON: 15 MIN. • **TOTAL: 25 MIN.** • **SERVES 4**

8 ounces uncooked cavatappi pasta
8 ounces flank steak, trimmed
1¼ teaspoons black pepper, divided
1 teaspoon kosher salt, divided

3 tablespoons olive oil, divided
8 ounces sliced cremini mushrooms
½ cup low-fat buttermilk
2 cups arugula leaves (about 2 ounces)

1. Prepare the pasta according to the package directions in a large stockpot, omitting salt and fat. Drain and return to the stockpot.
2. Sprinkle the steak with ½ teaspoon each of the pepper and salt. Heat 1 tablespoon of the oil in a large nonstick skillet over medium-high. Add the steak, and cook to the desired degree of doneness, about 4 to 5 minutes per side for medium-rare. Remove and let rest 5 minutes. Cut the steak diagonally across the grain into thin slices.
3. Add the mushrooms to the skillet, and cook, stirring occasionally, until browned and the liquid evaporates, about 7 minutes.
4. Whisk together the buttermilk and remaining 2 tablespoons oil, ¾ teaspoon pepper, and ½ teaspoon salt in a large bowl. Add the pasta; toss to coat. Add the mushrooms, steak, and arugula; toss to coat.

(**SERVING SIZE:** about 1½ cups): **CALORIES** 410; **FAT** 15g (sat 3g, unsat 10g); **PROTEIN** 22g; **CARB** 47g; **FIBER** 3g; **SUGARS** 5g (added sugars 0g); **SODIUM** 577mg; **CALC** 9% DV; **POTASSIUM** 20% DV

The larger size of the Israeli couscous gives this salad more chew, and the olives add a hit of brininess. Serve it by itself or paired with seared fish or shrimp.

Cut the sweet potatoes into ½-inch cubes so that they cook evenly and quickly—larger pieces may take longer in the oven.

CHICKEN *and* SNAP PEA PASTA SALAD

Using fresh mint in this recipe is worth it—the flavor brightens the entire dish.

HANDS-ON: 15 MIN. • TOTAL: 15 MIN. • SERVES 6

8   ounces uncooked whole-grain orecchiette
    pasta
6   tablespoons canola mayonnaise (such as
    Hellmann's)
1½ tablespoons fresh lemon juice
2   teaspoons chopped fresh mint
1½ teaspoons grated garlic

¾   teaspoon kosher salt
¾   teaspoon black pepper
12 ounces shredded skinless rotisserie
    chicken breast (about 2½ cups)
8   ounces sugar snap peas, trimmed and cut
    into 1-inch pieces (about 2½ cups)
1   cup halved cherry tomatoes

1. Prepare the pasta according to the package directions, omitting salt and fat. Drain,
   and rinse under cold running water to cool quickly.
2. Whisk together the mayonnaise, lemon juice, mint, garlic, salt, and pepper in a
   bowl. Add the cooled pasta, chicken, sugar snap peas, and tomatoes; toss to coat.

(**SERVING SIZE:** about 1½ cups): **CALORIES** 341; **FAT** 14g (sat 1g, unsat 12g); **PROTEIN** 22g; **CARB** 33g; **FIBER** 5g;
SUGARS 4g (added sugars 0g); **SODIUM** 517mg; **CALC** 4% DV; **POTASSIUM** 13% DV

ROTISSERIE CHICKEN

Rotisserie chicken is a
key ingredient for busy
weeknight cooks—you'll
save time without
spending much more
than you would to buy
raw chicken. To quickly
shred the chicken, take
the whole breast off,
and then shred the
meat into pieces. If
you're managing your
sodium intake closely,
look for rotisserie
chicken labeled
"naked," which means
it doesn't have any salt
or pepper added to it.

◄ FARRO-SWEET POTATO SALAD

HANDS-ON: 30 MIN. • TOTAL: 30 MIN. • SERVES 4

Cooking spray
2   small sweet potatoes (about 6 ounces
    each), peeled and cubed
¼   cup olive oil, divided
¾   teaspoon black pepper, divided
½   teaspoon kosher salt, divided

2   (8½-ounce) packages precooked farro
1½ tablespoons country-style Dijon mustard
1   tablespoon red wine vinegar
4   large eggs
½   cup chopped fresh flat-leaf parsley leaves
    (optional)

1. Preheat the oven to 425°F. Line a rimmed baking sheet with aluminum foil and coat
   with cooking spray. Toss the potatoes with 1 tablespoon of the oil and ¼ teaspoon
   each of the pepper and salt. Place on the prepared pan. Roast the potatoes until
   golden and tender, about 15 minutes, stirring halfway through.
2. While the potatoes roast, prepare the farro according to the package directions; set
   aside. Whisk together the mustard, vinegar, 2 tablespoons of the oil, ¼ teaspoon of
   the pepper, and the remaining ¼ teaspoon salt in a large bowl; set aside.
3. Cool the potatoes on the baking sheet on a wire rack 5 minutes. While potatoes cool,
   heat remaining 1 tablespoon oil in a large nonstick skillet over medium-high. Add
   eggs to the skillet, 1 at a time; cook 2 minutes. Sprinkle with remaining ¼ teaspoon
   pepper. Cook, covered, to desired degree of doneness, about 1 minute more.
4. Add the farro, potatoes, and, if desired, parsley to the dressing, and toss to coat.
   Divide the salad among 4 plates; top with the eggs.

(**SERVING SIZE:** 1¼ cups salad and 1 egg): **CALORIES** 380; **FAT** 19g (sat 3g, unsat 14g); **PROTEIN** 12g; **CARB** 47g;
FIBER 7g; **SUGARS** 4g (added sugars 0g); **SODIUM** 497mg; **CALC** 7% DV; **POTASSIUM** 12% DV

CHAPTER 4

MEATLESS MAIN DISHES

BUTTERNUT SQUASH *and* BLACK BEAN RICE BOWL

This flavor-packed bowl uses butternut squash as its base, giving this Mexican-inspired dish a decidedly fall flair. Be sure to spread the squash in an even layer on the baking sheet so every piece gets a roasty finish.

HANDS-ON: 30 MIN. • **TOTAL: 30 MIN.** • **SERVES 4**

3 cups prechopped butternut squash (about 17 ounces)
1 tablespoon canola oil
¾ teaspoon kosher salt
¼ teaspoon black pepper
½ teaspoon chili powder
1 (15-ounce) can no-salt-added black beans, drained and rinsed

½ cup refrigerated salsa
2 (8.8-ounce) packages precooked microwavable brown rice (such as Uncle Ben's)
¼ cup low-fat sour cream (optional)
Chopped fresh cilantro (optional)

1. Preheat the oven to 425°F. Toss the squash with the canola oil, salt, pepper, and chili powder. Spread in an even layer on an aluminum foil–lined rimmed baking sheet, and bake in the preheated oven until tender and beginning to brown, about 15 minutes.
2. Place the beans and salsa in a microwavable bowl, and microwave on HIGH until hot, about 1 minute.
3. Heat the rice according to the package directions. Divide the rice, squash, and beans among 4 bowls. Top with the sour cream and cilantro, if desired.

(**SERVING SIZE:** about ½ cup rice, about ½ cup squash, and about ⅓ cup beans): **CALORIES** 337; **FAT** 6g (sat 0g, unsat 4g); **PROTEIN** 12g; **CARB** 63g; **FIBER** 10g; **SUGARS** 2g (added sugars 0g); **SODIUM** 529mg; **CALC** 10% DV; **POTASSIUM** 14% DV

COCONUT–BROWN RICE BOWLS
with BRUSSELS SPROUTS *and* SOY

The tangy, salty, slightly sweet dressing helps this bowl come together. It doesn't take long to thinly slice the Brussels sprouts, but be on the lookout for preshaved sprouts in your grocery store to save yourself some time; some larger supermarkets carry them.

HANDS-ON: 15 MIN. • TOTAL: 15 MIN. • SERVES 4

COCONUT MILK

There are two very different types of coconut milks in the supermarket, and each has its own purpose. The carton variety in the dairy case next to the soy milk, cow's milk, and nut milks has been diluted with water and is meant to be a drinkable milk. The canned version found on the same aisle as the soy sauce is rich and creamy, and makes appearances in a variety of dishes, including soups, sauces, and desserts. You need to shake the canned variety before using it to reincorporate it since the coconut milk and the cream separate when it sits.

3 tablespoons well-shaken canned coconut milk
2 tablespoons seasoned rice vinegar
2 tablespoons lower-sodium soy sauce
8 ounces fresh Brussels sprouts, trimmed and shaved (about 4 cups)
2 (8.8-ounce) packages precooked microwavable brown rice (such as Uncle Ben's)

1½ cups frozen shelled edamame, thawed
1 medium-sized red Fresno chile, thinly sliced crosswise
¼ teaspoon black pepper
1 medium-sized ripe avocado, diced
¼ teaspoon kosher salt
Sriracha chili sauce (optional)
Fresh cilantro leaves (optional)

1. Stir together the coconut milk, vinegar, and soy sauce in a small bowl. Remove ¼ cup of the mixture, and toss with the Brussels sprouts in a large bowl.
2. Prepare the rice according to the package directions; add to the Brussels sprouts. Fold in the edamame, sliced chile, and black pepper until combined. Sprinkle the avocado with the salt, and place on the Brussels sprouts mixture.
3. Drizzle the remaining dressing over the mixture. If desired, serve with Sriracha and cilantro.

(**SERVING SIZE:** 2 cups): **CALORIES** 390; **FAT** 15g (sat 3g, unsat 11g); **PROTEIN** 14g; **CARB** 55g; **FIBER** 11g; **SUGARS** 5g (added sugars 0g); **SODIUM** 672mg, **CALC** 7% DV; **POTASSIUM** 14% DV

SOUTHWESTERN BURRITO BOWL

Tossing the rice with some of the spiced dressing stretches out the flavor and amps up plain brown rice. If there are leftovers, you can serve it as a side dish with steak or grilled chicken.

HANDS-ON: 15 MIN. • TOTAL: 15 MIN. • SERVES 4

1   cup fresh yellow corn kernels (from about 2 ears)
1   (8.8-ounce) package precooked microwavable brown rice (such as Uncle Ben's)
¼   cup olive oil
2   tablespoons fresh lime juice (from 1 lime)
2   teaspoons honey
¾   teaspoon ancho chile powder
1   teaspoon kosher salt
½   teaspoon black pepper
1   cup drained and rinsed no-salt-added black beans
1   cup drained refrigerated pico de gallo
1   medium-sized ripe avocado, sliced
Fresh cilantro leaves (optional)
Light sour cream, lime wedges (optional)

1. Heat a medium or large cast-iron skillet over high. Add the corn; cook, stirring occasionally, until lightly charred, about 3 minutes. Set aside. Prepare the rice according to the package directions.
2. Whisk together the olive oil, lime juice, honey, chile powder, salt, and pepper in a small bowl; remove and reserve ¼ cup of the dressing mixture. Toss the remaining 2 tablespoons dressing with the rice; divide among 4 bowls. Divide the beans, corn, pico de gallo, and avocado among the bowls. Drizzle with the reserved dressing. If desired, sprinkle with the cilantro, and serve with the sour cream and lime wedges.

(**SERVING SIZE:** 6 tablespoons rice, ¼ cup beans, ¼ cup corn, ¼ cup pico, ¼ of the avocado, and 1 tablespoon dressing): **CALORIES** 532; **FAT** 23g (sat 3g, unsat 18g); **PROTEIN** 11g; **CARB** 76g; **FIBER** 10g; **SUGARS** 8g (added sugars 3g); **SODIUM** 698mg; **CALC** 4% DV; **POTASSIUM** 14% DV

PEARL COUSCOUS *with* CHICKPEAS *and* KALE

After simmering the couscous, it should still look wet when you remove the skillet lid. That's a good thing. You want some liquid left over in the pan. If not, the couscous will be overcooked and the kale won't wilt as well.

HANDS-ON: 15 MIN. • **TOTAL: 30 MIN.** • **SERVES 4**

¼ cup olive oil
½ cup chopped yellow onion (from 1 small onion)
1 cup uncooked Israeli (pearl) couscous (about 5 ounces)
½ teaspoon ground turmeric
2 cups water

1¼ teaspoons kosher salt
½ teaspoon black pepper
1 (15-ounce) can no-salt-added chickpeas (garbanzo beans), drained and rinsed
5 ounces baby kale, roughly chopped
Chopped fresh cilantro (optional)

Heat the oil in a large skillet over medium-high. Add the onion, and cook, stirring occasionally, until softened, about 4 minutes. Add the couscous and turmeric; cook, stirring often, until lightly toasted, 2 to 3 minutes. Stir in the water, salt, and pepper; bring to a boil. Cover and reduce the heat to medium-low. Simmer until the liquid is almost absorbed, about 12 minutes. Stir in the chickpeas and kale; cover and cook until the kale is wilted and the chickpeas are heated through, 2 to 3 minutes. Sprinkle with the cilantro, if desired.

(**SERVING SIZE:** 1¼ cups): **CALORIES** 377; **FAT** 15g (sat 2g, unsat 13g); **PROTEIN** 12g; **CARB** 49g; **FIBER** 6g; **SUGARS** 2g (added sugars 0g); **SODIUM** 646mg; **CALC** 17% DV; **POTASSIUM** 12% DV

QUICK-BRAISED BUTTER BEANS
with GOAT CHEESE POLENTA

This warm, hearty dish pairs creamy butter beans with polenta that has a subtle goat cheese flavor. It's sure to satisfy.

HANDS-ON: 15 MIN. • **TOTAL: 15 MIN.** • **SERVES 4**

2   tablespoons olive oil, divided
2   tablespoons sliced garlic (about 6 garlic cloves)
2   teaspoons paprika
2   teaspoons chopped fresh oregano
1   (26.46-ounce) container no-salt-added chopped tomatoes (such as Pomì)
2   (15-ounce) cans no-salt-added butter beans, rinsed and drained (such as Eden Organic)

¼   teaspoon black pepper
⅝   teaspoon kosher salt, divided
2   cups roughly chopped baby spinach (about 2 ounces)
3   cups water
¾   cup uncooked polenta (such as Bob's Red Mill Corn Grits/Polenta)
1   ounce creamy goat cheese, softened

1. Heat 1½ tablespoons of the oil in a large nonstick skillet over medium-high. Add the garlic, paprika, and oregano; cook, stirring constantly, until fragrant, about 1 minute. Add the tomatoes; reduce the heat to medium, and cook, stirring often, until reduced slightly, about 5 minutes.

2. Add the beans, pepper, and ½ teaspoon of the salt; cook, stirring occasionally, until the beans are coated, about 2 minutes. Add the spinach, and cook, stirring constantly, until wilted, about 2 minutes. Remove from the heat, and cover to keep warm.

3. Bring the water to a boil in a medium saucepan over high. Gradually whisk in the polenta, and cook, stirring occasionally, until the polenta pulls away from sides of the pan, about 5 minutes. Stir in the goat cheese and the remaining ⅛ teaspoon salt. Serve the beans over the polenta, and drizzle with the remaining ½ tablespoon oil.

(SERVING SIZE: ¾ cup polenta and 1 cup butter beans): **CALORIES** 396; **FAT** 10g (sat 2g, unsat 7g); **PROTEIN** 16g; **CARB** 60g; **FIBER** 12g; **SUGARS** 6g (added sugars 0g); **SODIUM** 410mg; **CALC** 7% DV; **POTASSIUM** 14% DV

WILTED KALE *over* WHITE BEAN PUREE

Soaking the shallot and garlic in sherry vinegar and hot water helps to soften the texture and mellow the flavor a bit so that they don't overwhelm the puree. You can substitute any hearty green for the kale, if you like. Serve this dish with crusty bread, naan, or pita bread to dip in the flavorful puree.

HANDS-ON: 15 MIN. • **TOTAL: 15 MIN.** • **SERVES 4**

2   tablespoons chopped shallots (from 1 shallot)
1   teaspoon chopped garlic (about 1 garlic clove)
1   tablespoon sherry vinegar
1   tablespoon hot water
3   tablespoons olive oil, divided
2   bunches (about 16 ounces) Lacinato kale, tough stems removed

1   teaspoon kosher salt, divided
2   teaspoons fresh lemon juice (from 1 lemon)
2   (15-ounce) cans no-salt-added cannellini beans, drained and rinsed
½   teaspoon black pepper
¼   cup pine nuts, toasted
¼   cup golden raisins

NO-SALT-ADDED BEANS

No-salt-added beans are readily available in grocery stores. Using them in recipes allows you to control the sodium and also season to the saltiness (or lack thereof) that suits your tastebuds.

1. Toss together the shallots, garlic, vinegar, and hot water in a small bowl, and let stand 10 minutes.
2. While the shallot mixture stands, heat 1 tablespoon of the oil in a large nonstick skillet over medium-high. Add the kale, in batches, and cook just until wilted after each addition, about 2 minutes. Sprinkle evenly with ¼ teaspoon of the salt, and drizzle with the lemon juice.
3. Place the shallot mixture, beans, and remaining 2 tablespoons oil and ¾ teaspoon salt in a food processor; add the pepper. Process until smooth, about 30 seconds, stopping to scrape down the sides as necessary.
4. Spread the bean puree on each of 4 plates. Top with the kale, pine nuts, and raisins.

(**SERVING SIZE:** ¾ cup bean mixture, 1 cup kale, 1 tablespoon pine nuts, and 1 tablesoon raisins): **CALORIES** 385; **FAT** 18g (sat 2g, unsat 15g); **PROTEIN** 14g; **CARB** 47g; **FIBER** 11g; **SUGARS** 9g (added sugars 0g); **SODIUM** 584mg; **CALC** 21% DV; **POTASSIUM** 16% DV

WHITE BEAN *and* ASPARAGUS FARRO

The velvety buttermilk dressing is a lovely pairing for the toothsome farro and the crisp asparagus. Substitute couscous or barley for the farro, if you like.

HANDS-ON: 15 MIN. • **TOTAL: 15 MIN.** • **SERVES 4**

1 cup uncooked quick-cooking farro (such as Trader Joe's 10-Minute Farro)
⅔ cup whole buttermilk
⅓ cup canola mayonnaise (such as Hellmann's)
1½ tablespoons fresh lemon juice (from 1 lemon)
1¼ teaspoons kosher salt
½ teaspoon black pepper
¼ cup chopped fresh dill, divided
1 pound fresh asparagus, thinly sliced on diagonal (about 2 cups)
1 (15-ounce) can no-salt-added cannellini beans, drained and rinsed
1 shallot, thinly sliced (about ⅓ cup)

1. Bring a large pot of water to a boil over high. Add the farro; cook until tender, about 10 minutes. Drain.
2. Whisk together the buttermilk, mayonnaise, lemon juice, salt, pepper, and 2 tablespoons of the dill in a large bowl. Add the cooked farro, asparagus, beans, and shallots to the dressing; toss to coat. Sprinkle with the remaining 2 tablespoons dill.

(**SERVING SIZE:** 1¼ cups): **CALORIES** 365; **FAT** 9g (sat 1g, unsat 6g); **PROTEIN** 16g; **CARB** 59g; **FIBER** 12g; **SUGARS** 6g (added sugars 0g); **SODIUM** 833mg; **CALC** 13% DV; **POTASSIUM** 16% DV

QUINOA *with* BLISTERED TOMATO SAUCE

The tangy tomato sauce is a tasty partner over any grain or pasta. Serve this with garlic bread or a simple side salad.

HANDS-ON: 15 MIN. • **TOTAL: 15 MIN.** • **SERVES 4**

2   tablespoons olive oil
4   cups cherry tomatoes (about 20 ounces)
2   garlic cloves, sliced
½   teaspoon smoked paprika
¼   teaspoon black pepper
½   teaspoon kosher salt, divided
½   cup unsalted chicken stock (such as Swanson)

3   tablespoons heavy cream
2   (8-ounce) packages precooked microwavable quinoa (such as Simply Balanced)
1.5 ounces Parmesan cheese, shaved (about ⅓ cup)
2   tablespoons chopped fresh flat-leaf parsley (optional)

1. Heat the oil in a large nonstick skillet over medium-high. Add the tomatoes, and cook until the tomatoes burst and begin to brown, about 5 minutes. Reduce the heat to medium, and add the garlic, paprika, pepper, and ¼ teaspoon of the salt, and cook until the garlic softens, about 1 minute. Add the chicken stock, and bring to a simmer, stirring constantly. Stir in the cream, and cook until thickened, about 1 minute.

2. Cook the quinoa according to the package directions; stir in the remaining ¼ teaspoon salt. Divide among 4 bowls. Top with the tomato-cream sauce, Parmesan, and, if desired, parsley.

(**SERVING SIZE:** 1 cup quinoa, ¾ cup cream sauce, and about 1 tablespoon parmesan): **CALORIES** 312; **FAT** 16g (sat 6g, unsat 10g); **PROTEIN** 11g; **CARB** 32g; **FIBER** 5g; **SUGARS** 5g (added sugars 0g); **SODIUM** 457mg; **CALC** 18% DV; **POTASSIUM** 17% DV

PAPPARDELLE *with* VEGETABLE RIBBONS, TOMATOES, *and* BURRATA

Tossing the carrot ribbons in the hot pasta water softens them a bit, but they still retain some bite. The olive oil and the juice from the lemon and tomatoes combine to create a light sauce that adds brightness while allowing the flavor of the fresh vegetables to shine.

HANDS-ON: 15 MIN. • TOTAL: 15 MIN. • SERVES 4

8 ounces uncooked pappardelle pasta
2 large carrots (about 8 ounces), peeled
1 medium zucchini (about 8 ounces)
1 pint cherry tomatoes, halved
1 teaspoon lemon zest plus 2 tablespoons fresh juice (from 1 lemon)
2 tablespoons extra-virgin olive oil
1⅛ teaspoons kosher salt
¼ teaspoon black pepper
4 ounces burrata cheese, torn
¼ cup unsalted dry-roasted pistachios, chopped
¼ cup loosely packed fresh flat-leaf parsley leaves

1. Cook the pasta according to the package directions, omitting salt and fat.
2. While the pasta cooks, using a vegetable peeler, shave long ribbons from the carrots and zucchini to equal 2 cups each. Just before draining the pasta, add the carrot ribbons, and stir 30 seconds. Drain the pasta mixture, and place in a large bowl with the zucchini ribbons, tomatoes, lemon zest, lemon juice, olive oil, salt, and pepper. Toss gently to coat.
3. Divide the mixture among 4 serving plates; top with the torn burrata, pistachios, and parsley.

(**SERVING SIZE:** 1¼ cups): **CALORIES** 452; **FAT** 19g (sat 6g, unsat 10g); **PROTEIN** 16g; **CARB** 53g; **FIBER** 5g; **SUGARS** 7g (added sugars 0g); **SODIUM** 657mg; **CALC** 22% DV; **POTASSIUM** 16% DV

BURRATA

This super-creamy, semi-soft Italian cheese has a rich, luscious, buttery flavor. It looks like a ball of fresh mozzarella, but when you cut into it, the solid outer curd gives way to a hollow interior filled with soft curd and fresh cream. You'll find it in 4- to 8-ounce bundles in the specialty cheeses section of the grocery store.

Spiralized sweet
potatoes can be
found in Whole Foods,
Trader Joe's, and large
supermarkets. If you
can't find them in your
grocery store, here's
how to make them
to get an amount
equivalent to the 2
(10.7-ounce) packages
used in this recipe:
Peel 2 large sweet
potatoes (about 14
ounces each); cut the
sweet potatoes into
long noodles using a
julienne peeler or a
spiralizer.

SWEET POTATO NOODLES
with EDAMAME and TAHINI-MISO SAUCE

Be sure to use a gentle hand when tossing the noodles with the dressing
to prevent them from breaking.

HANDS-ON: 15 MIN. • **TOTAL: 15 MIN.** • **SERVES 4**

3 tablespoons water
2 tablespoons tahini
2 tablespoons white miso
2 tablespoons honey
1 teaspoon grated fresh ginger
½ teaspoon kosher salt
2 (10.7-ounce) packages sweet potato
  noodles (spiralized sweet potatoes; such
  as Veggie Noodle Co.)

1 cup frozen shelled edamame, thawed
¼ cup thinly sliced scallions (white and
  green parts only; about 3 scallions)
1 tablespoon toasted white and black
  sesame seeds

Stir together the water, tahini, miso, honey, ginger, and salt in a small bowl until
smooth. Place the noodles and edamame in a large bowl; drizzle with the tahini
mixture, and toss until well coated. Top with the scallions and sesame seeds. Serve
at room temperature or cold.

(**SERVING SIZE:** 1⅔ cups): **CALORIES** 289; **FAT** 7g (sat 1g, unsat 6g); **PROTEIN** 10g; **CARB** 48g; **FIBER** 8g; **SUGARS** 18g
(added sugars 9g); **SODIUM** 567mg; **CALC** 10% DV; **POTASSIUM** 17% DV

This noodle bowl is also tasty cold, making these leftovers a welcome lunch the next day. Garnish with fresh cilantro, if you like.

PAN-ROASTED CAULIFLOWER PASTA with PINE NUTS and ARUGULA

Be sure to cut larger cauliflower florets in half so they cook evenly in the pan.

HANDS-ON: 15 MIN. • **TOTAL: 15 MIN.** • **SERVES 4**

12 ounces uncooked whole-grain penne pasta
3 tablespoons extra-virgin olive oil, divided
1 (10-ounce) package fresh cauliflower florets
2 tablespoons refrigerated garlic paste
¼ teaspoon crushed red pepper (optional)
⅝ teaspoon kosher salt
½ teaspoon black pepper
1 (5-ounce) package baby arugula
3 tablespoons fresh lemon juice
¼ cup pine nuts, toasted

1. Cook the pasta according to the package directions, omitting salt and fat. Drain, reserving ½ cup cooking water.
2. Heat 1 tablespoon of the oil in a large high-sided skillet over medium-high. Add the cauliflower to the pan, and cook, without stirring, until light golden, about 2 minutes. Stir and cook, without stirring, until fully golden, about 2 more minutes. Transfer to a plate.
3. Add the garlic paste, remaining 2 tablespoons oil, and, if desired, crushed red pepper. Cook, stirring constantly, until fragrant, about 1 minute. Add the pasta; stir to coat. Add the cauliflower; stir in the cooking water, salt, and pepper. Cook, stirring occasionally, until thickened, about 1 minute. Transfer the mixture to a bowl; add the arugula and lemon juice, and stir until the arugula wilts. Top with the pine nuts.

(SERVING SIZE: 3 cups): **CALORIES** 534; **FAT** 23g (sat 3g, unsat 19g); **PROTEIN** 14g; **CARB** 71g; **FIBER** 10g; **SUGARS** 6g (added sugars 0g); **SODIUM** 661mg; **CALC** 11% DV; **POTASSIUM** 21% DV

◄ SOBA NOODLES and EDAMAME BOWL

HANDS-ON: 15 MIN. • **TOTAL: 15 MIN.** • **SERVES 4**

6 ounces uncooked soba noodles
1½ cups frozen shelled edamame, thawed
1 cup matchstick carrots
3 tablespoons white miso
3 tablespoons seasoned rice vinegar
1½ tablespoons sesame oil
1½ tablespoons water
1 cup thinly sliced red cabbage (from ¼ head)
1 teaspoon toasted sesame seeds
Lime wedges (optional)

1. Bring a large pot of water to a boil over high. Add noodles and edamame; cook until tender, about 3 minutes, adding carrots during last 1 minute of cook time. Drain.
2. Whisk together the miso, rice vinegar, sesame oil, and water in a bowl. Add the noodle mixture and cabbage. Sprinkle with sesame seeds. Serve with lime wedges, if desired.

(SERVING SIZE: about 1 cup): **CALORIES** 330; **FAT** 8g (sat 1g, unsat 6g); **PROTEIN** 17g; **CARB** 52g; **FIBER** 6g; **SUGARS** 8g (added sugars 0g); **SODIUM** 688mg; **CALC** 6% DV; **POTASSIUM** 5% DV

CHERRY TOMATO, OLIVE, *and* SPINACH PASTA

While the pasta cooks, you can prepare the rest of the ingredients for this speedy dish. The olives and feta add wonderful briny flavor to the creamy beans and fresh tomatoes.

HANDS-ON: 15 MIN. • TOTAL: 15 MIN. • SERVES 4

6   ounces uncooked whole-wheat farfalle pasta

3   tablespoons extra-virgin olive oil

¼   cup finely chopped red onion (from 1 small onion)

2   tablespoons red wine vinegar

¼   teaspoon kosher salt

¼   teaspoon black pepper

1   (15-ounce) can no-salt-added white beans, drained and rinsed

2½ cups baby spinach, roughly chopped (about 2½ ounces)

2   cups multicolored cherry tomatoes, halved

4   ounces pitted kalamata olives, quartered (about ¾ cup)

2   ounces crumbled feta cheese (about ¼ cup)

1. Cook the pasta according to the package directions, omitting salt and fat, until al dente, about 11 minutes; drain. Place in a large bowl.

2. Whisk together the olive oil, onion, vinegar, salt, and pepper in a small bowl; add to the pasta. Add the beans, spinach, tomatoes, olives, and feta, and toss to combine.

(**SERVING SIZE:** 2 cups): **CALORIES** 476; **FAT** 23g (sat 5g, unsat 17g); **PROTEIN** 17g; **CARB** 51g; **FIBER** 9g; **SUGARS** 5g (added sugars 0g); **SODIUM** 796mg; **CALC** 17% DV; **POTASSIUM** 12% DV

Broccolini is a wonderful—and colorful—textural contrast to the tortellini. The red pepper flakes add a tiny hit of heat. Use whatever brand of cheese tortellini you prefer or can find, and feel free to use varieties with different fillings to change this dish up.

CARAMELIZED CABBAGE STROGANOFF

You can spread the cabbage on anything flat to cool—a baking sheet, cutting board, large serving dish, or aluminum foil.

HANDS-ON: 20 MIN. • TOTAL: 20 MIN. • SERVES 4

8   ounces uncooked egg noodles
2   tablespoons canola oil
3   cups roughly chopped cabbage
1   teaspoon kosher salt, divided

1   tablespoon all-purpose flour
½   cup unsalted vegetable stock
½   cup low-fat sour cream
½   teaspoon black pepper

1. Cook the noodles according to the package directions, omitting salt and fat. Drain, reserving ½ cup cooking water.
2. Heat the oil in a large nonstick skillet over medium-high. Add the cabbage to the pan; sprinkle with ½ teaspoon salt. Cook, stirring occasionally, until golden, about 7 minutes. Spread in a single layer on a baking sheet, and cool 10 minutes.
3. Reduce the heat to medium. Add the flour to the pan, and cook, stirring constantly, until fragrant, about 1 minute. Add the stock; bring to a simmer. Cook, stirring constantly, until slightly thickened, about 2 minutes. Stir in the sour cream, pepper, and remaining ½ teaspoon salt; cook, stirring constantly, until smooth and bubbly, about 1 minute. Stir in the cabbage, and cook until the cabbage is hot, about 2 minutes. If the mixture is too thick, stir in the reserved cooking water, 3 tablespoons at a time, until the desired consistency is reached. Serve over the hot egg noodles.

(SERVING SIZE: ¾ cup noodles and about ¾ cup cabbage mixture): **CALORIES** 353; **FAT** 13g (sat 3g, unsat 8g); **PROTEIN** 11g; **CARB** 48g; **FIBER** 4g; **SUGARS** 7g (added sugars 0g); **SODIUM** 600mg; **CALC** 10% DV; **POTASSIUM** 5% DV

◀ TORTELLINI *with* SPICY BROCCOLINI

HANDS-ON: 10 MIN. • TOTAL: 20 MIN. • SERVES 4

12 ounces refrigerated cheese tortellini
2   tablespoons olive oil, divided
12 ounces Broccolini
1   tablespoon water
½   cup thinly sliced red onion

2   teaspoons sliced garlic
¼   teaspoon crushed red pepper
¼   teaspoon kosher salt
¼   teaspoon black pepper
    Parmesan cheese, shaved (optional)

1. Cook the tortellini according to the package directions, omitting salt and fat.
2. Meanwhile, heat 1 tablespoon oil in a large nonstick skillet over medium-high. Add the Broccolini and water; cook, covered, until tender, about 4 minutes. Add the onion, garlic, crushed red pepper, salt, and black pepper, and cook, uncovered until the Broccolini just begins to brown and the onion is tender, about 4 minutes.
3. Drain the pasta well, and toss with the remaining 1 tablespoon oil. Divide among 4 bowls, and top with the Broccolini mixture. Top with shaved Parmesan, if desired.

(SERVING SIZE: 1 cup pasta and ¾ cup Broccolini mixture): **CALORIES** 360; **FAT** 13g (sat 4g, unsat 8g); **PROTEIN** 15g; **CARB** 48g; **FIBER** 4g; **SUGARS** 6g (added sugars 0g); **SODIUM** 531mg; **CALC** 19% DV; **POTASSIUM** 9% DV

BUTTERNUT *and* GNOCCHI SKILLET

Make sure you spread the gnocchi in the skillet to cook so they each have the needed room to brown in the pan. Top with hazelnuts instead of walnuts, if you like.

HANDS-ON: 15 MIN. • TOTAL: 15 MIN. • SERVES 4

PREPARED PESTO

Refrigerated pesto is a powerhouse ingredient for the quick cook, adding a hefty dose of flavor and richness. Toss it with pasta or roasted potatoes, use it on pizzas, as a sandwich spread by itself or stirred into mayonnaise, or serve over grilled chicken or shrimp.

3   cups ½-inch cubed butternut squash (about 1 pound)
2   tablespoons olive oil
12 ounces whole-wheat potato gnocchi (such as Gia Russa)
¾   cup unsalted vegetable stock (such as Swanson)
1   (5-ounce) package baby spinach, roughly chopped
¼   cup refrigerated basil pesto
1   ounce Parmesan cheese, shaved (about ¼ cup)
¼   cup chopped walnuts, toasted
Fresh basil leaves (optional)

1. Place the squash in a steamer basket set over ½ inch of simmering water in a medium saucepan; cover and cook until tender, about 5 minutes.
2. Meanwhile, heat the oil in a large skillet over medium. Add the gnocchi to the skillet; cook, stirring occasionally, until lightly browned, about 2 minutes. Stir in the vegetable stock. Cover and cook until the gnocchi is tender and the liquid is absorbed, about 4 minutes. Stir in the squash, spinach, and pesto; cook, stirring occasionally, until the spinach is wilted, about 1 minute. Top with the Parmesan and walnuts. Sprinkle with basil, if desired.

(**SERVING SIZE:** about 1 cup): **CALORIES** 405; **FAT** 21g (sat 4g, unsat 15g); **PROTEIN** 10g; **CARB** 45g; **FIBER** 10g; **SUGARS** 4g (added sugars 0g); **SODIUM** 626mg; **CALC** 19% DV; **POTASSIUM** 12% DV

SPAGHETTI SQUASH *with* CHARRED MUSHROOMS *and* RICOTTA

Thanks to the spaghetti squash base, this earthy dish feels rich without being too heavy. If you have trouble finding the oyster mushrooms, use shiitake or a mixed blend instead.

HANDS-ON: 30 MIN. • TOTAL: 30 MIN. • SERVES 4

1   (2- to 3-pound) spaghetti squash, halved lengthwise and seeded
½   cup water
1   teaspoon kosher salt, divided
1   teaspoon black pepper, divided
¼   cup olive oil, divided

1   pound fresh oyster mushrooms, cut into large pieces
8   ounces part-skim ricotta cheese
1   cup lower-sodium marinara sauce (such as Dell'Amore), warmed
¼   cup fresh basil leaves

1. Place 1 squash half, cut side down, in an 11- x 7-inch microwavable baking dish; add ¼ cup water, and cover with plastic wrap. Microwave on HIGH until tender, 10 to 12 minutes. Remove carefully, and repeat with the remaining squash half. Using a fork, scrape the flesh from the squash halves to make spaghetti-like strands, and place in a bowl. Sprinkle with ½ teaspoon each of the salt and pepper. Cover with aluminum foil to keep warm.

2. While the squash cooks, heat a large cast-iron skillet over medium-high; add 2 tablespoons of the oil, and swirl to coat. Add the mushrooms, and cook, stirring occasionally, until browned and tender, about 7 minutes. Stir in the remaining ½ teaspoon each of the salt and pepper. Stir the mushrooms into the squash.

3. Stir together the ricotta and the remaining 2 tablespoons oil in a small bowl. Swirl the marinara sauce and ricotta mixture into the squash. Top with the basil. Serve immediately.

(**SERVING SIZE:** about 1½ cups): **CALORIES** 331; **FAT** 19g (sat 5g, unsat 13g); **PROTEIN** 13g; **CARB** 33g; **FIBER** 7g; **SUGARS** 12g (added sugars 0g); **SODIUM** 617mg; **CALC** 24% DV; **POTASSIUM** 24% DV

SPAGHETTI SQUASH

This aptly named vegetable is a wonderful substitute for pasta—tender, sweet, and filling—and has significantly fewer calories and carbs. Cooking it in the microwave (as we've done in this recipe) has speedier results, but you can also prepare it in the oven. Here's how: Place the halved, deseeded squash halves, cut sides down, in a baking dish. Fill the dish with ½ cup of water, and bake at 350°F for 45 to 50 minutes or until tender. Remove the squash from the oven, turn the cut sides up, and let cool for 10 minutes. Then, scrape the insides with a fork to remove the spaghetti-like strands.

SWEET POTATOES
with BLACK BEANS *and* CORN

Steaming the potatoes in the microwave is much quicker than baking them in the oven. Pair these stuffed potatoes with a simple, fresh salad.

HANDS-ON: 10 MIN. • **TOTAL: 15 MIN.** • **SERVES 4**

4   (6-ounce) sweet potatoes
¼   cup water
1   (15-ounce) can no-salt-added black beans, drained and rinsed
1   cup frozen corn kernels (about 4 ounces), thawed
1   cup chopped tomato (about 6 ounces)
½   cup finely chopped red onion (from 1 medium onion)

2   teaspoons fresh lime juice (from 1 lime)
1   teaspoon ground cumin
¾   teaspoon kosher salt
½   teaspoon black pepper
3   ounces Monterey Jack cheese, shredded (about ¾ cup), divided
Light sour cream (optional)
Diced avocado (optional)
Fresh cilantro leaves (optional)

1. Preheat the broiler to high with the oven rack 5 inches from the heat. Prick the potatoes several times with a fork. Place the potatoes in a shallow microwavable dish; add the water. Cover with plastic wrap. Microwave on HIGH until the potatoes are tender, about 11 minutes. Cool in the dish 2 minutes. Cut a lengthwise slit in the potatoes. Push the ends to open slightly.
2. Stir together the black beans, corn, tomato, red onion, lime juice, cumin, salt, pepper, and ½ cup of the cheese in a medium bowl.
3. Place the sweet potatoes in a broiler-safe pan. Spoon the black bean mixture into the sweet potatoes, and top evenly with the remaining ¼ cup shredded cheese. Broil until warmed through and the cheese is melted, 2 to 3 minutes. If desired, dollop with sour cream, and top with avocado and cilantro.

(**SERVING SIZE:** 1 stuffed sweet potato): **CALORIES** 367; **FAT** 7g (sat 4g, unsat 3g); **PROTEIN** 16g; **CARB** 63g; **FIBER** 12g; **SUGARS** 11g (added sugars 0g); **SODIUM** 599mg; **CALC** 27% DV; **POTASSIUM** 31% DV

JACKFRUIT "CRAB" CAKES

Unripe jackfruit tastes like briny artichoke hearts and has a firm, meaty texture. (See the box at right for more information.) Use the large holes of a box grater to quickly shred the hard-cooked eggs. You can serve the cakes with a homemade dipping sauce, if you like: Combine ¼ cup fat-free Greek yogurt, 2 tablespoons stoneground mustard, 1 teaspoon fresh lemon juice, and ¼ teaspoon each of salt and pepper.

HANDS-ON: 20 MIN. • TOTAL: 20 MIN. • SERVES 4

2 (14-ounce) cans jackfruit in brine, drained and rinsed

5 large hard-cooked eggs, peeled and shredded

¼ cup canola mayonnaise (such as Hellmann's)

2 tablespoons chopped fresh dill

½ teaspoon black pepper

¾ cup panko (Japanese-style breadcrumbs), divided

3 tablespoons olive oil

1. Finely chop the jackfruit. Combine the jackfruit, eggs, mayonnaise, dill, pepper, and ½ cup of the panko in a large bowl; stir well to combine. Shape into 8 (3-inch) patties.

2. Heat the oil in a large nonstick skillet over medium-high; sprinkle 1 side of each cake with 1½ teaspoons panko, pressing to adhere. Place the cakes in the pan, panko side down. Cook until golden, about 4 minutes. Sprinkle the remaining panko on the cakes, and flip. Cook until golden brown, about 4 minutes. Serve immediately.

(SERVING SIZE: 2 cakes): **CALORIES** 371; **FAT** 25g (sat 3g, unsat 20g); **PROTEIN** 9g; **CARB** 22g; **FIBER** 3g; **SUGARS** 1g (added sugars 0g); **SODIUM** 648mg; **CALC** 9% DV; **POTASSIUM** 3% DV

Jackfruit grows prolifically in hot, tropical climates like southeast Asia, South America, and the Caribbean. The starchy unripe green fruit is a bit stringy and tastes similar to artichoke hearts—you'll find it in curries and as a vegan meat substitute in the U.S. (often referred to as "vegan pulled pork"). The ripe fruit has a sweet, bright, banana-like flavor and often makes appearances in desserts or is eaten fresh on its own. You can find it canned and fresh at Asian markets and Whole Foods.

SPICY LETTUCE CUPS ▶

HANDS-ON: 15 MIN. • **TOTAL: 15 MIN.** • **SERVES 4**

¼ cup extra-virgin olive oil
3 tablespoons fresh lime juice (from 2 limes)
1 tablespoon honey
1 tablespoon sambal oelek (ground fresh chili paste)
¾ teaspoon kosher salt
2 cups broccoli slaw

¾ cup lightly salted dry-roasted peanuts, chopped (about 3½ ounces)
1½ cups sliced fresh mango (from 1 medium mango)
1 medium-sized ripe avocado, sliced
Fresh cilantro leaves (optional)
8 large Bibb lettuce leaves (from 1 head)

Whisk together the olive oil, lime juice, honey, sambal oelek, and salt in a bowl; remove and reserve ¼ cup of dressing mixture. Toss together the broccoli slaw, peanuts, and remaining dressing mixture in a bowl. Divide the broccoli mixture, mango, avocado, and, if desired, cilantro among the lettuce leaves. Drizzle with the reserved dressing.

(SERVING SIZE: 2 lettuce cups): CALORIES 423; **FAT** 34g (sat 5g, unsat 26g); **PROTEIN** 10g; **CARB** 26g; **FIBER** 8g; **SUGARS** 15g (added sugars 4g); **SODIUM** 545mg; **CALC** 6% DV; **POTASSIUM** 12% DV

LEEK *and* MANCHEGO FRITTATA

A lightly dressed arugula salad is served with the cheesy frittata. It is slightly bitter, a little tart, and very fresh—the perfect complement to the entrée.

HANDS-ON: 15 MIN. • **TOTAL: 15 MIN.** • **SERVES 4**

8 large eggs
⅓ cup 2% reduced-fat milk
¼ teaspoon black pepper
½ teaspoon kosher salt, divided
2 tablespoons olive oil, divided
1 large leek, sliced (about 1 cup sliced)

1 teaspoon chopped garlic (from 1 garlic clove)
1 ounce Manchego cheese, shredded (about ¼ cup)
4 cups arugula (about 3 ounces)
2 teaspoons fresh lemon juice (from 1 lemon)

1. Preheat the broiler with the oven rack 6 inches from the heat. Whisk together the eggs, milk, pepper, and ¼ teaspoon of the salt in a large bowl; set aside.
2. Heat 1 tablespoon of the oil in a 10-inch ovenproof nonstick skillet over medium-high. Add the sliced leek, and cook, stirring constantly, until softened and beginning to brown, about 6 minutes. Add the garlic, and cook, stirring constantly, 1 minute. Reduce the heat to medium-low, and slowly pour the egg mixture into the pan; sprinkle with the cheese. Cook, stirring constantly, until the mixture just begins to set, about 1 minute. Continue to cook, without stirring, until the mixture is just set, about 6 more minutes. Transfer the pan to the preheated oven, and broil until the top is lightly brown, about 2 minutes.
3. Toss together the arugula, lemon juice, and remaining 1 tablespoon oil and ¼ teaspoon salt. Cut the frittata into 4 wedges, and serve with the salad.

(SERVING SIZE: ¼ frittata and 1 cup salad): CALORIES 266; **FAT** 20g (sat 6g, unsat 12g); **PROTEIN** 16g; **CARB** 6g; **FIBER** 1g; **SUGARS** 3g (added sugars 0g); **SODIUM** 463mg; **CALC** 21% DV; **POTASSIUM** 8% DV

These lettuce cups are wonderfully multi-textured: the fresh lettuce and slaw provide crispness, the buttery avocado lends creaminess, the mango adds just the right amount of sweet acidity, and the peanuts give good crunchiness. Look for the colorful broccoli slaw variety that has carrots and red cabbage in it.

MUSHROOM *and* SWISS CHARD TARTINE

Use rustic, not sandwich, bread for this savory toast. You can substitute sliced cremini mushrooms if you can't find the wild mushroom blend.

HANDS-ON: 15 MIN. • **TOTAL: 15 MIN.** • **SERVES 2**

1 tablespoon olive oil

4 ounces sliced gourmet wild mushroom blend

2 ounces green Swiss chard, torn (about 2 cups)

2 garlic cloves, sliced

¼ teaspoon kosher salt

⅛ teaspoon crushed red pepper

1 teaspoon fresh lemon juice (from 1 lemon)

4 ounces whole-milk ricotta cheese (about ½ cup)

4 (1-ounce) whole-wheat rustic bread slices, toasted

⅛ teaspoon cracked black pepper

1. Heat the olive oil in a large nonstick skillet over medium-high. Add the mushrooms; cook, stirring occasionally, until tender and browned, about 4 minutes. Add the chard, garlic, salt, and crushed red pepper; cook, stirring often until the chard is tender, 1 to 2 minutes. Drizzle with the lemon juice.

2. Spread the ricotta evenly on the toasts; top evenly with the mushroom mixture. Sprinkle with the cracked black pepper.

(**SERVING SIZE:** 2 toasts): **CALORIES** 340; **FAT** 16g (sat 6g, unsat 9g); **PROTEIN** 14g; **CARB** 34g; **FIBER** 4g; **SUGARS** 7g (added sugars 0g); **SODIUM** 549mg; **CALC** 22% DV; **POTASSIUM** 10% DV

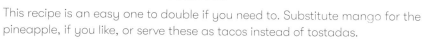

BLACK BEAN TOSTADAS *with* PINEAPPLE SALSA

This recipe is an easy one to double if you need to. Substitute mango for the pineapple, if you like, or serve these as tacos instead of tostadas.

HANDS-ON: 12 MIN. • TOTAL: 12 MIN. • SERVES 2

1 cup chopped fresh pineapple (from 1 small pineapple)
¼ cup chopped red onion (from 1 small onion)
2 tablespoons chopped fresh cilantro
1 tablespoon fresh lime juice (from 1 lime)
1 (15-ounce) can no-salt-added black beans, undrained
2 teaspoons hot sauce (such as Valentina)
2 teaspoons olive oil
¼ teaspoon kosher salt
4 corn tostada shells
1 ounce queso fresco (fresh Mexican cheese), crumbled (about 2 tablespoons)

1. Stir together the pineapple, red onion, cilantro, and lime juice in a small bowl. Set aside.
2. Heat a large nonstick skillet over medium. Add the beans, hot sauce, oil, and salt; cook, stirring often and mashing the beans, until thickened, about 4 minutes.
3. Spread ¼ cup of the black bean mixture on each tostada shell; top with the pineapple mixture, and sprinkle with the queso fresco.

(SERVING SIZE: 2 tostadas): CALORIES 404; FAT 15g (sat 4g, unsat 10g); PROTEIN 16g; CARB 56g; FIBER 13g; SUGARS 10g (added sugars 0g); SODIUM 574mg; CALC 21% DV; POTASSIUM 18% DV

TOSTADA SHELLS

These crispy shells are pretty widely available these days—you'll usually find them in the international aisle—but you can always make them yourself. Simply brush both sides of each corn tortilla with oil or spray with cooking spray and sprinkle with a little salt. Place the oiled tortillas in a single layer on a baking sheet and bake at 450°F for 5 minutes on each side or until crisp.

PEACH *and* BURRATA PIZZA

The pizza is at its prime when you use fresh in-season peaches. The optional arugula and balsamic glaze push it over the edge.

HANDS-ON: 15 MIN. • **TOTAL: 30 MIN.** • **SERVES 4**

1 pound refrigerated fresh whole-wheat pizza dough
Cooking spray
1 tablespoon all-purpose flour
1½ tablespoons extra-virgin olive oil, divided
2½ cups fresh peach slices (from 2 peaches)

1 cup halved cherry tomatoes
4 ounces burrata cheese, torn
¼ teaspoon kosher salt
¼ teaspoon black pepper
Baby arugula (optional)
Balsamic glaze (optional)

1. Place the dough in a bowl coated with cooking spray, turning to coat all sides. Cover and let stand 15 minutes. Place a rectangular pizza stone or baking sheet in a cold oven; preheat the oven to 500°F. (Do not remove the pizza stone while the oven preheats.)
2. Sprinkle the flour on parchment paper. Place the dough on the parchment, and roll into a 15- x 8-inch rectangle or oval. Pierce the dough well with a fork. Place the parchment and dough on the preheated stone; bake at 500°F until lightly browned, 5 to 7 minutes.
3. Brush the pizza crust with 1 tablespoon of the oil; top with the peaches, tomatoes, and burrata; sprinkle with the salt and pepper. Bake until the toppings are heated through and the cheese is melted, 3 to 4 minutes. Drizzle with the remaining 1½ teaspoons oil. If desired, top with arugula and balsamic glaze.

(**SERVING SIZE:** 2 slices): **CALORIES** 420; **FAT** 16g (sat 5g, unsat 9g); **PROTEIN** 13g; **CARB** 60g; **FIBER** 6g; **SUGARS** 10g (added sugars 1g); **SODIUM** 673mg; **CALC** 16% DV; **POTASSIUM** 8% DV

SEITAN SATAY KEBABS

The nutty, tangy dipping sauce elevates these skewers to something special.

HANDS-ON: 15 MIN. • TOTAL: 15 MIN. • SERVES 4

2   tablespoons canola oil
1   tablespoon seasoned rice vinegar
1   tablespoon fresh lime juice (from 1 lime)
2   teaspoons lower-sodium soy sauce
2   teaspoons minced garlic

1   teaspoon Sriracha chili sauce
1   (1-pound) package chicken-style seitan (such as Tofurky Slow-Roasted Chick'n)
2   tablespoons creamy peanut butter
2   tablespoons water

1. Preheat the grill to medium-high (400°F to 450°F) or heat a grill pan over medium-high. Stir together the oil, vinegar, lime juice, soy sauce, garlic, and Sriracha in a bowl. Remove and reserve 2 tablespoons of the mixture. Pour the remaining 2½ tablespoons into a ziplock plastic bag; add the seitan. Let stand at room temperature about 5 minutes.
2. Stir the peanut butter and water into the reserved vinegar mixture. Set aside.
3. Remove the seitan strips from the marinade, and thread onto 8 (8-inch) skewers. Grill, uncovered, until charred, about 5 minutes, turning halfway through grilling. Serve with the peanut sauce.

(SERVING SIZE: 2 kebabs and 1 tablespoon sauce): CALORIES 200; FAT 9g (sat 1g, unsat 8g); PROTEIN 20g; CARB 11g; FIBER 1g; SUGARS 1g (added sugars 0g); SODIUM 638mg; CALC 4% DV; POTASSIUM 0% DV

RICOTTA *and* ZUCCHINI FLATBREAD ▶

Whole-wheat naan is widely available in large supermarkets. It can burn quickly under the broiler, so be sure to keep your eye on it.

HANDS-ON: 15 MIN. • TOTAL: 15 MIN. • SERVES 4

2   whole-wheat naan (about 8.8 ounces)
2   tablespoons olive oil, divided
4½ ounces part-skim ricotta cheese
⅜   teaspoon kosher salt
¼   teaspoon black pepper
2   small zucchini, cut into thin ribbons (about 10 ounces)

1½ cups cherry tomatoes (about 12 ounces), halved
1   ounce crumbled goat cheese (about ¼ cup)
2   tablespoons fresh basil leaves (optional)

1. Preheat the broiler with the oven rack 5 inches from the heat. Brush the naan with 1 tablespoon oil; place on a baking sheet. Broil until lightly toasted, 1 minute per side.
2. Spread the ricotta over the warm naan. Sprinkle with the salt and pepper. Top with the zucchini, tomatoes, and goat cheese. Return to the oven, and broil just until the topping begins to brown, about 3 minutes. Drizzle with the remaining 1 tablespoon olive oil, and, if desired, top with the basil. Cut each naan in half.

(SERVING SIZE: ½ naan): CALORIES 310; FAT 14g (sat 5g, unsat 9g); PROTEIN 13g; CARB 35g; FIBER 4g; SUGARS 6g (added sugars 1g); SODIUM 590mg; CALC 12% DV; POTASSIUM 12% DV

Serve these flatbreads as a main dish or an appetizer garnished with sliced scallions.

TOFU *and* PEPPER STIR-FRY

The key with any stir-fry is to have all your ingredients prepped and ready to go since the process is more hands-on than other cooking methods. Two medium-sized bell peppers will yield about 3 cups of slices.

HANDS-ON: 15 MIN. • TOTAL: 15 MIN. • SERVES 4

2 (8.8-ounce) packages precooked microwavable brown rice (such as Uncle Ben's)
1 tablespoon canola oil
12 ounces extra-firm tofu, drained, patted dry, and diced
1 medium-sized red bell pepper, cut into strips
1 medium-sized green bell pepper, cut into strips

1 small yellow onion, sliced
3 tablespoons lower-sodium soy sauce
1 tablespoon hoisin sauce
2 tablespoons water
2 tablespoons fresh cilantro leaves
1 tablespoon Sriracha chili sauce (optional)

1. Prepare the rice according to the package directions.
2. Meanwhile, heat the oil in a large nonstick skillet over medium-high. Add the tofu, and cook, stirring often, until beginning to brown, about 3 minutes. Add the bell peppers, onion, soy sauce, hoisin, and water. Cook, stirring often, until the peppers and onion soften and begin to brown, about 5 minutes.
3. Place the rice on a large rimmed serving platter. Top with the tofu mixture, and sprinkle with the cilantro. Serve with Sriracha, if desired.

(**SERVING SIZE:** 1 cup rice and 1 cup tofu mixture): **CALORIES** 322; **FAT** 11g (sat 1g, unsat 10g); **PROTEIN** 15g; **CARB** 44g; **FIBER** 5g; **SUGARS** 4g (added sugars 0g); **SODIUM** 516mg; **CALC** 8% DV; **POTASSIUM** 4% DV

TOFU *and* SPINACH—STUFFED SHELLS

Pureeing the tofu with the ricotta helps add creaminess to these cheesy stuffed shells without the saturated fat or calories. Sprinkle with Parmesan and fresh basil, if you like.

HANDS-ON: 30 MIN. • TOTAL: 30 MIN. • SERVES 4

12 uncooked large pasta shells (about 4 ounces)
10 ounces firm tofu, drained and patted dry
6 ounces part-skim ricotta cheese
¾ teaspoon kosher salt
½ teaspoon black pepper
1 teaspoon olive oil
4 cups loosely packed baby spinach
2 cups lower-sodium tomato-basil marinara sauce (such as Amy's)

1. Preheat the oven to 375°F. Cook the pasta shells according to the package directions, omitting salt and fat. Drain and set aside.

2. While the pasta shells cook, place the tofu, ricotta, salt, and pepper in a food processor, and process until smooth, about 30 seconds. Transfer to a medium bowl, and set aside.

3. Heat the oil in a large nonstick skillet over medium. Add the spinach, and cook, stirring often, until wilted, about 1 minute. Using a rubber spatula, fold the spinach into the ricotta mixture.

4. Place 1 cup of the marinara sauce in a 9-inch square glass baking dish. Spoon about 2 tablespoons filling into each pasta shell, and place in the baking dish. Spoon the remaining marinara over the shells, and bake in the preheated oven until the sauce is hot and bubbly, about 15 minutes.

(**SERVING SIZE:** 3 shells): **CALORIES** 288; **FAT** 9g (sat 3g, unsat 6g); **PROTEIN** 17g; **CARB** 34g; **FIBER** 4g; **SUGARS** 6g (added sugars 0g); **SODIUM** 548mg; **CALC** 28% DV; **POTASSIUM** 4% DV

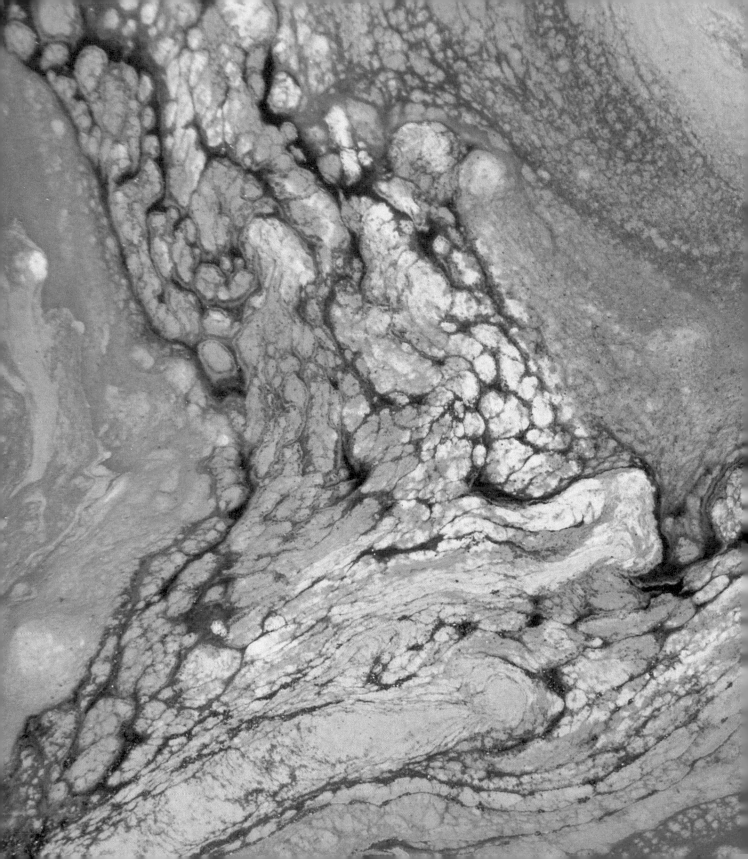

CHAPTER 5

FISH & SHELLFISH

MISO COD *with* BABY BOK CHOY SLAW

The sweet miso sauce is a delicious pairing for the flaky fish and crunchy bok choy. Teriyaki-style microwavable rice would complement this dish, so look for it at your supermarket. Substitute halibut for cod, if you like.

HANDS-ON: 15 MIN. • TOTAL: 15 MIN. • SERVES 4

You'll find bok choy in mature and baby forms. Mature bok choy has dark green leaves and white stems, while baby bok choy is naturally smaller and light green. It's more tender—use cut fresh stalks in salads and slaw (as in this recipe). The stems of mature bok choy are best when cooked. Previously only found in Asian markets, bok choy is now widely available in most supermarkets.

1   tablespoon white miso
1   tablespoon olive oil
1   tablespoon honey
2   tablespoons rice vinegar, divided
4   (6-ounce) skinless cod fillets
Cooking spray
2   teaspoons lower-sodium soy sauce
1   teaspoon sesame oil
3½ cups thinly sliced baby bok choy (from 3 baby bok choy)
2   cups precooked microwavable brown rice (such as Uncle Ben's)
Chopped fresh cilantro (optional)

1. Preheat the broiler with the oven rack 6 inches from the heat. Whisk together the miso, olive oil, honey, and 1 tablespoon of the rice vinegar. Place the cod on a baking sheet coated with cooking spray; brush the fillets with the miso mixture. Broil until cooked through, about 6 minutes.
2. Whisk together the soy sauce, sesame oil, and remaining 1 tablespoon rice vinegar in a medium bowl. Add the bok choy; toss to coat.
3. Microwave the rice according to the package directions. Serve with the cod and bok choy. Sprinkle with cilantro, if desired.

(**SERVING SIZE:** 1 fillet, ¾ cup bok choy, and ½ cup rice): **CALORIES** 307; **FAT** 7g (sat 1g, unsat 5g); **PROTEIN** 34g; **CARB** 27g; **FIBER** 3g; **SUGARS** 6g (added sugars 4g); **SODIUM** 370mg; **CALC** 9% DV; **POTASSIUM** 20% DV

GRILLED GROUPER *with* HEARTS *of* PALM SALAD *and* LEMON-THYME VINAIGRETTE

The versatile homemade vinaigrette flavors the salad and the fish. Serve this with microwavable steamed new potatoes for a complete meal.

HANDS-ON: 15 MIN. • **TOTAL: 15 MIN.** • **SERVES 4**

- 2 tablespoons red wine vinegar
- 2 tablespoons fresh lemon juice (from 1 lemon)
- 1 tablespoon chopped fresh thyme
- ¼ cup extra-virgin olive oil
- 1 (14-ounce) can hearts of palm, drained and cut crosswise into ½-inch slices
- 4 (6-ounce) skinless grouper fillets
- ¼ teaspoon kosher salt
- ¼ teaspoon black pepper
- Cooking spray
- 2 heads radicchio, halved lengthwise

1. Whisk together the red wine vinegar, lemon juice, and thyme in a small bowl. Gradually add the oil, whisking constantly, until the mixture is emulsified. Place the hearts of palm in a bowl, and add 2 tablespoons of the vinaigrette; toss to coat. Set aside the remaining vinaigrette.
2. Sprinkle the grouper evenly with the salt and pepper. Heat a large grill pan over medium-high; coat the pan with cooking spray. Add the fish; cook 5 minutes. Turn the fish, and add the radicchio to the grill pan; cook until the fish flakes easily with a fork and the radicchio is browned and tender, about 5 minutes.
3. Cut the radicchio into wedges. Divide the radicchio and hearts of palm mixture evenly among 4 plates. Top with the fish fillets, and drizzle with the remaining vinaigrette.

(**SERVING SIZE:** about ⅓ cup salad and 1 fillet): **CALORIES** 303; **FAT** 16g (sat 2g, unsat 13g); **PROTEIN** 35g; **CARB** 3g; **FIBER** 2g; **SUGARS** 1g (added sugars 0g); **SODIUM** 562mg; **CALC** 8% DV; **POTASSIUM** 24% DV

Add mushrooms, shredded carrots, or any veggies you have on hand for even more color and crunch.

STEAMED HALIBUT *with* LEMONY LEEKS

This recipe may not have many ingredients, but the result is a wonderfully delicate dish. Covering the leeks while they soften allows them to steam in their own juices—you don't want any caramelization to overwhelm this gentle dish.

HANDS-ON: 15 MIN. • **TOTAL 25 MIN.** • **SERVES 4**

2   tablespoons unsalted butter
1   tablespoon chopped fresh thyme
12 ounces thinly sliced leeks, white and very light green parts only (from 4 large leeks, about 4 cups sliced), rinsed
½   teaspoon kosher salt, divided

¼   cup water
1½ teaspoons lemon zest plus 2 tablespoons fresh juice (from 1 lemon)
4   (6-ounce) skin-on halibut fillets
½   teaspoon black pepper

1. Cook the butter and thyme in a large skillet over medium until the butter is foamy, about 2 minutes. Stir in the sliced leeks and ¼ teaspoon of the salt. Cover and cook, stirring occasionally, until soft, 8 to 10 minutes. Stir in the water, zest, and juice.
2. Sprinkle the halibut with the pepper and remaining ¼ teaspoon salt. Nestle the halibut into the leek mixture. Cover and increase the heat to medium-high. Cook until the fish flakes easily with a fork, about 10 minutes. Spoon the leek mixture into 4 shallow bowls; top with the fillets.

(SERVING SIZE: about ⅔ cup leek mixture and 1 fillet): **CALORIES** 261; **FAT** 8g (sat 4g, unsat 3g); **PROTEIN** 33g; **CARB** 13g; **FIBER** 2g; **SUGARS** 4g (added sugars 0g); **SODIUM** 374mg; **CALC** 7% DV; **POTASSIUM** 26% DV

LEEKS

While they resemble large, sturdy green onions, leeks have a mild, slightly sweet onion flavor. Be sure to thoroughly rinse leeks because dirt can easily get trapped in their many layers.

TERIYAKI SALMON RICE BOWLS

HANDS-ON: 20 MIN. • **TOTAL: 20 MIN.** • **SERVES 4**

1½ tablespoons extra-virgin olive oil, divided
1   red bell pepper, thinly sliced
4   (4-ounce) skinless salmon fillets
½   teaspoon table salt
¼   teaspoon black pepper

¼   cup lower-sodium teriyaki sauce, divided
2   (8.8-ounce) packages precooked microwavable brown rice (such as Uncle Ben's)
2   scallions, sliced

1. Heat 1½ teaspoons of the oil in a medium skillet over medium-high. Add the bell pepper to the pan; sauté 2 minutes. Remove the bell pepper from the pan; set aside.
2. Add the remaining 1 tablespoon oil to the pan. Sprinkle the salmon with the salt and pepper. Add to the pan; cook 3 minutes. Turn the salmon, and brush with 2 tablespoons of the teriyaki sauce. Cook 3 minutes.
3. While the salmon cooks, microwave the rice according to the package directions.
4. Divide the rice among 4 bowls. Top each with the bell pepper and salmon fillets; drizzle the remaining 2 tablespoons teriyaki sauce over the bowls. Sprinkle with the scallions.

(SERVING SIZE: ⅔ cup rice, ⅓ cup bell pepper, 1 fillet, and ½ tablespoon teriyaki sauce): **CALORIES** 470; **FAT** 23g (sat 4g, unsat 16g); **PROTEIN** 29g; **CARB** 38g; **FIBER** 3g; **SUGARS** 4g (added sugars 1g); **SODIUM** 693mg; **CALC** 2% DV; **POTASSIUM** 15% DV

SKIN-ON SALMON

To get a crispy skin on the salmon, start by cooking the fish on the skin side first, and finish on the flesh side until the fish is cooked through. This helps keep the fish moist. Be sure to purchase thicker fillets instead of fillets from the thinner tail end.

SEARED SALMON *with* GINGER-CORN SALSA ▶

HANDS-ON: 15 MIN. • TOTAL: 15 MIN. • SERVES 4

2   tablespoons olive oil, divided
4   (6-ounce) skin-on salmon fillets
1   teaspoon kosher salt, divided
¾   teaspoon black pepper, divided

2   cups fresh corn kernels (about 3 ears)
2   teaspoons grated fresh ginger
2   tablespoons chopped fresh cilantro
1   tablespoon red wine vinegar

1. Heat 1 tablespoon of the oil in a large nonstick skillet over medium-high. Sprinkle the salmon evenly with ½ teaspoon each of the salt and pepper. Add the fish to the pan, skin sides down, and cook until the skin is browned, 3 to 4 minutes. Turn and cook to the desired degree of doneness, 3 to 4 minutes for medium. Remove from the pan.
2. Heat the remaining 1 tablespoon oil in the pan over medium-high. Add the corn, ginger, and remaining ½ teaspoon salt and ¼ teaspoon pepper. Cook, stirring often, until the corn is slightly tender, 2 to 3 minutes. Remove from the heat, and stir in the cilantro and vinegar. Serve the salsa over the salmon.

(SERVING SIZE: 1 fillet and ½ cup salsa): CALORIES 370; FAT 19g (sat 3g, unsat 14g); PROTEIN 36g; CARB 15g; FIBER 2g; SUGARS 5g (added sugars 0g); SODIUM 567mg; CALC 2% DV; POTASSIUM 30% DV

SALMON *with* MINT, LEMON, *and* PEAS

This simple recipe leaves very little for you to clean up. To add richness, serve it with a side of low-fat Greek yogurt mixed with lemon juice and fresh herbs.

HANDS-ON: 15 MIN. • TOTAL: 15 MIN. • SERVES 4

4   (6-ounce) skinless salmon fillets
¼   teaspoon black pepper
½   teaspoon kosher salt, divided
2   lemons
8   dill sprigs
2   (8.8-ounce) packages precooked microwavable brown rice

1   cup frozen sweet peas, thawed
2   tablespoons chopped fresh mint
1   tablespoon chopped fresh flat-leaf parsley
1   tablespoon extra-virgin olive oil

1. Preheat the oven to 425°F. Line a rimmed baking sheet with heavy-duty aluminum foil, and place a lightly greased wire rack on the prepared baking sheet. Place the salmon fillets on the rack; sprinkle evenly with the pepper and ¼ teaspoon of the salt. Cut 4 slices from 1 lemon, and cut the slices into half-moons. Place 2 dill sprigs and 2 lemon pieces on each fillet. Roast in the preheated oven until the salmon reaches the desired degree of doneness, 10 to 12 minutes for medium.
2. While the salmon roasts, microwave the rice according to the package directions; transfer to a bowl. Fluff with a fork, and stir in the peas, mint, parsley, oil, and the remaining ¼ teaspoon salt. Juice the remaining lemon to equal 2 teaspoons; stir the lemon juice into the rice mixture. Serve immediately with the salmon.

(SERVING SIZE: 1 fillet and 1¼ cups rice mixture): CALORIES 470; FAT 17g (sat 2g, unsat 14g); PROTEIN 40g; CARB 40g; FIBER 4g; SUGARS 2g (added sugars 0g); SODIUM 365mg; CALC 3% DV; POTASSIUM 26% DV

SNAPPER VERACRUZ

Scoring the skin on the fish helps keep the fillets from curling up as they cook.

HANDS-ON: 15 MIN. • TOTAL: 15 MIN. • SERVES 4

2   tablespoons olive oil
4   (6-ounce) skin-on snapper fillets
¼   teaspoon black pepper
2   cups pico de gallo

¼   cup chopped green olives
1   tablespoon drained capers, chopped
2   (8.8-ounce) packages precooked microwavable brown rice

1. Heat the oil in a large nonstick skillet over medium-high. Using a very sharp knife, cut 3 (⅛-inch-deep) slits in the skin side of the fillets. Sprinkle the fish evenly with the pepper. Add the fillets to the pan, skin sides down, and cook until the skin is lightly browned, 3 to 4 minutes. Remove from the pan.
2. Add the pico de gallo, olives, and capers to the pan, and bring to a boil, stirring occasionally. Place the fillets in the pan, skin sides up. Reduce the heat to medium, and simmer until the fish is opaque and flakes easily with a fork, 2 to 3 minutes.
3. Microwave the rice according to the package directions. Spoon the rice onto 4 plates. Top with the fillets and sauce.

(SERVING SIZE: 1 cup rice, 1 fillet, and ½ cup sauce): **CALORIES** 435; **FAT** 13g (sat 2g, unsat 11g); **PROTEIN** 40g; **CARB** 43g; **FIBER** 3g; **SUGARS** 4g (added sugars 0g); **SODIUM** 681mg; **CALC** 6% DV; **POTASSIUM** 21% DV

SWEET *and* SOUR SWORDFISH *and* PINEAPPLE SKEWERS

Grilling the pineapple and fish caramelizes them, while the bell peppers cook until just tender, adding a nice crunch. Brush the glaze on towards the end so it doesn't burn. Serve with rice pilaf and lime wedges.

HANDS-ON: 15 MIN. • TOTAL: 15 MIN. • SERVES 4

1½ pounds skinless swordfish fillets, cut into 1½-inch cubes
3   cups prechopped fresh pineapple chunks
3   red bell peppers, cut into 1-inch pieces
Cooking spray

3   tablespoons sweet chili sauce
2   tablespoons red wine vinegar
¾   teaspoon kosher salt
½   teaspoon black pepper

1. Heat a grill pan over high. Thread the swordfish, pineapple, and bell peppers alternately onto 8 (7-inch) wooden skewers, and coat with cooking spray.
2. Whisk together the chili sauce, vinegar, salt, and pepper in a small bowl.
3. Add the skewers to the pan; grill 3 minutes per side. Coat evenly with half of the chili sauce mixture. Grill just until the fish is cooked through, about 2 minutes. Serve with the remaining chili sauce mixture.

(SERVING SIZE: 2 skewers): **CALORIES** 347; **FAT** 12g (sat 3g, unsat 7g); **PROTEIN** 35g; **CARB** 24g; **FIBER** 4g; **SUGARS** 17g (added sugars 0g); **SODIUM** 505mg; **CALC** 3% DV; **POTASSIUM** 32% DV

GRILLED SWORDFISH *with* SALSA VERDE *and* RADISH SALAD

The homemade salsa verde offers big flavor and color in this dish. If you're not a cilantro fan, substitute basil or parsley. You can also cut the swordfish into chunks, and serve it over black beans or with tortillas to make tacos.

HANDS-ON: 15 MIN. • TOTAL: 15 MIN. • SERVES 4

SWORDFISH

White-fleshed swordfish has a mild flavor and firm, meaty texture that makes it a great fish option for grilling, either as a steak or on skewers, since it can stand up to the heat. It's also tasty broiled and sautéed.

1   bunch fresh cilantro, stems removed (about 1½ cups firmly packed leaves)
1   tablespoon water
3   tablespoons olive oil, divided
1   tablespoon plus 2 teaspoons fresh lime juice (from 2 limes), divided
¾   teaspoon kosher salt, divided
½   teaspoon black pepper, divided
4   ounces radishes, trimmed and thinly sliced (about 1 cup sliced)
½   cup matchstick carrots
3   scallions, thinly sliced
½   teaspoon sugar
½   jalapeño chile, seeded and minced
4   (6-ounce) swordfish steaks (1 inch thick)
Cooking spray

1. Preheat the grill to medium-high (400°F to 450°F). Process the cilantro, water, 2 tablespoons of the oil, 1 tablespoon of the lime juice, and ¼ teaspoon each of the salt and black pepper in a blender until smooth, about 1 minute. Set aside.
2. Stir together the radishes, carrots, scallions, sugar, jalapeño, ¼ teaspoon of the salt, and the remaining 1 tablespoon oil and 2 teaspoons lime juice in a small bowl. Set aside.
3. Sprinkle the swordfish steaks evenly with the remaining ¼ teaspoon each salt and black pepper. Place the swordfish on a grill grate coated with cooking spray, and grill until the fish flakes easily with a fork, about 5 minutes per side.
4. Place the swordfish steaks on 4 plates. Top with the salsa verde and radish salad.

(**SERVING SIZE:** 1 swordfish steak, 2 tablespoons salsa verde, and ¼ cup radish salad): **CALORIES** 356; **FAT** 22g (sat 4g, unsat 16g); **PROTEIN** 34g; **CARB** 5g; **FIBER** 2g; **SUGARS** 2g (added sugars 1g); **SODIUM** 521mg; **CALC** 4% DV; **POTASSIUM** 27% DV

BROILED RED SNAPPER
with CAULIFLOWER and CAPERS

Briny capers and sweet raisins are a fantastic combination in this sheet pan supper. Be sure to watch closely as the dish broils under the high heat—it can go from perfectly cooked to burnt in seconds. You can use sea bass, salmon, or grouper in place of the red snapper, if you like.

HANDS-ON: 20 MIN. • TOTAL: 20 MIN. • SERVES 4

1 (2¼-pound) head cauliflower, cut into florets
3 tablespoons olive oil, divided
¾ teaspoon kosher salt, divided
½ teaspoon black pepper, divided
4 (6-ounce) skin-on red snapper fillets

2 tablespoons drained capers
3 tablespoons golden raisins
2 tablespoons sherry vinegar
¼ cup chopped mixed fresh herbs (such as parsley, chives, and basil; optional)

1. Preheat the broiler with the oven rack 6 inches from the heat. Spread the cauliflower florets in a single layer on a rimmed baking sheet; brush with 2 tablespoons of the oil, and sprinkle with ¼ teaspoon each of the salt and pepper. Broil until tender-crisp and golden brown, 10 to 12 minutes.

2. Drizzle the fish evenly with the remaining 1 tablespoon oil; sprinkle with the remaining ½ teaspoon salt and remaining ¼ teaspoon pepper. Place the fish fillets, skin sides up, on the cauliflower, and add the capers to the cauliflower. Broil until the fish is opaque, 5 to 7 minutes.

3. Add the raisins to the cauliflower mixture, and broil just until the raisins are plump and hot, about 30 seconds. Drizzle the fish and cauliflower mixture evenly with the vinegar. Divide among 4 plates. Sprinkle with the herbs, if desired, and drizzle with any pan drippings.

(SERVING SIZE: 1 fillet and 1 cup cauliflower mixture): CALORIES 348; FAT 13g (sat 2g, unsat 10g); PROTEIN 40g; CARB 18g; FIBER 6g; SUGARS 9g (added sugars 0g); SODIUM 647mg; CALC 12% DV; POTASSIUM 44% DV

BUYING RED SNAPPER

Most of the red snapper from the U.S. is sold with the skin on. That's a good thing since it holds the fillets together, but also because of the potential for mislabeling. Some fish labeled as red snapper may actually be rockfish, which has a different texture and flavor. The skin of a red snapper should be bright red or metallic and the flesh should be moist and reflective without any signs of drying or gaping (when the layers of muscle start to separate). Be sure to buy from a trusted source.

TILAPIA *and* NAPA CABBAGE TACOS

Mild-flavored tilapia offers a non-fishy filling for these tacos. If you have the time, lightly char the corn tortillas in your skillet. Serve this with black beans on the side.

HANDS-ON: 15 MIN. • **TOTAL: 15 MIN.** • **SERVES 4**

2   cups shredded napa cabbage (about ½ medium head)
½   cup chopped white onion (about 2¾ ounces)
¼   cup fresh lime juice (from 3 limes)
¼   cup olive oil, divided
1   teaspoon kosher salt, divided

4   (4-ounce) skinless tilapia fillets
1   teaspoon smoked paprika
8   (6-inch) corn tortillas, warmed
2   radishes, thinly sliced (about ¼ cup)
Pickled onions (optional)
Lime wedges (optional)

1. Toss together the cabbage, onion, lime juice, 2 tablespoons of the oil, and ½ teaspoon of the salt in a medium bowl. Set aside.

2. Heat 1 tablespoon of the oil in a large nonstick skillet over medium-high. Sprinkle the tilapia evenly with the paprika and remaining ½ teaspoon salt. Cook 2 fillets until golden brown and cooked through, 2 to 3 minutes per side. Repeat with the remaining 1 tablespoon oil and 2 fillets.

3. Cut each fillet into 2 pieces, and place 1 piece on each tortilla. Top evenly with the cabbage slaw and sliced radishes. Top with pickled onions, and serve with lime wedges, if desired.

(**SERVING SIZE:** 2 tacos): **CALORIES** 383; **FAT** 17g (sat 3g, unsat 13g); **PROTEIN** 27g; **CARB** 35g; **FIBER** 5g; **SUGARS** 3g (added sugars 0g); **SODIUM** 565mg; **CALC** 8% DV; **POTASSIUM** 12% DV

TUNA POKE BOWL

Pronounced POH-key, this Hawaiian salad is made with "sushi-grade" tuna, which means that it's the highest-quality fish offered at the market. You should seek out a reputable fishmonger or retailer, and don't be afraid to ask where the fish came from and how long it's been there. Use a very sharp knife to cut the tuna so that you don't rip the flesh.

HANDS-ON: 15 MIN. • TOTAL: 15 MIN. • SERVES 4

- 4 ounces uncooked bean thread noodles (cellophane noodles)
- ¼ cup ponzu sauce
- 3 tablespoons seasoned rice vinegar
- 2 tablespoons mirin
- 2 teaspoons toasted sesame oil
- 1 teaspoon wasabi paste (optional)
- 12 ounces sushi-grade tuna, cut into ½-inch cubes
- 1½ cups chopped English cucumber (about 7½ ounces)
- 1 ripe small avocado, chopped
- Chopped scallions (optional)
- Black sesame seeds (optional)

1. Soak the bean thread noodles according to the package directions. Drain and rinse under cold water; drain well. Using kitchen shears, cut the noodles into 2-inch pieces.
2. Whisk together the ponzu, rice vinegar, mirin, sesame oil, and, if desired, wasabi paste in a medium bowl. Toss together 2 tablespoons of the ponzu mixture and the tuna. Divide the noodles among 4 bowls; top with the tuna, cucumber, and avocado. Drizzle evenly with the remaining sauce. Sprinkle with scallions and sesame seeds, if desired.

(**SERVING SIZE:** 1 cup noodle mixture and about ⅓ cup tuna): **CALORIES** 324; **FAT** 9g (sat 1g, unsat 7g); **PROTEIN** 22g; **CARB** 36g; **FIBER** 3g; **SUGARS** 7g (added sugars 2g); **SODIUM** 767mg; **CALC** 2% DV; **POTASSIUM** 18% DV

SEARED TUNA *with* WHITE BEAN RAGOUT

Cooking spray is a great substitute for oil when searing—the tuna will get a nice crust. For this dish, the tuna is seared quickly on the outside while the interior remains virtually raw. The result is a silky smooth texture that pairs perfectly with the spicy, creamy white bean ragout.

HANDS-ON: 15 MIN. • TOTAL: 15 MIN. • SERVES 4

FRESH TUNA

When buying tuna steaks that have already been cut, make sure the flesh is moist but not wet and shiny. Cut steaks that are old and should be avoided will look dull, matte, and/or brown, and may show signs of gaping (when the layers of muscle start to separate). Tuna steaks will have a dark line running through them (called the bloodline). It's edible but also has a stronger fishy flavor than the rest of the flesh. Remove it if you like.

2 tablespoons olive oil, divided
¼ cup chopped red onion
¼ cup chopped celery
2 garlic cloves, minced
2 (15-ounce) cans no-salt-added cannellini beans, drained and rinsed
2 teaspoons lemon zest (from 1 lemon)
¼ teaspoon crushed red pepper
¾ teaspoon kosher salt, divided
1 tablespoon chopped fresh flat-leaf parsley
4 (6-ounce) tuna steaks
¼ teaspoon black pepper

1. Heat 1 tablespoon of the oil in a large skillet over medium-high. Add the onion and celery; cook, stirring often, until softened, about 5 minutes. Stir in the garlic, and cook 1 minute. Add the beans, lemon zest, crushed red pepper, and ½ teaspoon of the salt; cook, stirring occasionally, until the beans are heated through, about 2 minutes. Remove from the heat, and stir in the parsley.

2. Heat the remaining 1 tablespoon oil in a large cast-iron skillet over medium-high. Sprinkle the tuna with the black pepper and remaining ¼ teaspoon salt. Cook the tuna to the desired degree of doneness, about 2 minutes per side for medium. Thinly slice against the grain. Divide the bean mixture among 4 plates, and top with the tuna steaks.

(**SERVING SIZE:** ¾ cup beans and 1 tuna steak): **CALORIES** 417; **FAT** 9g (sat 1g, unsat 8g); **PROTEIN** 52g; **CARB** 30g; **FIBER** 9g; **SUGARS** 2g (added sugars 0g); **SODIUM** 508mg; **CALC** 8% DV; **POTASSIUM** 34% DV

MUSSELS *with* COCONUT-CURRY SAUCE

Despite the name, the sauce isn't overly coconutty, but has a nice balance of acidic, spicy, salty, and sweet. Be sure to serve this flavorful dish with grilled bread to sop up all the amazing sauce. See page 186 for tips on buying mussels.

HANDS-ON: 10 MIN. • **TOTAL: 15 MIN.** • **SERVES 4**

2 tablespoons olive oil

2 tablespoons chopped shallots

3 tablespoons red curry paste

1 (3-inch) lemongrass stalk, lightly crushed with the side of a knife

1 cup unsweetened coconut milk

½ cup dry white wine (such as sauvignon blanc)

2 tablespoons fresh lime juice (from 1 lime)

¼ teaspoon kosher salt

2 pounds mussels, scrubbed and debearded

2 tablespoons chopped fresh cilantro

Grilled crusty bread slices (optional)

Heat the oil in a Dutch oven over medium. Add the shallots; cook, stirring often, until tender, 1 to 2 minutes. Stir in the curry paste and lemongrass; cook, stirring constantly, until fragrant, about 20 seconds. Add the coconut milk, wine, lime juice, and salt; stir to combine. Bring to a simmer. Add the mussels; cover and simmer until the mussels open, 4 to 6 minutes. Remove and discard any mussels that do not open. Discard the lemongrass. Sprinkle with the cilantro. Serve with grilled bread, if desired.

(**SERVING SIZE:** about 14 mussels and ½ cup sauce): **CALORIES** 295; **FAT** 10g (sat 2g, unsat 6g); **PROTEIN** 33g; **CARB** 12g; **FIBER** 0g; **SUGARS** 1g (added sugars 0g); **SODIUM** 461mg; **CALC** 20% DV; **POTASSIUM** 4% DV

BRODETTO *with* MUSSELS, SCALLOPS, *and* SHRIMP

Brodetto, a classic Italian tomato-based fish stew, is quick, easy, impressive, and deeply gratifying. Since the seafood all cooks differently, the order and timing in which they are added is key, so follow the recipe closely.

HANDS-ON: 15 MIN.   •   TOTAL: 15 MIN.   •   SERVES 4

1   (15-ounce) can no-salt-added cannellini beans, drained and rinsed
1   (14.5-ounce) can no-salt-added diced tomatoes, undrained
1¼ cups seafood stock (such as Kitchen Basics)
3   garlic cloves, crushed

½   teaspoon crushed red pepper
¼   teaspoon kosher salt
1   pound mussels, scrubbed and debearded
8   ounces sea scallops
8   ounces peeled and deveined raw medium shrimp
½   cup fresh basil leaves (optional)

Stir together the beans, tomatoes, stock, garlic, red pepper, and salt in a large Dutch oven with a tight-fitting lid. Bring to a boil over high, stirring occasionally. Add the mussels; cover and cook until the mussels open, about 3 minutes. Remove and discard any mussels that do not open. Stir in the scallops and shrimp; cover and cook until the scallops and shrimp are opaque, 2 to 3 minutes. Stir in the basil, if desired. Serve immediately.

(**SERVING SIZE:** 2 cups): **CALORIES** 278; **FAT** 3g (sat 0g, unsat 2g); **PROTEIN** 37g; **CARB** 24g; **FIBER** 5g; **SUGARS** 3g (added sugars 0g); **SODIUM** 527mg; **CALC** 13% DV; **POTASSIUM** 17% DV

BUYING MUSSELS

Always buy fresh mussels and use them within a day. Choose tightly closed mussels with shells that have no chips or cracks. If a mussel is open, tap it on the counter. If it doesn't close, trash it. Once home, remove the mussels from the packaging, and store them wrapped in a moist towel in the fridge. Don't store mussels in plastic—it prevents them from breathing. Wait to clean the mussels until right before cooking them.

BUCATINI *and* CLAMS

Bucatini is a thick spaghetti-like pasta with a hole running through the center—ideal for trapping flavorful sauces like the one in this recipe. Crushed red pepper provides a little punch of spice, while the parsley adds freshness. Pair this with grilled bread and a simply dressed salad.

HANDS-ON: 15 MIN. • **TOTAL: 15 MIN.** • **SERVES 4**

12 ounces uncooked bucatini pasta
2½ tablespoons olive oil
1 ounce pancetta, diced
3 garlic cloves, smashed
½ cup dry white wine (such as sauvignon blanc)
1 teaspoon kosher salt

½ teaspoon black pepper
24 littleneck clams, scrubbed
1½ tablespoons fresh lemon juice (from 1 lemon)
2 tablespoons chopped fresh flat-leaf parsley
⅛ teaspoon crushed red pepper

1. Cook the pasta according to the package directions. Drain, reserving ½ cup cooking water.

2. Heat the oil in a large skillet over medium. Add the pancetta and garlic; cook, stirring often, until the garlic is lightly browned and the pancetta is rendered, 3 to 4 minutes. Add the wine, salt, and black pepper, stirring and scraping to loosen the browned bits from bottom of the pan. Add the clams; cover and cook just until the clams open, 6 to 8 minutes. Remove and discard any clams that do not open.

3. Add the pasta, and toss to coat. Add the cooking water, ¼ cup at a time, if necessary to coat the pasta. Cook, stirring occasionally, until the sauce begins to thicken, 1 to 2 minutes. Remove from the heat. Stir in the lemon juice, and sprinkle with the parsley and red pepper.

(**SERVING SIZE:** 2 cups): **CALORIES** 482; **FAT** 13g (sat 3g, unsat 8g); **PROTEIN** 20g; **CARB** 67g; **FIBER** 3g; **SUGARS** 2g (added sugars 0g); **SODIUM** 631mg; **CALC** 5% DV; **POTASSIUM** 7% DV

15-MINUTE FIDEOS ▶

Ask the fishmonger to cut the grouper into 1-inch cubes for you and remove the shells and veins from the shrimp. You'll want to purchase clams that are the same size so that they cook evenly. Adding the clams to the stock while it comes to a boil helps speed up the process.

HANDS-ON: 15 MIN. • **TOTAL: 15 MIN.** • **SERVES 4**

6 ounces uncooked vermicelli, broken into 1-inch pieces
1 tablespoon olive oil
12 medium-sized littleneck clams, scrubbed
2 cups unsalted chicken stock
8 garlic cloves, sliced (about 2 tablespoons)
1 tablespoon tomato paste
¾ teaspoon kosher salt
½ teaspoon black pepper
8 ounces skinless grouper fillets, cut into 1-inch chunks
8 peeled and deveined raw medium shrimp
Lemon wedges
Chopped fresh parsley (optional)

Heat the vermicelli and oil in a large skillet with a tight-fitting lid over medium-high. Cook, stirring often, until toasted, 2 to 3 minutes. Add the clams, stock, garlic, tomato paste, salt, and pepper; stir to combine. Increase the heat to high, and bring to a boil. Add the grouper and shrimp; cover and cook until the clams open, the fish is opaque and flaky, and the shrimp is just opaque, about 6 minutes. Remove and discard any clams that do not open. Serve immediately with lemon wedges and sprinkle with parsley, if desired.

(**SERVING SIZE:** about 1½ cups): **CALORIES** 285; **FAT** 5g (sat 1g, unsat 4g); **PROTEIN** 24g; **CARB** 36g; **FIBER** 2g; **SUGARS** 3g (added sugars 0g); **SODIUM** 479mg; **CALC** 5% DV; **POTASSIUM** 12% DV

CRAB COBB SALAD LETTUCE CUPS

Lemon juice and bacon lend full flavor to this crab salad. Don't buy pasteurized crabmeat, as its flavor is not ideal for this salad.

HANDS-ON: 15 MIN. • **TOTAL: 15 MIN.** • **SERVES 4**

1 pound fresh jumbo lump crabmeat, drained
¼ cup canola mayonnaise (such as Hellmann's)
2 tablespoons fresh lemon juice (from 1 lemon)
½ teaspoon black pepper
8 Boston lettuce leaves
1 ripe avocado, diced
1 medium tomato, diced
2 center-cut bacon slices, cooked and crumbled

1. Carefully pick through the crabmeat to remove any bits of shell, taking care to leave the crabmeat in large pieces. Gently stir together the crabmeat, mayonnaise, lemon juice, and pepper in a bowl.
2. Place 2 lettuce leaves on each of 4 plates. Divide the crab mixture evenly among the lettuce leaves. Top evenly with the avocado, tomato, and bacon.

(**SERVING SIZE:** 2 lettuce cups): **CALORIES** 336; **FAT** 21g (sat 2g, unsat 17g); **PROTEIN** 29g; **CARB** 7g; **FIBER** 4g; **SUGARS** 1g (added sugars 0g); **SODIUM** 590mg; **CALC** 12% DV; **POTASSIUM** 10% DV

BAKED OYSTERS *with* ITALIAN BREADCRUMBS *and* HORSERADISH

Baked oysters are a classic. This version gets some spice from the fresh horseradish and texture from the whole-wheat panko. You can add some heat with a splash of hot sauce, if you like. Purchase your oysters from a reliable source when they're in season to ensure freshness. You can have the fishmonger shuck them for you, but you'll need to cook them as soon as you get home.

HANDS-ON: 10 MIN. • TOTAL: 15 MIN. • SERVES 4

1½ tablespoons olive oil
1 teaspoon minced garlic
1 cup whole-wheat panko (Japanese-style breadcrumbs)
¼ cup grated fresh horseradish
1½ tablespoons chopped fresh flat-leaf parsley
1 tablespoon lemon zest (from 1 lemon)
½ teaspoon kosher salt
¼ teaspoon black pepper
24 oysters on the half shell
Lemon wedges

1. Preheat the oven to 450°F. Heat the oil in a medium nonstick skillet over medium. Add the garlic, and cook, stirring constantly, until beginning to brown, about 2 minutes. Remove from the heat; stir in the panko, horseradish, parsley, lemon zest, salt, and pepper.
2. Place the oysters on a rimmed baking sheet. Top evenly with the breadcrumb mixture. Bake in the preheated oven until the oyster edges curl and the breadcrumbs are lightly browned. Serve immediately with lemon wedges.

(SERVING SIZE: 6 oysters): **CALORIES** 188; **FAT** 7g (sat 1g, unsat 5g); **PROTEIN** 9g; **CARB** 23g; **FIBER** 5g; **SUGARS** 3g (added sugars 0g); **SODIUM** 340mg; **CALC** 9% DV; **POTASSIUM** 8% DV

SHUCKING OYSTERS

Before shucking, scrub the shell with a stiff vegetable brush and rinse under cold water. This will keep loose dirt and debris from getting on the meat. To protect your hands, wear a rubber shucking glove or use a towel to hold the oyster steady in case the knife slips or the shell cracks. With the flat shell on top and the hinged point of the shell toward you, work an oyster knife into the hinge. Using lots of pressure, pry the top and bottom shell apart until you hear the hinge pop.

SEARED SCALLOPS *with* BACON *and* ORANGES

Serve this company-worthy platter with a green salad, and you're set for an elegant, fuss-free meal. For a more affordable (but equally tasty) option, try using shrimp in place of the scallops.

HANDS-ON: 20 MIN.   •   TOTAL: 20 MIN.   •   SERVES 4

BUYING SCALLOPS

When buying scallops, it's best to purchase dry scallops instead of wet. Why? Wet scallops are treated with a sodium solution that's used to preserve them as soon as they're caught. While it does just that, it also plumps them up so they look great raw but shrink as the liquid cooks out. This extra liquid in the pan prevents them from getting a good browned crust and leaves behind smaller scallops and more sodium.

4   center-cut bacon slices
3   large navel oranges, divided
1½ pounds sea scallops
½   teaspoon black pepper
½   teaspoon kosher salt, divided
1   tablespoon apple cider vinegar
2   teaspoons chopped fresh thyme

1. Place the bacon in a large cast-iron skillet over medium-high; cook 6 minutes or until crisp, turning once after 3 minutes. Remove from the pan with a slotted spoon; coarsely chop.
2. While the bacon cooks, cut 1 orange in half; squeeze the juice from both halves into a bowl. Peel and section the remaining 2 oranges over the bowl to collect the juices. Place the orange sections in a separate bowl.
3. Increase the heat to high. Pat the scallops dry; sprinkle evenly with the pepper and ¼ teaspoon salt. Add the scallops to the drippings in the pan; cook 2 minutes on each side or until golden brown. Transfer the scallops to a platter; cover with aluminum foil to keep warm. Add the orange juice, vinegar, and remaining ¼ teaspoon salt to the pan. Cook 2 minutes or until simmering, scraping the pan to loosen the browned bits. Drizzle the orange juice mixture evenly over the scallops; top evenly with the bacon, orange sections, and thyme.

CALORIES 191; FAT 2g (sat 1g, unsat 1g); PROTEIN 23g; CARB 18g; FIBER 2g; SUGARS 10g (added sugars 0g); SODIUM 601mg; CALC 6% DV; POTASSIUM 10% DV

SEARED SCALLOPS *with* HERBED ORZO

There's no need to cut the cherry tomatoes in half before adding them to the skillet. Heat will make them burst, and their flavorful juice makes a wonderful sauce. Be sure to purchase dry-packed scallops (see page 194 for more information), which sear the best.

HANDS-ON: 15 MIN. • TOTAL: 15 MIN. • SERVES 4

6 ounces uncooked whole-wheat orzo pasta
¼ cup thinly sliced fresh basil, divided
3 tablespoons olive oil, divided
1 teaspoon kosher salt, divided
½ teaspoon black pepper, divided

1 cup prechopped yellow onion
6 garlic cloves, thinly sliced
2 pints cherry tomatoes
1 pound sea scallops

1. Cook the orzo according to the package directions, omitting salt and fat. Drain. Place the orzo in a bowl with 2 tablespoons of the basil, 1 tablespoon of the oil, ½ teaspoon of the salt, and ¼ teaspoon of the pepper; stir to combine. Set aside.

2. Heat 1 tablespoon of the oil in a large nonstick skillet over medium-high. Add the onion and garlic; cook, stirring often, until lightly browned, about 2 minutes. Add the tomatoes, ¼ teaspoon of the salt, and the remaining 2 tablespoons basil and ¼ teaspoon pepper. Cook, stirring often, until the tomatoes burst and the sauce thickens slightly, about 5 minutes. (Use the back of a wooden spoon to break up the tomatoes, if necessary.)

3. Heat the remaining 1 tablespoon oil in a large cast-iron skillet over medium-high. Pat the scallops dry, and sprinkle the scallops evenly with the remaining ¼ teaspoon salt. Place the scallops in the pan in a single layer; cook until browned, about 2 minutes per side. Divide the orzo mixture among 4 plates. Top with the scallops. Spoon the sauce over the orzo mixture and around the scallops.

(**SERVING SIZE:** ½ cup orzo mixture, 3 to 4 scallops, and ½ cup sauce): **CALORIES** 367; **FAT** 12g (sat 2g, unsat 9g); **PROTEIN** 22g; **CARB** 47g; **FIBER** 6g; **SUGARS** 6g (added sugars 0g); **SODIUM** 676mg; **CALC** 6% DV; **POTASSIUM** 22% DV

FUSILLI *with* SCALLOPS *and* PESTO

Buttery scallops paired with a savory pesto pasta makes a rich, satisfying meal. The cherry tomatoes add color, texture, and sweetness.

HANDS-ON: 10 MIN. • **TOTAL: 15 MIN.** • **SERVES 4**

6 ounces uncooked whole-wheat fusilli pasta
1 pint red and yellow cherry tomatoes, halved
½ cup jarred refrigerated basil pesto (such as Buitoni)

2 teaspoons olive oil
1 pound sea scallops
¼ teaspoon kosher salt
¼ teaspoon black pepper
2 tablespoons thinly sliced fresh chives

1. Cook the pasta according to the package directions, omitting salt and fat. Drain. Toss with the tomatoes and pesto.
2. While the pasta cooks, heat the oil in a large nonstick skillet over medium-high. Pat the scallops dry. Sprinkle the scallops with the salt and pepper. Add to the hot oil in the pan, and cook until golden brown, 2 to 3 minutes per side.
3. Divide the pasta among 4 shallow bowls or plates; top with the scallops and chives.

(**SERVING SIZE:** 1½ cups pasta and 4 scallops): **CALORIES** 420; **FAT** 18g (sat 3g, unsat 14g); **PROTEIN** 23g; **CARB** 41g; **FIBER** 6g; **SUGARS** 5g (added sugars 0g); **SODIUM** 584mg; **CALC** 11% DV; **POTASSIUM** 17% DV

GRILLED SCALLOPS *with* HERBED POTATOES *and* ASPARAGUS

Seek out fresh sea scallops. Frozen are easy to find, but they have a rubbery texture when cooked. Grilling the scallops quickly allows them to develop a nice crust while the interior remains creamy.

HANDS-ON: 15 MIN. • TOTAL: 15 MIN. • SERVES 4

12 ounces baby gold potatoes, quartered (about 3 cups)
1 tablespoon water
1 pound sea scallops
1 pound thick asparagus, trimmed
1 tablespoon olive oil
½ teaspoon black pepper, divided

2 tablespoons unsalted butter, melted
3 tablespoons chopped fresh flat-leaf parsley
1 tablespoon chopped fresh dill
1 garlic clove, grated
½ teaspoon kosher salt
Lemon wedges (optional)

1. Preheat the grill to medium-high (400°F to 450°F). Combine the potatoes and water in a medium-sized microwavable bowl; cover tightly with plastic wrap. Microwave on HIGH until the potatoes are tender when pierced with a fork, about 4 minutes. Spread the potatoes in a single layer on a plate lined with paper towels. Let stand 2 minutes.

2. Pat the scallops dry. Brush the scallops and asparagus with the oil; sprinkle evenly with ¼ teaspoon of the pepper.

3. Place the potatoes, scallops, and asparagus on a lightly greased grill grate. Grill, covered, until the scallops are opaque and the potatoes are lightly charred, about 2 minutes per side. Cut the asparagus into 2-inch pieces. Combine the asparagus, potatoes, butter, parsley, dill, garlic, salt, and remaining ¼ teaspoon pepper in a bowl; toss to coat. Serve the asparagus mixture with the scallops and, if desired, lemon wedges.

(**SERVING SIZE:** about ¾ cup asparagus mixture and 3 to 4 scallops): **CALORIES** 236; **FAT** 10g (sat 4g, unsat 5g); **PROTEIN** 17g; **CARB** 22g; **FIBER** 3g; **SUGARS** 1g (added sugars 0g); **SODIUM** 454mg; **CALC** 9% DV; **POTASSIUM** 11% DV

GRILLED SHRIMP
with SMASHED CUCUMBER SALAD

This dish shows that a handful of fresh ingredients can create a meal that shines. Smashing the cucumbers allows the salt cure to better penetrate and flavor the skins. The oil and vinegar mixed with the fresh cucumber juices creates a delicately flavored cucumber dressing.

HANDS-ON: 15 MIN. • **TOTAL: 25 MIN.** • **SERVES 4**

2 (8-ounce) English cucumbers
½ teaspoon kosher salt
6 tablespoons extra-virgin olive oil
3 tablespoons rice vinegar
2 tablespoons honey

Cooking spray
1¼ pounds peeled and deveined raw large shrimp
3 tablespoons torn fresh basil

1. Cut the cucumbers lengthwise into quarters. Cut the quarters into 1-inch pieces. Place the cucumbers, cut sides up, on a cutting board. Lightly smash the cucumbers with a mallet or small pan just until the skins are broken. (Do not beat the cucumbers to a pulp.) Transfer the smashed cucumbers to a bowl; add the salt, and toss to combine. Let stand until the juices begin to release, about 10 minutes.
2. Whisk together the oil, vinegar, and honey in a small bowl. Pour half of the oil mixture over the smashed cucumbers.
3. Heat a grill pan lightly coated with the cooking spray over high. Add the shrimp to the pan; grill until opaque, about 5 minutes, turning the shrimp about halfway through grilling time.
4. Using a slotted spoon, divide the cucumbers evenly among 4 shallow bowls, reserving the cucumber liquid in the bowl. Top the cucumbers evenly with the shrimp. Stir the basil and remaining oil mixture into the reserved cucumber liquid; pour over the shrimp.

(**SERVING SIZE:** about 1¼ cups): **CALORIES** 344; **FAT** 22g (sat 3g, unsat 17g); **PROTEIN** 24g; **CARB** 13g; **FIBER** 1g; **SUGARS** 10g (added sugars 9g); **SODIUM** 493mg; **CALC** 12% DV; **POTASSIUM** 10% DV

BBQ SHRIMP *with* POLENTA

Simple to prepare, the homemade barbecue sauce gives both the shrimp and polenta a hearty flavor boost. Warm it just until the sugar and spices dissolve.

HANDS-ON: 15 MIN. • **TOTAL: 15 MIN.** • **SERVES 4**

⅔ cup no-salt-added ketchup
¼ cup water
3 tablespoons apple cider vinegar
2 tablespoons light brown sugar
½ teaspoon garlic powder
½ teaspoon onion powder
1 teaspoon black pepper
¼ teaspoon kosher salt

2 tablespoons canola oil, divided
1 (18-ounce) tube plain polenta, cut into 8 slices
1¼ pounds peeled and deveined raw large shrimp
1 tablespoon chopped fresh flat-leaf parsley (optional)

1. Whisk together the ketchup, water, vinegar, brown sugar, garlic powder, onion powder, pepper, and salt in a small saucepan. Cook over medium-high, whisking occasionally, until warmed and bubbling, about 5 minutes.
2. Heat 1 tablespoon of the oil in a large skillet over high. Add the polenta rounds; cook until browned, about 3 minutes per side. Remove from the pan, and keep warm.
3. Heat the remaining 1 tablespoon oil in the pan over medium-high. Add the shrimp; cook, stirring occasionally, just until opaque and pink, 3 to 4 minutes. Place the polenta rounds on 4 plates, and top with the shrimp. Drizzle with the barbecue sauce. Sprinkle with the parsley, if desired.

(**SERVING SIZE:** 2 polenta rounds, about 5 shrimp, and about ¼ cup sauce): **CALORIES** 351; **FAT** 9g (sat 1g, unsat 7g); **PROTEIN** 26g; **CARB** 41g; **FIBER** 2g; **SUGARS** 17g (added sugars 7g); **SODIUM** 612mg; **CALC** 10% DV; **POTASSIUM** 19% DV

SPICY SHRIMP NOODLE BOWL

This colorful bowl offers a wonderful mix of textures and spice. Adding the ingredients in stages ensures they don't overcook—the vegetables stay slightly crisp while the shrimp reach a perfect doneness. If you can't find snow peas, use sugar snaps.

HANDS-ON: 15 MIN. • **TOTAL: 15 MIN.** • **SERVES 4**

RICE STICK NOODLES

Banh pho noodles are available in dried and fresh forms. While dried are more widely available at Asian markets and some grocery stores, you're only likely to find fresh at Asian markets. The dried variety cook up to a wonderfully chewy texture that's almost as good as fresh.

8 ounces uncooked wide rice stick noodles (banh pho)
4 cups unsalted chicken stock (such as Swanson)
3 tablespoons sambal oelek (ground fresh chile paste)
1 pound peeled and deveined raw medium shrimp
2 cups shredded napa cabbage (about 6 ounces)
1 cup fresh snow peas, cut into 1-inch pieces
¾ cup matchstick carrots
¼ cup loosely packed fresh cilantro leaves
⅜ teaspoon kosher salt
3 scallions, thinly sliced (optional)

1. Cook the noodles according to the package directions; drain.
2. Stir together the chicken stock and sambal oelek in a 3-quart saucepan. Bring to a boil over high. Add the shrimp, and cook 3 minutes. Add the cabbage, snow peas, and carrots; cook just until the shrimp are cooked through, about 2 minutes. Stir in the noodles, cilantro, salt, and, if desired, scallions. Serve immediately.

(**SERVING SIZE:** 1½ cups): **CALORIES** 279; **FAT** 2g (sat 0g, unsat 1g); **PROTEIN** 26g; **CARB** 37g; **FIBER** 5g; **SUGARS** 3g (added sugars 0g); **SODIUM** 780mg; **CALC** 12% DV; **POTASSIUM** 5% DV

SHRIMP *and* BROWN RICE COLLARD GREEN WRAPS

Blanching the collard greens helps them become tender and pliable enough to wrap and eat with ease. Use the biggest leaves you can find, but if you only have small ones, just place 1½ or 2 leaves beside each other, fill, and wrap.

HANDS-ON: 20 MIN. • **TOTAL: 20 MIN.** • **SERVES 4**

6 large collard green leaves (about 12 ounces)

2 (8.8-ounce) packages precooked microwaveable brown rice (such as Uncle Ben's)

1 tablespoon olive oil, divided

1 tablespoon fresh lime juice (from 1 lime; optional)

1¼ pounds peeled and deveined raw large shrimp

¼ teaspoon kosher salt

¼ teaspoon black pepper

1 medium-sized ripe avocado, sliced

½ cup pico de gallo

1. Bring a stockpot of water to a boil over high. Remove the collard green leaves from the stems, keeping the leaves intact. Drop the leaves into the boiling water; boil 30 seconds. Drain and plunge the leaves into a bowl of ice and water to stop the cooking process. Gently remove the leaves, and pat dry with paper towels. Tear 2 leaves in half.

2. Microwave the rice according to the package directions. Place the rice in a large bowl. Add 1 teaspoon of the oil and, if desired, the lime juice, and stir to combine.

3. Heat the remaining 2 teaspoons oil in a large skillet over medium-high. Add the shrimp; cook, stirring occasionally, just until opaque and pink, 3 to 4 minutes. Add the shrimp, salt, and pepper to the rice; stir to combine.

4. Arrange 1½ collard green leaves beside each other, slightly overlapping the leaves to create a solid surface. Divide the shrimp mixture evenly among the centers of the leaves, leaving a 2-inch border at the ends of the leaves. Top evenly with the avocado and pico de gallo. Fold the top and bottom ends of the leaves up and over the filling, and roll up burrito-style. Cut each roll in half, and serve immediately.

(**SERVING SIZE:** 1 wrap): **CALORIES** 426; **FAT** 15g (sat 2g, unsat 12g); **PROTEIN** 30g; **CARB** 46g; **FIBER** 8g; **SUGARS** 3g (added sugars 0g); **SODIUM** 547mg; **CALC** 21% DV; **POTASSIUM** 16% DV

SALSA VERDE SHRIMP TOSTADAS

Melty cheese–topped shrimp tostadas get a wonderful hit of brightness from the fresh slaw.

HANDS-ON: 10 MIN. • **TOTAL: 15 MIN.** • **SERVES 4**

4   (6-inch) corn tortillas
Cooking spray
2   teaspoons olive oil
12 ounces peeled and deveined raw large
    shrimp
½   cup salsa verde

3   ounces Monterey Jack cheese, shredded
    (about ¾ cup)
3   cups angel hair slaw (about 8 ounces)
¼   cup chopped fresh cilantro
3   tablespoons fresh lime juice (from 2 limes)

1. Preheat the oven to 450°F. Coat both sides of the tortillas with the cooking spray; arrange in a single layer on a baking sheet. Bake in the preheated oven until crisp, about 10 minutes, turning after 5 minutes.

2. Meanwhile, heat the oil in a large skillet over medium-high. Add the shrimp, and cook, stirring occasionally, until opaque, 3 to 4 minutes. Remove from the heat. Toss the shrimp with the salsa verde.

3. Top the tortillas evenly with the shrimp mixture. Sprinkle evenly with the cheese. Bake at 450°F until the cheese melts, 3 to 4 minutes.

4. Toss together the slaw, cilantro, and lime juice; pile evenly on top of the tostadas. Serve immediately.

(**SERVING SIZE:** 1 tostada): **CALORIES** 269; **FAT** 11g (sat 5g, unsat 5g); **PROTEIN** 22g; **CARB** 18g; **FIBER** 3g; **SUGARS** 5g (added sugars 0g); **SODIUM** 541mg; **CALC** 24% DV; **POTASSIUM** 7% DV

SHRIMP *with* PARMESAN-CHIVE GRITS

Whisking the grits constantly for the first 45 seconds helps prevent lumps from forming. You can vary the flavor of the grits by using smoked Gouda or sharp Cheddar in place of the Parmesan.

HANDS-ON: 15 MIN. • **TOTAL: 25 MIN.** • **SERVES 2**

- 2 cups water
- ½ cup uncooked stone-ground grits
- 1 ounce Parmesan cheese, shredded (about ¼ cup)
- 1 tablespoon unsalted butter
- ¼ teaspoon kosher salt
- ⅓ cup chopped fresh chives, divided
- ½ tablespoon olive oil
- ½ pound unpeeled raw large shrimp, peeled and deveined
- ¼ teaspoon cayenne pepper (optional)

1. Bring the water to a boil in a medium saucepan over high. Whisk in the grits; cook, whisking constantly, until smooth, about 45 seconds. Return to a boil; cover and reduce the heat to medium-low. Cook until tender, about 20 minutes. Whisk in the Parmesan, butter, salt, and ¼ cup of the chives.
2. While the grits cook, heat the oil in a medium nonstick skillet over medium-high. Add the shrimp and, if desired, cayenne; cook, stirring occasionally, until the shrimp are opaque, about 3 minutes. Serve the shrimp over the grits, and sprinkle with the remaining chives.

(**SERVING SIZE:** 1 cup grits and 8 shrimp): **CALORIES** 367; **FAT** 15g (sat 7g, unsat 7g); **PROTEIN** 24g; **CARB** 33g; **FIBER** 2g; **SUGARS** 1g (added sugars 0g); **SODIUM** 650mg; **CALC** 25% DV; **POTASSIUM** 6% DV

CHICKEN *and* SHRIMP JAMBALAYA

This recipe capitalizes on smart, fresh convenience products (rotisserie chicken, microwavable rice, prechopped produce) that help get this Cajun-flavored dish on the table quickly. You can find trinity mix by the prechopped onions in the produce section.

HANDS-ON: 15 MIN. • **TOTAL: 15 MIN.** • **SERVES 4**

2 (8.8-ounce) packages precooked microwavable brown rice (such as Uncle Ben's)

2 tablespoons olive oil

1 pound unpeeled raw large shrimp, peeled and deveined

8 ounces prechopped trinity mix (onion, celery, and green bell pepper)

1 tablespoon chopped fresh garlic (about 2 cloves)

1 cup canned crushed tomatoes

6 ounces rotisserie chicken breast meat, shredded (about 1 cup)

2 teaspoons hot sauce (such as Crystal)

1½ teaspoons Cajun seasoning (such as Tony Chachere's)

½ teaspoon black pepper

Sliced scallions (optional)

1. Microwave the rice according to the package directions. Set aside.
2. Heat the oil in a large skillet over medium-high. Add the shrimp; cook, stirring occasionally, until cooked through, about 3 minutes. Using a slotted spoon, transfer the shrimp to a plate; set aside. Add the trinity mix to the pan; cook, stirring occasionally, until tender, about 4 minutes. Add the garlic; cook, stirring often, until fragrant, about 30 seconds.
3. Reduce the heat to medium-low. Stir in the tomatoes, chicken, hot sauce, Cajun seasoning, and pepper. Simmer, stirring occasionally, until slightly thickened, about 5 minutes. Stir in the shrimp and rice. Sprinkle with scallions, if desired.

(**SERVING SIZE:** 2 cups): **CALORIES** 403; **FAT** 12g (sat 1g, unsat 9g); **PROTEIN** 33g; **CARB** 44g; **FIBER** 5g; **SUGARS** 4g (added sugars 0g); **SODIUM** 694mg; **CALC** 10% DV; **POTASSIUM** 19% DV

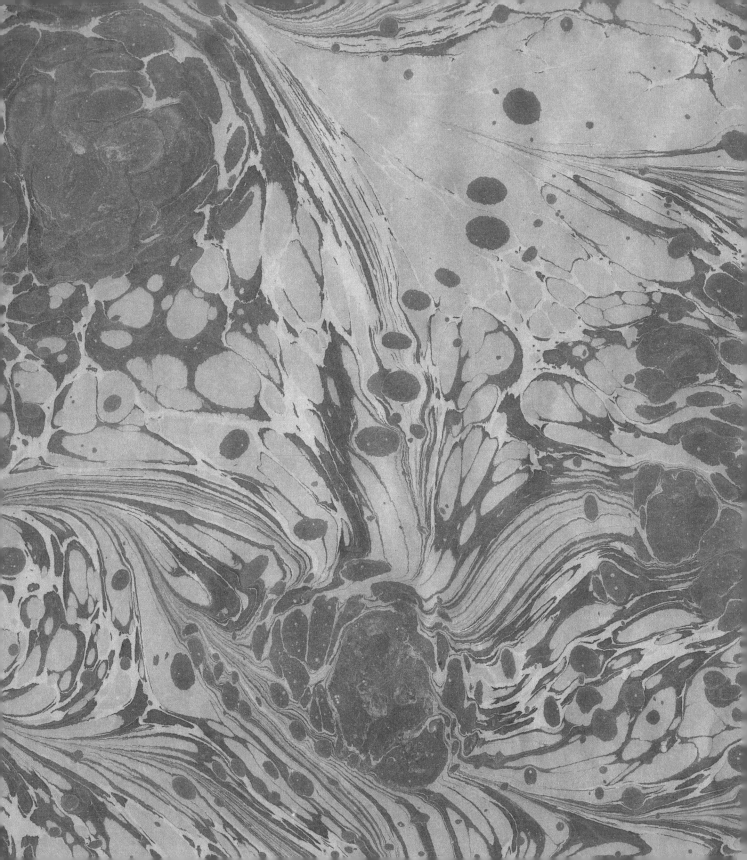

CHAPTER 6

MEATS & POULTRY

SHEET PAN FAJITAS

This is a wonderfully mess-free way to make fajitas. The steak cooks nicely while the vegetables remain crisp-tender. If you'd like your vegetables more tender, cook them by themselves under the broiler for about 2 minutes, and then add the steak, and cook another 5 minutes. The homemade crema adds just the right amount of creaminess to round out the flavors and textures. Serve with pico de gallo too, if desired.

HANDS-ON: 5 MIN. • **TOTAL: 15 MIN.** • **SERVES 4**

1 (1-pound) sirloin steak, trimmed and cut into ¼- to ½-inch-thick slices

1 (16-ounce) container fresh fajita vegetable mix (sliced onions and tri-color bell peppers; about 3 cups)

1 tablespoon olive oil

2 tablespoons salt-free fajita seasoning (such as Mrs. Dash)

1 teaspoon kosher salt, divided

Cooking spray

2 large limes

½ medium-sized ripe avocado

⅓ cup light sour cream

8 (6-inch) corn tortillas

2 tablespoons fresh cilantro leaves

1. Preheat the broiler with the oven rack 6 inches from the heat. Toss together the steak slices, vegetable mix, olive oil, fajita seasoning, and ¾ teaspoon of the salt in a medium bowl. Spread the steak mixture in an even layer on a large rimmed baking sheet coated with cooking spray.
2. Broil in the preheated oven until the steak is the desired degree of doneness and the vegetables are tender-crisp, about 5 minutes.
3. While the steak cooks, juice 1 lime to measure 1 to 2 tablespoons. Process the avocado, sour cream, 1 tablespoon of the lime juice, and the remaining ¼ teaspoon salt in a mini processor until smooth, adding additional lime juice to reach desired consistency if necessary.
4. Heat the tortillas according to the package directions. Cut the remaining lime into wedges. Divide the steak mixture among the warm tortillas, and dollop with the avocado mixture. Sprinkle with the cilantro and serve with lime wedges.

(**SERVING SIZE:** 2 tortillas, ¾ cup steak mixture, and 2 tablespoons avocado mixture): **CALORIES** 387; **FAT** 15g (sat 4g, unsat 9g); **PROTEIN** 29g; **CARB** 35g; **FIBER** 6g; **SUGARS** 7g (added sugars 0g); **SODIUM** 577mg; **CALC** 8% DV; **POTASSIUM** 25% DV

AVOCADO

When buying avocado, look for fruit that's firm but gives a little when gently squeezed. If it's hard, it's not ready yet—let it ripen a little more. You can speed up ripening by placing an avocado in a paper bag with an apple or banana and storing it at room temperature. If it's ripe but you're not ready to eat it, put it in the refrigerator; it should last about a week without browning. When the avocado skin starts to shrivel and becomes very soft, it's ripened too much and may be brown inside.

STEAK *and* POBLANO QUESADILLA ▶

HANDS-ON: 25 MIN. • **TOTAL: 25 MIN.** • **SERVES 4**

12 ounces flank steak
¼ teaspoon kosher salt
¼ teaspoon black pepper
1 tablespoon olive oil
2 medium-sized poblano chiles (about 6 ounces), sliced

3½ ounces reduced-fat Monterey Jack cheese, shredded (about ⅞ cup)
4 (8-inch) whole-wheat flour tortillas
Cooking spray
¼ cup fresh pico de gallo
Reduced-fat sour cream (optional)

1. Sprinkle the steak with salt and pepper. Heat the oil in a large skillet over medium-high. Add the steak, and cook until desired degree of doneness, 4 to 5 minutes per side for medium-rare. Remove from the pan, and let rest 5 minutes. Add poblanos to the pan; cook, stirring often, until lightly browned and tender, 3 to 5 minutes.
2. Cut the steak across the grain into thin slices. Sprinkle half of the cheese evenly over half of each tortilla; top evenly with the steak, poblanos, and remaining cheese. Fold each tortilla in half over the filling. Lightly coat the tortillas with cooking spray.
3. Heat the same pan over medium. Place 2 quesadillas in the pan, and cook until the cheese melts and the tortilla is lightly browned, 2 to 3 minutes per side. Repeat with the remaining quesadillas. Cut each quesadilla into 3 wedges. Top evenly with pico de gallo, and, if desired, serve with sour cream.

(SERVING SIZE: 3 wedges): CALORIES 329; **FAT** 14g (sat 5g, unsat 7g); **PROTEIN** 28g; **CARB** 22g; **FIBER** 1g; **SUGARS** 1g (added sugars 0g); **SODIUM** 580mg; **CALC** 25% DV; **POTASSIUM** 8% DV

HERBED STEAKS *with* HORSERADISH CREAM

Pair this easy-but-impressive dish with asparagus and mashed potatoes.

HANDS-ON: 10 MIN. • **TOTAL: 15 MIN.** • **SERVES 4**

4 (4-ounce, about 1-inch-thick) beef tenderloin steaks
1 tablespoon olive oil
1 teaspoon kosher salt, divided
1 teaspoon black pepper, divided

2 tablespoons chopped fresh herbs, divided (such as rosemary, thyme, and oregano)
¼ cup reduced-fat sour cream
½ teaspoon prepared horseradish
Cooking spray

1. Preheat the grill to medium-high (400°F to 450°F). Rub the steaks evenly with the olive oil. Sprinkle evenly with ¾ teaspoon each of the salt and pepper. Gently pat the herbs onto both sides of each steak (about ½ tablespoon per steak).
2. Stir together the sour cream, horseradish, and remaining ¼ teaspoon each salt and pepper. Set aside.
3. Place the steaks on a grill grate coated with cooking spray, and grill, uncovered, 3 to 5 minutes. Turn the steaks, and grill until the desired degree of doneness, 3 to 5 minutes for medium-rare. Serve the steaks with the horseradish cream.

(SERVING SIZE: 1 steak and about 1 tablespoon cream): CALORIES 201; **FAT** 11g (sat 4g, unsat 7g); **PROTEIN** 23g; **CARB** 2g; **FIBER** 0g; **SUGARS** 1g (added sugars 0g); **SODIUM** 535mg; **CALC** 5% DV; **POTASSIUM** 10% DV

Sautéing the poblanos in the same pan as you used to sear the steak maximizes the flavor and the oil used in the recipe. If you'd prefer a milder chile, you can substitute bell peppers for the poblano.

This complete meal is a tasty mix of sweet and savory flavors. Caramelizing the pineapple is an easy way to add flavor and color to the dish.

GRILLED STEAK *with* PINEAPPLE RICE

HANDS-ON: 20 MIN. • **TOTAL: 20 MIN.** • **SERVES 4**

¼ cup lower-sodium soy sauce
½ teaspoon freshly ground black pepper
4 (4-ounce) beef tenderloin fillets
Cooking spray
1 (8-ounce) can pineapple slices in juice,
   drained

6 scallions
2 (8.8-ounce) packages precooked
   microwavable brown rice (such as
   Uncle Ben's)
⅞ teaspoon kosher salt

1. Place the soy sauce, pepper, and beef in a large ziplock plastic bag. Massage
   the sauce into the beef; let stand at room temperature 7 minutes, turning the
   bag occasionally.
2. While the steak marinates, heat a large grill pan over medium-high. Coat the pan
   with cooking spray. Arrange the pineapple and scallions in the pan; cook 5 minutes
   or until well charred, turning to char evenly. Cut the scallions and pineapple into
   bite-sized pieces. Microwave the rice according to the package directions; stir in
   the pineapple, scallions, and salt. Keep warm.
3. Heat a grill pan over medium-high. Coat pan with cooking spray. Remove the beef
   from the marinade; discard the marinade. Add the beef to the pan; cook 3 minutes
   on each side or until the desired degree of doneness. Serve the beef with the rice mixture.

(**SERVING SIZE:** 3 ounces beef and about ¾ cup rice): **CALORIES** 382; **FAT** 10g (sat 3g, unsat 5g); **PROTEIN** 31g;
CARB 44g; **FIBER** 4g; **SUGARS** 6g (added sugars 0g); **SODIUM** 645mg; **CALC** 5% DV; **POTASSIUM** 15% DV

PEPPER-ROSEMARY FLANK STEAK

Be sure to let the steak rest before cutting into it. This allows the juices inside to
redistribute back into the meat instead of running all over your cutting board.

HANDS-ON: 5 MIN. • **TOTAL: 20 MIN.** • **SERVES 6**

2 tablespoons olive oil
1½ tablespoons lower-sodium Worcestershire
   sauce
1 tablespoon lemon zest (from 1 lemon)
1 tablespoon coarsely ground black pepper

2 teaspoons finely chopped fresh rosemary
1¼ teaspoons kosher salt
2 garlic cloves, minced
1 (1½-pound) flank steak, trimmed
Cooking spray

1. Preheat the grill to medium-high (400°F to 450°F) or heat a grill pan over medium
   high. Stir together the olive oil, Worcestershire, lemon zest, pepper, rosemary, salt,
   and garlic in a small bowl; rub the mixture into the steak.
2. Place the steak on a grill grate coated with cooking spray, and grill, uncovered, until
   the desired degree of doneness, about 5 minutes per side for medium-rare. Transfer
   the steak to a cutting board, and let rest 5 minutes. Cut the steak across the grain
   into thin slices.

(**SERVING SIZE:** 3 ounces): **CALORIES** 205; **FAT** 11g (sat 3g, unsat 6g); **PROTEIN** 25g; **CARB** 2g; **FIBER** 0g; **SUGARS** 0g
(added sugars 0g); **SODIUM** 497mg; **CALC** 4% DV; **POTASSIUM** 12% DV

CORIANDER STEAK *with* SWEET POTATO *and* SNAP PEAS

Cooking the sweet potatoes in the microwave helps this dish get to the table fast. Choose the smallest sweet potatoes you can find to ensure they cook quickly.

HANDS-ON: 15 MIN. • **TOTAL: 15 MIN.** • **SERVES 4**

3   tablespoons olive oil, divided
1   (1-pound) flank steak
2   teaspoons coarsely cracked coriander seeds
1¼ teaspoons kosher salt, divided
¾   teaspoon black pepper, divided
2   small sweet potatoes (about 8 ounces), halved lengthwise

2   tablespoons water
¼   cup plain 2% low-fat Greek yogurt
¼   cup whole buttermilk
2   teaspoons chopped fresh tarragon
2   teaspoons fresh lemon juice (from 1 lemon)
8   ounces fresh sugar snap peas, trimmed

1. Heat 1 tablespoon of the oil in a large cast-iron skillet over medium-high. Rub the steak all over with 1 tablespoon of the oil; rub with the coriander seeds and ½ teaspoon each of the salt and pepper. Cook until the desired degree of doneness, 4 to 5 minutes per side for medium-rare. Let rest 5 minutes before slicing across the grain.

2. While the steak cooks, place the potatoes and water in a medium-sized microwave-safe bowl. Cover with plastic wrap; pierce with the tip of a knife to vent. Microwave at HIGH until tender, about 5 minutes. Fluff the flesh of the potatoes with a fork; sprinkle with ¼ teaspoon each salt and pepper.

3. Whisk together the yogurt, buttermilk, tarragon, lemon juice, and remaining ½ teaspoon salt.

4. Heat the remaining 1 tablespoon oil in the pan over medium-high. Add the sugar snap peas; cook, stirring occasionally, until tender and lightly charred, about 3 minutes. Divide the snap peas and potato halves evenly among 4 plates; drizzle with the tarragon dressing, and serve with the sliced steak.

(SERVING SIZE: 3 ounces steak, ½ cup snap peas, 1 sweet potato half, and 2 tablespoons dressing): **CALORIES** 338; **FAT** 17g (sat 4g, unsat 11g); **PROTEIN** 28g; **CARB** 17g; **FIBER** 4g; **SUGARS** 5g (added sugars 0g); **SODIUM** 701mg; **CALC** 10% DV; **POTASSIUM** 17% DV

CORIANDER

Coriander is the aromatic seed of the cilantro plant. It has a mild, sweet flavor, so it sometimes takes a lot for the flavor to assert itself. You can find it in stores both whole and ground. Ground coriander can lose its flavor quickly, so if you don't plan on using it often, you may want to purchase whole seeds, which are easy to smash or grind.

MUFFIN PAN BBQ MEAT LOAVES

Using a muffin pan makes meat loaf a more doable weeknight option since the smaller servings cook more quickly. The meat mixture is on the sticky side so you may want to coat your hands with cooking spray or use gloves when rolling it into balls. Sprinkle with chopped fresh parsley, if you like.

HANDS-ON: 10 MIN. • TOTAL: 30 MIN. • SERVES 6

1¼ pounds 85⁄15 lean ground round
½ cup dry breadcrumbs
½ cup prechopped green pepper and onion mix
½ teaspoon kosher salt
½ teaspoon black pepper
1 large egg, lightly beaten
6 tablespoons lower-sodium barbecue sauce, divided
Cooking spray

1. Preheat the oven to 450°F. Place the beef, breadcrumbs, pepper and onion mix, salt, black pepper, egg, and 3 tablespoons of the barbecue sauce in a large bowl, and gently combine using your hands.
2. Spray a 6-cup muffin pan with cooking spray. Gently roll the meat mixture into 6 equal-sized balls, and place 1 in each muffin cup. Top each with ½ tablespoon barbecue sauce. Bake in the preheated oven until no longer pink in the centers, about 20 minutes.

(**SERVING SIZE:** 1 meat loaf): **CALORIES** 288; **FAT** 16g (sat 6g, unsat 7g); **PROTEIN** 20g; **CARB** 15g; **FIBER** 1g; **SUGARS** 7g (added sugars 3g); **SODIUM** 311mg; **CALC** 5% DV; **POTASSIUM** 10% DV

LAMB SKEWERS
with TZATZIKI DIPPING SAUCE ▶

HANDS-ON: 15 MIN. • TOTAL: 15 MIN. • SERVES 4

1   (1-pound) lamb top round, cut into ¾-inch cubes
2   tablespoons extra-virgin olive oil, divided
2   teaspoons finely chopped garlic (from 2 cloves), divided
1   medium-sized red onion (about 8 ounces), cut into large pieces
2   cups grape tomatoes
⅓   cup plain whole-milk Greek yogurt
¼   small English cucumber (about 1½ to 2 ounces), peeled, seeded, and grated
1   tablespoon fresh lemon juice (from 1 lemon)
1   teaspoon kosher salt, divided
¼   teaspoon black pepper
8   pita bread wedges (optional)

1. Toss together the lamb, 1 tablespoon of the oil, and 1 teaspoon of the garlic in a medium bowl until evenly coated.
2. Heat a large grill pan over high. Thread the lamb, red onion, and tomatoes alternately onto 8 (6-inch) skewers. Add the skewers to the grill pan; cook until desired degree of doneness, turning often, about 6 minutes for medium-rare. Remove the skewers from the grill pan.
3. Stir together the yogurt, grated cucumber, lemon juice, remaining 1 teaspoon garlic, and ½ teaspoon salt in a bowl. Place the skewers on a serving plate. Sprinkle with the pepper and remaining ½ teaspoon salt; drizzle with the remaining 1 tablespoon oil. Serve with the cucumber dipping sauce, and, if desired, the pita wedges.

(SERVING SIZE: 2 skewers and 2 tablespoons dipping sauce): CALORIES 245; FAT 14g (sat 4g, unsat 10g); PROTEIN 21g; CARB 8g; FIBER 2g; SUGARS 4g (added sugars 0g); SODIUM 544mg; CALC 5% DV; POTASSIUM 15% DV

QUINOA—GROUND PORK MEATBALLS

Combining quinoa with ground pork creates a juicy, tender meatball that has a nice chew. Snuggling the meatballs into the dish helps keep them moist.

HANDS-ON: 15 MIN. • TOTAL: 15 MIN. • SERVES 4

1   (9-ounce) package precooked microwavable quinoa (such as Suzie's)
1   large egg, lightly beaten
16 ounces lean ground pork
1   cup lower-sodium tomato-basil marinara sauce
2   teaspoons minced garlic (from 2 cloves)
½   teaspoon kosher salt
¼   teaspoon black pepper
Cooking spray

Preheat the oven to 425°F. Combine all the ingredients except the cooking spray; shape the mixture into 20 (2-inch) balls. Place balls in an 8-inch square baking dish coated with cooking spray. Bake until browned and cooked through, 15 to 18 minutes.

(SERVING SIZE: 5 meatballs): CALORIES 321; FAT 15g (sat 5g, unsat 9g); PROTEIN 28g; CARB 19g; FIBER 3g; SUGARS 3g (added sugars 0g); SODIUM 468mg; CALC 3% DV; POTASSIUM 11% DV

Lamb is widely available, but if you can't find it or prefer not to use it, you can substitute beef. Both work nicely with the bright tzatziki sauce.

PORK LO MEIN

Pork tenderloin is the ideal meat for this sweet and savory dish—it stands up to the bold flavors and becomes very tender when stir-fried. Chinese lo mein noodles are the most traditional choice for this recipe, but you can substitute regular egg noodles if desired. If you can't find Fresno chiles, use a jalapeño instead.

HANDS-ON: 15 MIN. • TOTAL: 15 MIN. • SERVES 4

8   ounces uncooked lo mein noodles
2   tablespoons canola oil
1   red Fresno chile, seeded and finely chopped (about 2 tablespoons)
½   tablespoon finely chopped fresh ginger
12 ounces pork tenderloin, cut into ½-inch-thick slices

½   cup sliced shiitake mushrooms
1½ tablespoons oyster sauce
1½ tablespoons unseasoned rice vinegar
1   tablespoon granulated sugar
¼   teaspoon kosher salt
¼   cup chopped scallions (optional)
Lime wedges (optional)

1. Cook the noodles according to the package directions, omitting salt and fat; drain.
2. Heat the oil in a large skillet over medium. Add the chile and ginger; cook, stirring constantly, 30 seconds. Add the pork slices to the pan; cook, stirring often, until the pork begins to brown, about 3 minutes. Add the mushrooms to the pan, and cook, stirring often, until the mushrooms are just tender and the pork is browned, about 2 minutes.
3. Stir together the oyster sauce, rice vinegar, sugar, and salt; add to the pan, stirring to coat the pork and mushrooms. Remove the pan from the heat, and stir in the noodles. If desired, top with the scallions, and serve with the lime wedges.

(**SERVING SIZE:** 1 cup): **CALORIES** 344; **FAT** 10g (sat 1g, unsat 7g); **PROTEIN** 24g; **CARB** 39g; **FIBER** 2g; **SUGARS** 4g (added sugars 0g); **SODIUM** 529mg; **CALC** 2% DV; **POTASSIUM** 13% DV

RICE VINEGAR

Unseasoned rice vinegar is often labeled "natural" rice vinegar. Unlike seasoned rice vinegar, it doesn't have any salt or sugar added, which allows you to better control the flavor of the dish.

CHORIZO, MUSHROOM, *and* QUINOA BOWL

Cooking the vegetables in the fat that cooks out of the chorizo is a smart way to flavor every element of this dish. If you can't find poblanos, you can use a bell pepper and add some diced jalapeño for heat.

HANDS-ON: 25 MIN. • **TOTAL: 25 MIN.** • **SERVES 4**

2   tablespoons canola oil
6   ounces chopped dry-cured Spanish chorizo
16 ounces cremini mushrooms, halved
1½ cups chopped poblano chiles (from 2 large chiles)
¾   teaspoon kosher salt

½   teaspoon black pepper
12 ounces fresh baby spinach (about 12 cups)
2   (8.5-ounce) packages precooked microwavable quinoa and brown rice blend with garlic (such as Seeds of Change)

1. Heat the oil in a large nonstick skillet over medium-high. Add the chorizo, and cook, stirring occasionally, until the chorizo starts to brown, about 4 minutes. Using a slotted spoon, transfer the chorizo to a plate lined with paper towels; set aside. Reserve the drippings in the pan.

2. Add the mushrooms to the pan; cook, stirring occasionally, until the mushrooms have softened and are starting to brown, about 8 minutes. Return the chorizo to the pan; add the chopped poblano, salt, and pepper, and cook, stirring occasionally, until starting to soften, about 4 minutes. Stir in the spinach; cover and cook until the spinach is slightly wilted, about 3 minutes. Remove from the heat.

3. Microwave the quinoa and rice blend according to the package directions. Serve the chorizo mixture over the quinoa-rice mixture.

(**SERVING SIZE:** 1 cup quinoa-rice mixture and 1¼ cups chorizo mixture): **CALORIES** 452; **FAT** 20g (sat 5g, unsat 13g); **PROTEIN** 19g; **CARB** 51g; **FIBER** 6g; **SUGARS** 3g (added sugars 0g); **SODIUM** 772mg; **CALC** 12% DV; **POTASSIUM** 15% DV

POBLANOS

These chiles are larger than most hot chiles, look like an elongated green bell pepper, and have a mild-medium heat. When fully ripe, they turn dark red-brown. They can be dried and are then referred to as an ancho chile. If poblanos are smoked and dried, they're referred to as chipotles.

ITALIAN SAUSAGE PUTTANESCA

This recipe is a keeper. It's a well-rounded mix of flavors from salty olives, briny capers, spicy sausage, and sweet tomatoes. The anchovies give it depth without adding fishy flavor.

HANDS-ON: 15 MIN. • **TOTAL: 15 MIN.** • **SERVES 4**

12 ounces uncooked whole-wheat spaghetti
6 ounces spicy Italian sausage, casings removed
3 cups multicolored cherry tomatoes
¼ cup olive oil
3 garlic cloves, smashed

2 anchovy fillets
10 pitted Castelvetrano olives, halved
¼ cup chopped fresh basil
3 tablespoons drained capers
Shaved Parmesan cheese (optional)
Basil leaves (optional)

1. Cook the pasta according to the package directions, omitting salt and fat. Drain, reserving 1 cup cooking water.
2. Heat a large skillet over medium-high. Add the sausage; cook, stirring to crumble, until browned, about 6 minutes. Using a slotted spoon, remove the sausage from the pan. Add the tomatoes, olive oil, garlic, and anchovies to the pan, and cook, stirring often, until the tomatoes begin to burst, about 3 minutes. Add the pasta, sausage, olives, basil, and capers; toss to coat. Add the reserved cooking water, ¼ cup at a time, if needed to reach the desired consistency. If desired, top with the shaved Parmesan and basil leaves.

(**SERVING SIZE:** about 2 cups): **CALORIES** 537; **FAT** 23g (sat 4g, unsat 17g); **PROTEIN** 21g; **CARB** 69g; **FIBER** 9g; **SUGARS** 5g (added sugars 0g); **SODIUM** 779mg; **CALC** 6% DV; **POTASSIUM** 21% DV

GRILLED PORK TENDERLOIN
with CHERRY-GINGER GLAZE

Turning the pork helps it cook thoroughly while also allowing a nice crust to form. The sweet, slightly spicy, sticky glaze also works on pork chops or chicken.

HANDS-ON: 10 MIN. • **TOTAL: 20 MIN.** • **SERVES 4**

½ teaspoon kosher salt
¼ teaspoon black pepper
2 teaspoons lower-sodium soy sauce, divided
1½ teaspoons grated fresh ginger, divided

1 (1-pound) pork tenderloin, trimmed
⅓ cup cherry preserves
1 tablespoon fresh lime juice (from 1 lime)
Cooking spray

1. Preheat the grill to medium-high (400°F to 450°F). Stir together the salt, pepper, and 1 teaspoon each of the soy sauce and grated ginger in a small bowl; rub the mixture over the tenderloin.
2. Stir together the cherry preserves, lime juice, and remaining 1 teaspoon soy sauce and ½ teaspoon grated ginger in a small bowl.
3. Place the pork on a grill grate coated with cooking spray, and grill, covered, until a thermometer inserted into the thickest portion registers 145°F, 10 to 12 minutes, turning several times with the tongs and brushing the pork with 2 tablespoons of the cherry preserve mixture during the last 5 minutes of grilling. Transfer the pork to a plate; tent with aluminum foil, and let rest 5 minutes. Cut the pork into slices, and serve with the remaining cherry glaze.

(**SERVING SIZE:** 3 ounces pork and about 1 tablespoon glaze): **CALORIES** 194; **FAT** 2g (sat 1g, unsat 1g); **PROTEIN** 24g; **CARB** 18g; **FIBER** 0g; **SUGARS** 16g (added sugars 8g); **SODIUM** 396mg; **CALC** 1% DV; **POTASSIUM** 13% DV

TRIMMING PORK TENDERLOIN

Pork tenderloin often has a thin, shiny silver membrane running along the surface of the meat. Leaving it on can cause the tenderloin to toughen and lose shape during cooking, so be sure to remove it. Stretch the membrane with one hand so it's tight, and then use your other hand to slip the knife underneath the skin.

SEARED PORK CHOPS *and* SOUR CREAM MASHED POTATOES

When making the gravy, be sure to whisk vigorously to avoid clumping.
Serve this with a simple salad or steamed green beans.

HANDS-ON: 15 MIN. • TOTAL: 15 MIN. • SERVES 4

1   tablespoon olive oil
4   (4-ounce) boneless center-cut pork chops
1½ tablespoons chopped fresh thyme, divided
⅞   teaspoon kosher salt, divided
¾   teaspoon black pepper, divided
1   cup unsalted chicken stock (such as Swanson)

2   tablespoons all-purpose flour
2   cups frozen steam-and-mash cut russet potatoes (such as Ore Ida Steam n' Mash)
¼   cup reduced-fat sour cream
2   tablespoons water
1   tablespoon unsalted butter

1. Heat the oil in a large skillet over medium-high. Sprinkle the pork with 1 tablespoon of the thyme and ⅜ teaspoon each of the salt and pepper. Add the pork to the pan; cook until a meat thermometer inserted into the thickest portion registers 145°F, about 3 minutes per side. Remove the chops from the pan, and keep warm. Add the stock, flour, and ⅛ teaspoon of the salt to the pan, and whisk vigorously until the flour is dissolved. Set aside, and keep warm.

2. While the pork cooks, place the potatoes in a medium-sized microwave-safe bowl; cover with plastic wrap, and poke holes with a knife to vent. Microwave at HIGH until tender, about 10 minutes. Add the sour cream, water, butter, and remaining ⅜ teaspoon each of the salt and pepper; mash until desired consistency. Sprinkle the pork chops with the remaining ½ tablespoon thyme. Serve the pork chops with the mashed potatoes and gravy.

(**SERVING SIZE:** 1 pork chop, about ½ cup mashed potatoes, and about ¼ cup gravy): **CALORIES** 276; **FAT** 13g (sat 5g, unsat 7g); **PROTEIN** 22g; **CARB** 16g; **FIBER** 2g; **SUGARS** 1g (added sugars 0g); **SODIUM** 674mg; **CALC** 7% DV; **POTASSIUM** 12% DV

ONE-SHEET PORK CHOPS, BRUSSELS SPROUTS, and APPLES

This is the ultimate mess-free weeknight meal in the fall. Removing the pork from the pan and hitting the vegetables and fruit with a little more heat gives them a roasty char.

HANDS-ON: 10 MIN. • **TOTAL: 30 MIN.** • **SERVES 4**

Galas have thin skin, crisp flesh, and a mild, sweet flavor that pairs well with bold flavors. They're wonderful to eat out of hand, but their shape and flavor hold up well under the high heat of the oven, as in this recipe. Select apples that are smooth-skinned and glossy. When ripe, Gala apples will be golden yellow with slight pink-orange stripes.

1½ teaspoons finely chopped fresh rosemary
1½ teaspoons salt-free lemon-pepper seasoning blend (such as Mrs. Dash)
1¼ teaspoons kosher salt
½ teaspoon black pepper
4 (6-ounce, 1-inch-thick) bone-in, center-cut pork chops

3 tablespoons olive oil, divided
1 pound fresh Brussels sprouts, trimmed and halved lengthwise
2 Gala apples (about 8 ounces each), cut into ½-inch wedges
Cooking spray

1. Preheat the oven to 425°F. Stir together the rosemary, seasoning blend, salt, and pepper in a small bowl. Rub the pork chops with 1½ tablespoons of the olive oil; rub both sides of each pork chop with the rosemary mixture (about ½ teaspoon per pork chop).

2. Toss together the Brussels sprouts, apples, and the remaining 1½ tablespoons olive oil and about 2½ teaspoons rosemary mixture.

3. Place the pork chops in the center of a large aluminum foil-lined rimmed baking sheet coated with cooking spray; spoon the Brussels sprouts mixture around the pork chops. Bake in the preheated oven 12 minutes; turn the pork chops, and bake until a meat thermometer inserted into the thickest portion registers 145°F, 8 to 10 minutes. Remove the pan; transfer the pork chops to a serving platter, and cover with foil to keep warm.

4. Increase the oven temperature to broil with the oven rack 6 inches from the heat. Spread the Brussels sprouts mixture in an even layer in the baking sheet. Broil until browned and slightly charred, 2 to 3 minutes. Serve immediately with the pork chops.

(**SERVING SIZE:** 1 pork chop and about 1 cup Brussels sprouts mixture): **CALORIES** 348; **FAT** 15g (sat 3g, unsat 11g); **PROTEIN** 30g; **CARB** 25g; **FIBER** 7g; **SUGARS** 14g (added sugars 0g); **SODIUM** 695mg; **CALC** 7% DV; **POTASSIUM** 28% DV

MU SHU PORK *and* RICE

The hoisin gives this dish a classic sweetness, while the cabbage and carrots lend it some crunch.

HANDS-ON: 15 MIN. • **TOTAL: 15 MIN.** • **SERVES 4**

2 (8.8-ounce) packages precooked microwavable brown rice (such as Uncle Ben's)

3 tablespoons canola oil, divided

6 ounces sliced shiitake mushroom caps

1 cup matchstick carrots

1½ teaspoons chopped fresh ginger

4 cups thinly sliced napa cabbage (from 1 small head)

¾ teaspoon kosher salt, divided

12 ounces boneless pork shoulder, trimmed and thinly sliced

3 tablespoons hoisin sauce

Sliced scallions (optional)

1. Microwave the rice according to the package directions. Heat 1½ tablespoons of the oil in a large skillet over medium-high. Add the mushrooms, carrots, and ginger; cook, stirring often, until just tender, about 4 minutes. Stir in the cabbage and ¼ teaspoon of the salt; cook, stirring occasionally, until the cabbage is wilted, about 2 minutes. Transfer the mixture to a bowl; set aside.

2. Wipe the pan clean. Heat the remaining 1½ tablespoons oil in the pan over medium-high. Add the pork and the remaining ½ teaspoon salt; cook, stirring occasionally, until the pork is browned and no longer pink, 3 to 4 minutes. Stir in the hoisin and cabbage mixture; cook until heated through, 1 to 2 minutes. Serve with the rice; garnish with the scallions, if desired.

(**SERVING SIZE:** ¾ cup rice and ⅔ cup pork mixture): **CALORIES** 456; **FAT** 20g (sat 3g, unsat 15g); **PROTEIN** 24g; **CARB** 49g; **FIBER** 6g; **SUGARS** 7g (added sugars 3g); **SODIUM** 665mg; **CALC** 9% DV; **POTASSIUM** 18% DV

CHORIZO, POTATO, *and* CORN TACOS

These tacos pack a lot of flavor. The crispy potatoes are a perfect pairing for the spicy chorizo, while the salsa verde and chopped cilantro add some freshness. Microwaving the potatoes gets them tender, so you can quickly brown them in the skillet.

HANDS-ON: 15 MIN.   •   TOTAL: 15 MIN.   •   SERVES 4

10 ounces quartered baby golden potatoes (about 3 cups)
1 tablespoon water
1 cup fresh corn kernels (from 1 large ear)
7 ounces fresh Mexican chorizo, casings removed
1 cup prechopped yellow onion (about 8 ounces)

⅜ teaspoon kosher salt
8 (6-inch) corn tortillas, warmed
¼ cup salsa verde
2 ounces Cotija cheese, crumbled (about ½ cup)
¼ cup chopped fresh cilantro
Lime wedges (optional)

1. Place the potatoes and water in a medium-sized microwave-safe bowl; cover tightly with plastic wrap. Microwave at HIGH until the potatoes are tender, about 4 minutes.
2. Heat a large cast-iron skillet over high. Add the corn, and cook, stirring occasionally, until lightly charred, about 3 minutes. Remove the corn from the pan, and set aside.
3. Return the pan to medium-high. Add the chorizo and onion, and cook, stirring until the chorizo is crumbled and cooked through and the onion is tender, about 6 minutes. Using a slotted spoon, transfer the mixture to a plate lined with paper towels; set aside. Reserve the drippings in the pan.
4. Add the potatoes and salt to the hot drippings, and, cook, turning occasionally, until lightly crisped, about 3 minutes. Divide the potatoes evenly among the tortillas; top evenly with the chorizo mixture, corn, salsa verde, crumbled Cotija, and cilantro. Serve with the lime wedges, if desired.

(**SERVING SIZE:** 2 tacos): **CALORIES** 480; **FAT** 27g (sat 8g, unsat 17g); **PROTEIN** 15g; **CARB** 48g; **FIBER** 6g; **SUGARS** 7g (added sugars 0g); **SODIUM** 753mg; **CALC** 18% DV; **POTASSIUM** 6% DV

CHORIZO

The two most common types of chorizo you'll find in stores are fresh Mexican chorizo and dried, cured Spanish chorizo. Mexican chorizo is highly spiced ground meat sausage that's most commonly sold fresh. You'll usually find it with the other raw meats and sausages in the grocery store. Spanish chorizo is usually sold in casings. It may be smoked or unsmoked, sweet or spicy. You'll usually find it with other cured and smoked sausages. It's important you use the one called for in the recipe, as the results are very different.

Using in-season produce is what will really make this bowl shine. Don't overcook the peas and tomatoes—you want them to maintain their color and texture.

GRILLED CHICKEN ENCHILADA FLATBREAD

Naan forms the base for this quick and healthy way to eat pizza. To save even more time, use shredded rotisserie chicken breast.

HANDS-ON: 15 MIN. • TOTAL: 25 MIN. • SERVES 4

Cooking spray
2 (6-ounce) boneless, skinless chicken breasts
½ cup green chile enchilada sauce
1 (8.8-ounce) package whole-grain naan

2½ ounces queso blanco cheese, crumbled (about ⅔ cup)
¼ teaspoon black pepper
2 tablespoons chopped fresh cilantro
Lime wedges (optional)

1. Heat a grill pan over medium-high; coat with cooking spray. Add the chicken to the grill pan. Grill the chicken until cooked through, about 5 minutes per side. Remove the chicken from the pan; let stand at least 5 minutes before cutting into thin slices.
2. Spread ¼ cup sauce over each flatbread. Top each evenly with the chicken, cheese, and pepper. Place the flatbreads in the grill pan, and cook until the cheese is melted, about 5 minutes. Sprinkle with the cilantro, and cut each flatbread in half. Serve with the lime wedges, if desired.

(SERVING SIZE: ½ naan): CALORIES 343; FAT 9g (sat 3g, unsat 4g); PROTEIN 30g; CARB 35g; FIBER 6g; SUGARS 2g (added sugars 0g); SODIUM 581mg; CALC 15% DV; POTASSIUM 9% DV

◄ CHICKEN SUCCOTASH BOWL

HANDS-ON: 15 MIN. • TOTAL: 15 MIN. • SERVES 4

3 tablespoons olive oil, divided
4 (6-ounce) boneless, skinless chicken breasts
1¼ teaspoons kosher salt, divided
½ teaspoon black pepper, divided
1¼ cups fresh yellow corn kernels

¾ cup vertically sliced red onion (from 1 small onion)
1¼ cups frozen green peas, thawed
1 cup halved grape tomatoes
Chopped fresh flat-leaf parsley (optional)

1. Heat 1 tablespoon of the oil in a large skillet over medium-high. Sprinkle the chicken with ½ teaspoon salt and ¼ teaspoon pepper. Add the chicken to the pan; cook until golden brown and cooked through, about 5 minutes per side. Remove the chicken from the pan; let stand at least 5 minutes. Cut into bite-sized cubes.
2. Return the pan to medium-high, and heat the remaining 2 tablespoons oil. Add the corn and onion, and cook, stirring occasionally, until tender and starting to brown, 5 to 7 minutes. Add the peas and tomatoes to the pan; cook, stirring occasionally, until thoroughly heated, about 3 minutes. Stir in the remaining ¾ teaspoon salt and ¼ teaspoon pepper. Divide the mixture among 4 serving bowls; top with the chicken, and, if desired, sprinkle with the parsley.

(SERVING SIZE: 1 cup succotash and 1 cup chicken): CALORIES 381; FAT 15g (sat 3g, unsat 11g); PROTEIN 43g; CARB 18g; FIBER 4g; SUGARS 7g (added sugars 0g); SODIUM 732mg; CALC 3% DV; POTASSIUM 25% DV

CUMIN-GRILLED CHICKEN *with* CHUNKY WATERMELON, TOMATO, *and* ONION SALAD

The fresh tomato and watermelon salad creates a light sauce for this meal, perfect for the hot days of summer. Be sure to pound the chicken so it cooks quickly and evenly on the grill.

HANDS-ON: 15 MIN. • TOTAL: 15 MIN. • SERVES 4

4 (6-ounce) boneless, skinless chicken breasts, pounded to 1-inch thickness
2 (½-inch-thick) slices red onion
¼ cup olive oil, divided
1½ teaspoons ground cumin
½ teaspoon black pepper
¾ teaspoon kosher salt, divided
2 cups ½-inch cubes seedless watermelon

2 cups halved yellow cherry tomatoes
½ cup loosely packed fresh cilantro leaves
1½ ounces feta cheese, crumbled (about ⅓ cup)
3 tablespoons fresh lime juice (from about 2 limes)

1. Preheat the grill to medium-high (400°F to 450°F). Brush both sides of the chicken and onion slices with 2 tablespoons of the oil; sprinkle the chicken evenly with the cumin, pepper, and ½ teaspoon of the salt. Place the chicken and onion slices on oiled grates, and grill, uncovered, until the chicken is cooked through and the onions are softened and lightly charred, 3 to 4 minutes per side.

2. Combine the watermelon, tomatoes, cilantro, and feta in a medium bowl. Chop the grilled red onions, and add to the watermelon mixture. Add the lime juice and remaining 2 tablespoons olive oil and ¼ teaspoon salt, and toss to coat. Serve the watermelon salad with the chicken.

(**SERVING SIZE:** 1 chicken breast and 1 cup salad): **CALORIES** 415; **FAT** 21g (sat 5g, unsat 14g); **PROTEIN** 42g; **CARB** 14g; **FIBER** 2g; **SUGARS** 9g (added sugars 0g); **SODIUM** 560mg; **CALC** 10% DV; **POTASSIUM** 26% DV

POUNDING CHICKEN

Pounding chicken breasts to an even thickness means they'll cook more quickly and evenly in the pan. To do this, you can place each breast between sheets of plastic wrap or in a ziplock bag with a little bit of water to prevent sticking, and then use a meat pounder, rolling pin, or heavy skillet to pound them to an even thickness.

SOUTHWEST-GRILLED CHICKEN BREAST *with* HEIRLOOM TOMATO SALSA

Feel free to leave in some of the jalapeño seeds if you'd like some heat.

HANDS-ON: 15 MIN. • **TOTAL: 15 MIN.** • **SERVES 4**

4 (6-ounce) boneless, skinless chicken breasts

2 teaspoons salt-free Southwest chipotle seasoning blend (such as Mrs. Dash)

1 teaspoon kosher salt, divided

Cooking spray

3 cups chopped heirloom tomatoes (about 2 medium tomatoes)

¼ cup finely chopped red onion (from 1 small onion)

2 tablespoons chopped fresh cilantro

2 tablespoons seeded finely chopped jalapeño chile (from 1 small chile)

2 tablespoons olive oil

1 tablespoon fresh lime juice (from 1 lime)

1 teaspoon honey

1. Preheat the grill to medium-high (400°F to 450°F). Sprinkle the chicken with the seasoning blend and ½ teaspoon salt. Place the chicken on a grill grate coated with cooking spray. Grill, uncovered, until cooked through, about 5 minutes per side.
2. Meanwhile, stir together the tomatoes, red onion, cilantro, jalapeño, oil, lime juice, honey, and remaining ½ teaspoon salt in a bowl. Serve the salsa over the chicken.

(**SERVING SIZE:** 1 chicken breast and about ¾ cup salsa): **CALORIES** 295; **FAT** 11g (sat 2g, unsat 8g); **PROTEIN** 39g; **CARB** 7g; **FIBER** 2g; **SUGARS** 5g (added sugars 1g); **SODIUM** 563mg; **CALC** 2% DV; **POTASSIUM** 25% DV

◄ CHILI CHICKEN *with* PEACH-LIME SAUCE

HANDS-ON: 10 MIN. • **TOTAL: 20 MIN.** • **SERVES 4**

1 medium lime

⅓ cup peach preserves

4 (6-ounce) boneless, skinless chicken breasts

1 teaspoon chili powder

¾ teaspoon kosher salt

¼ teaspoon black pepper

1 tablespoon olive oil

1 cup sliced peaches

1. Grate the zest from the lime to measure ½ teaspoon; squeeze the juice to measure 1 tablespoon. Stir together the zest, juice, and peach preserves.
2. Sprinkle the chicken with the chili powder, salt, and pepper. Heat the oil in a large nonstick skillet over medium-high. Add the chicken, and cook until cooked through, about 5 minutes per side. Remove the chicken from the pan.
3. Reduce the heat to medium; add the sliced peaches to the pan, and cook, stirring occasionally, until just starting to soften, about 2 minutes. Remove the pan from the heat; add the peach preserve mixture, and stir until smooth. Spoon the peach-lime sauce over the chicken.

(**SERVING SIZE:** 1 chicken breast and about 1½ tablespoons peach-lime sauce): **CALORIES** 319; **FAT** 8g (sat 1g, unsat 5g); **PROTEIN** 39g; **CARB** 22g; **FIBER** 1g; **SUGARS** 19g (added sugars 6g); **SODIUM** 456mg; **CALC** 1% DV; **POTASSIUM** 19% DV

Placing the breaded chicken on a wire rack that's in a baking sheet helps the heat circulate around the meat, cooking it thoroughly. It also prevents the crisp coating from getting soggy, which often happens when coated meats are placed directly on the baking sheet. You can line the baking sheet with aluminum foil to make cleanup a little quicker.

OVEN-FRIED PARMESAN CHICKEN

Toasting the breadcrumbs before breading the chicken is a key tip to making it look fried. If you can't find Italian panko, you can use regular panko instead.

HANDS-ON: 10 MIN. • **TOTAL: 30 MIN.** • **SERVES 4**

Cooking spray
¾ cup Italian-seasoned panko (Japanese-style breadcrumbs)
2 large egg whites
4 (6-ounce) boneless, skinless chicken breasts

¼ teaspoon kosher salt
¼ teaspoon black pepper
1½ ounces Parmesan cheese, grated (about ⅓ cup)
Chopped fresh flat-leaf parsley (optional)

1. Preheat the oven to 425°F. Place a wire rack coated with cooking spray in a rimmed baking sheet.
2. Heat a large skillet over medium-high. Add the panko; cook, stirring often, until golden brown, about 3 minutes. Transfer the panko to a shallow dish. Whisk the egg whites in a separate shallow dish just until foamy.
3. Sprinkle the chicken with the salt and pepper. Dredge the chicken in the egg whites, shaking off the excess. Dredge in the panko; press into the chicken to adhere. Coat the chicken on each side with cooking spray; arrange the chicken on the prepared wire rack placed in the rimmed baking sheet.
4. Bake in the preheated oven 18 minutes. Sprinkle evenly with the cheese, and bake until the chicken is cooked through, 5 to 10 minutes. If desired, sprinkle with the parsley.

(**SERVING SIZE:** 1 chicken breast): **CALORIES** 316; **FAT** 8g (sat 3g, unsat 4g); **PROTEIN** 45g; **CARB** 13g; **FIBER** 2g; **SUGARS** 1g (added sugars 0g); **SODIUM** 519mg; **CALC** 10% DV; **POTASSIUM** 18% DV

SPICY CHICKEN SATAY SKEWERS
with BOK CHOY SLAW

This colorful dish is sublime thanks to its flavorful sauce, crunchy slaw, and spicy skewers. You can slice the produce for the slaw and make the dressing the day before, and then mix them together just before serving.

HANDS-ON: 15 MIN. • **TOTAL: 15 MIN.** • **SERVES 4**

1¼ pounds boneless, skinless chicken thighs (about 6 thighs), cut into strips
1 tablespoon canola oil
¾ teaspoon kosher salt, divided
½ teaspoon black pepper, divided
⅓ cup peanut satay sauce
2 tablespoons sesame oil
2 teaspoons lower-sodium soy sauce

2 teaspoons unseasoned rice vinegar
4 cups thinly sliced baby bok choy (from 3 heads)
1 cup chopped mango (from 1 medium mango)
1 cup thinly sliced red cabbage (from 1 small head)
Chopped fresh cilantro (optional)

1. Heat a grill pan over medium-high. Thread the chicken onto 8 (6-inch) skewers; brush with the canola oil, and sprinkle with ½ teaspoon of the salt and ¼ teaspoon of the pepper. Place the skewers in the grill pan, and cook until the chicken is charred and cooked through, about 4 minutes per side. Drizzle with the satay sauce.

2. Whisk together the sesame oil, soy sauce, rice vinegar, and remaining ¼ teaspoon each salt and pepper in a large bowl. Add the bok choy, mango, and red cabbage; toss to coat. Sprinkle the chicken skewers and slaw with the cilantro, if desired.

(**SERVING SIZE:** 2 skewers and 1 cup slaw): **CALORIES** 342; **FAT** 18g (sat 4g, unsat 13g); **PROTEIN** 30g; **CARB** 15g; **FIBER** 3g; **SUGARS** 12g (added sugars 2g); **SODIUM** 639mg; **CALC** 10% DV; **POTASSIUM** 13% DV

LEMON-HONEY CHICKEN THIGHS

These sticky, saucy chicken thighs pair perfectly with any grilled vegetables, such as fresh zucchini or summer squash. Top with chopped tomato for a fresh finish. You can also use chicken breasts; just cook them a little longer, about 6 minutes per side.

HANDS-ON: 18 MIN. • **TOTAL: 18 MIN.** • **SERVES 4**

1½ tablespoons olive oil

8   (3-ounce) skinless, boneless chicken thighs

¾   teaspoon kosher salt

¼   teaspoon black pepper

¼   cup thinly sliced shallots

2   tablespoons water

1   tablespoon fresh lemon juice

1   tablespoon honey

1   tablespoon chopped fresh oregano

1. Heat the oil in a large skillet over medium-high. Sprinkle the chicken with the salt and pepper. Add the chicken to the pan; cook 4 to 5 minutes on each side or until browned and done. Transfer to a plate; keep warm.

2. Add the shallots to the pan; reduce the heat to medium, and cook 2 minutes or until beginning to brown and soften, stirring frequently. Add 2 tablespoons water, juice, and honey to the pan; bring to a boil. Cook 1 minute, scraping the pan to loosen the browned bits. Return the chicken to the pan, turning to coat. Sprinkle evenly with the fresh oregano, and serve immediately.

(**SERVING SIZE:** 2 thighs and about 4 teaspoons sauce): **CALORIES** 276; **FAT** 12g (sat 3g, unsat 8g); **PROTEIN** 34g; **CARB** 7g; **FIBER** 0g; **SUGARS** 5g (added sugars 4g); **SODIUM** 523mg; **CALC** 2% DV; **POTASSIUM** 13% DV

CHICKEN BIRYANI

This one-pot meal has a slight curry flavor that gets richness and moisture from the yogurt stirred in at the end. Serve it with naan.

HANDS-ON: 15 MIN. • **TOTAL: 15 MIN.** • **SERVES 6**

½   cup plain whole-milk yogurt
1   teaspoon kosher salt
1   teaspoon garam masala
½   teaspoon ground turmeric
10 ounces skinless rotisserie chicken, shredded into large pieces and warmed (about 2½ cups)
3½ tablespoons canola oil
1   cup prechopped yellow onion

1   (12-ounce) package fresh broccoli and cauliflower blend
2   (8.5-ounce) packages precooked microwavable basmati rice (such as Uncle Ben's)
¾   cup unsalted chicken stock
½   cup golden raisins (optional)
Chopped fresh cilantro (optional)

1. Stir together the yogurt, salt, garam masala, and turmeric in a medium bowl. Add the chicken; toss to coat. Set aside.

2. Heat the oil in a large skillet over medium-high. Add the onion; cook, stirring occasionally, until beginning to soften, about 2 minutes. Add the vegetable blend; cook, stirring occasionally, until almost tender, about 5 minutes. Stir in the rice and chicken stock, and bring to a simmer; cover and cook until the vegetables and rice are tender and the liquid is absorbed, about 4 minutes. Stir in the chicken-yogurt mixture, and cook until warmed through, about 1 minute. Sprinkle with the golden raisins and cilantro, if desired.

(**SERVING SIZE:** 1½ cups): **CALORIES** 330; **FAT** 14g (sat 2g, unsat 10g); **PROTEIN** 19g; **CARB** 33g; **FIBER** 2g; **SUGARS** 3g (added sugars 0g); **SODIUM** 527mg; **CALC** 8% DV; **POTASSIUM** 6% DV

TURMERIC

Ground turmeric is a key part of most jarred curry powders, and it is also used as a natural food coloring—in cheese, mustard, and chicken broth, for example. You can sometimes find fresh turmeric root in South Asian groceries; it looks like orange-colored ginger. However, most turmeric is sold ground. As with all ground spices, the fresher it is, the better. Keep a jar for up to a year before replacing it.

QUICK STEWED CHICKEN *and* RICE

Be sure not to overcook this comforting dish, as it will lose all its saucy goodness. You want to just warm all the ingredients.

HANDS-ON: 15 MIN. • TOTAL: 15 MIN. • SERVES 4

1 tablespoon canola oil
½ cup prechopped yellow onion
1 tablespoon finely chopped garlic (about 3 cloves)
2 teaspoons Cajun seasoning
⅓ cup unsalted chicken stock (such as Swanson)
1 teaspoon cornstarch
1 (14.5-ounce) can no-salt-added diced tomatoes

¼ teaspoon kosher salt
12 ounces skinless rotisserie chicken, coarsely shredded
2 (8.8-ounce) packages precooked microwavable jasmine rice
¼ cup chopped fresh flat-leaf parsley (optional)

1. Heat the oil in a large skillet over medium-high. Add the onion to the pan; cook, stirring often, until transparent, about 6 minutes. Add the garlic and Cajun seasoning to the pan; cook 1 minute, stirring constantly.
2. Whisk together the stock and cornstarch in a small bowl. Add the stock mixture, tomatoes, and salt to the pan; bring to a boil, stirring constantly. Add the chicken; cook until warmed through, about 1 minute.
3. Microwave the rice according to the package directions. Serve the chicken over the rice. Sprinkle with the parsley, if desired.

(**SERVING SIZE:** about 2 cups): **CALORIES** 451; **FAT** 11g (sat 2g, unsat 8g); **PROTEIN** 29g; **CARB** 60g; **FIBER** 2g; **SUGARS** 3g (added sugars 0g); **SODIUM** 484mg; **CALC** 6% DV; **POTASSIUM** 14% DV

MEDITERRANEAN CHICKEN *and* WHITE BEANS

Removing the chicken thighs from the pan before stirring in the spinach gives you more room to work, limiting the risk of making a mess on your stovetop.

HANDS-ON: 5 MIN. • **TOTAL: 20 MIN.** • **SERVES 4**

⅜ teaspoon kosher salt
½ teaspoon black pepper
8 boneless, skinless chicken thighs (about 1½ pounds)
1 tablespoon olive oil
1 (14.5-ounce) can stewed tomatoes, undrained

1 (15-ounce) can no-salt-added navy beans, drained
1 (5-ounce) package fresh baby spinach (about 5 cups)
1½ ounces feta cheese, crumbled (about ⅓ cup)

1. Combine the salt and pepper, and sprinkle evenly over 1 side of the chicken thighs. Heat 1½ teaspoons oil in a large skillet over medium-high. Place 4 thighs in the pan, seasoned side down; cook 3 minutes. Transfer the chicken to a plate. Repeat with the remaining 1½ teaspoons oil and 4 chicken thighs.

2. Return the chicken thighs, unseasoned side down, to the pan over medium. Add the tomatoes and beans; cover and simmer until the chicken is cooked through, 5 to 8 minutes. Remove the chicken to a serving platter. Remove the pan from the heat; add the baby spinach, stirring until wilted. Sprinkle the bean mixture and chicken with the crumbled feta, and serve immediately.

(**SERVING SIZE:** 2 thighs and about ¾ cup bean mixture): **CALORIES** 391; **FAT** 13g (sat 4g, unsat 8g); **PROTEIN** 42g; **CARB** 24g; **FIBER** 7g; **SUGARS** 4g (added sugars 0g); **SODIUM** 650mg; **CALC** 18% DV; **POTASSIUM** 24% DV

BABY SPINACH

Baby spinach is a helpful ingredient for the busy weeknight cook since the delicate, small stems don't need to be removed as they often do on mature spinach.

CLUB CHICKEN *and* QUINOA

You can vary this whole-grain main dish by layering it on top of greens, making a wrap, or stuffing it in tortillas or lettuce leaves.

HANDS-ON: 15 MIN. • **TOTAL: 15 MIN.** • **SERVES 4**

4   center-cut bacon slices
12 ounces skinless rotisserie chicken, shredded and warmed
½   cup halved cherry heirloom tomatoes
½   teaspoon black pepper
2   (8-ounce) packages precooked microwavable quinoa (such as Simply Balanced)

½   cup blue cheese yogurt dressing (such as Bolthouse Farms)
¼   cup chopped fresh flat-leaf parsley

1. Wrap the bacon in a single layer in paper towels. Microwave at HIGH until crispy, 3 to 4 minutes. Cool completely, and crumble.
2. Toss together the chicken, tomatoes, and pepper in a medium bowl. Microwave the quinoa according to the package directions. Transfer the quinoa to a platter; top with the chicken mixture. Drizzle with the dressing; sprinkle with the bacon and the parsley.

(SERVING SIZE: about 1½ cups): **CALORIES** 373; **FAT** 15g (sat 5g, unsat 9g); **PROTEIN** 33g; **CARB** 27g; **FIBER** 4g; **SUGARS** 3g (added sugars 0g); **SODIUM** 531mg; **CALC** 11% DV; **POTASSIUM** 15% DV

LEMON-DILL COUSCOUS *and* CHICKEN

To make slicing the chicken easier, you may want to prep the chicken as soon as you get home from the grocery store. To do this, you'll need to pull the breast off in one piece, which is easier to do when the bird is hot.

HANDS-ON: 15 MIN. • TOTAL: 30 MIN. • SERVES 4

- 3 tablespoons olive oil, divided
- 1 cup uncooked Israeli (pearl) couscous
- 1¾ cups water
- ½ cup sliced shallots (from 2 medium shallots)
- ¼ cup chopped fresh dill
- 2 teaspoons grated lemon zest plus 2 tablespoons fresh juice (from 1 lemon), divided
- ½ teaspoon kosher salt, divided
- 8 ounces skinless rotisserie chicken breast (about 2 breasts), sliced
- 4 ounces skinless rotisserie chicken thigh (about 1 thigh), sliced

1. Heat 1 tablespoon of the oil in a large skillet over medium-high. Add the couscous; cook, stirring often, until golden brown, about 5 minutes. Add the water and shallots; bring to a boil. Cover, reduce the heat to medium, and cook until tender, about 12 minutes. Drain any remaining liquid, if necessary. Toss together the couscous and dill in a medium bowl.
2. Whisk together the lemon juice, ¼ teaspoon salt, and remaining 2 tablespoons oil in a small bowl.
3. Transfer the couscous mixture to a platter, and top with the chicken slices. Drizzle with the lemon dressing, and sprinkle with the lemon zest and remaining ¼ teaspoon salt.

(**SERVING SIZE:** 3 ounces chicken and about ⅔ cup couscous): **CALORIES** 430; **FAT** 15g (sat 3g, unsat 11g); **PROTEIN** 29g; **CARB** 44g; **FIBER** 3g; **SUGARS** 3g (added sugars 0g); **SODIUM** 516mg; **CALC** 2% DV; **POTASSIUM** 9% DV

ONE-POT CHICKEN *and* ORZO

The chicken in this dish becomes fall-off-the-bone tender. Be sure you get the pan really hot before adding the chicken to prevent sticking.

HANDS-ON: 20 MIN. • **TOTAL: 30 MIN.** • **SERVES 6**

6 (5-ounce) skinless, bone-in chicken thighs
1 teaspoon kosher salt, divided
1 tablespoon olive oil
1 (8-ounce) package frozen chopped onions and garlic (such as Bird's Eye)
12 ounces uncooked orzo (about 1½ cups)

2 cups unsalted chicken stock (such as Swanson)
½ teaspoon black pepper
¾ cup canned crushed tomatoes with basil
Chopped fresh flat-leaf parsley (optional)

1. Sprinkle the chicken thighs evenly with ¼ teaspoon of the salt. Heat the oil in a large (12-inch) straight-sided skillet over medium-high; add the chicken, and cook until browned and almost cooked through, 4 to 5 minutes per side. Remove the chicken from the pan, and set aside.
2. Add the chopped onion-and-garlic blend to the pan, and cook, stirring often, until the vegetables begin to soften, 3 to 4 minutes. Add the orzo to the pan, and cook, stirring often, until the pasta begins to brown and the vegetables are soft, about 2 minutes.
3. Stir together the stock, pepper, and remaining ¾ teaspoon salt in a large glass measuring cup. Pour over the orzo mixture, and bring to a boil.
4. Cover; reduce the heat to low, and cook until the orzo has absorbed the liquid, 12 to 15 minutes. Add the chicken and tomatoes to the pan; cover and cook until the chicken is cooked through, about 5 minutes. Sprinkle with the parsley, if desired.

(**SERVING SIZE:** 1 chicken thigh and about ¾ cup orzo mixture): **CALORIES** 414; **FAT** 10g (sat 3g, unsat 6g); **PROTEIN** 29g; **CARB** 49g; **FIBER** 3g; **SUGARS** 5g (added sugars 0g); **SODIUM** 544mg; **CALC** 3% DV; **POTASSIUM** 10% DV

TURKEY BOLOGNESE
over WHOLE-WHEAT FETTUCCINE

Don't be tempted to stir the meat too often when you're browning it—overstirring will cause it to steam instead and you'll lose the extra flavor that browning adds. You can toss the sauce together with the pasta for a more cohesive dish or pour it over the noodles for an easy-to-serve option.

HANDS-ON: 15 MIN. • TOTAL: 30 MIN. • SERVES 4

1   tablespoon olive oil
1   pound ground turkey
½   cup chopped yellow onion
2   garlic cloves, minced
1   (24-ounce) jar lower-sodium tomato-basil marinara sauce
½   teaspoon kosher salt
½   teaspoon black pepper
8   ounces uncooked whole-wheat fettuccine noodles
Torn fresh basil (optional)

1. Heat the oil in a large skillet over medium-high. Add the turkey, onion, and garlic, and cook, stirring to break up the turkey, until the turkey is cooked and the onion is soft, 8 to 10 minutes. Add the marinara sauce, salt, and pepper. Bring the mixture to a boil; reduce the heat to low, and simmer, stirring occasionally, until slightly thickened, about 10 minutes.
2. While the turkey mixture simmers, cook the pasta according to the package directions, omitting salt and fat; drain. Serve the Bolognese over the pasta. If desired, sprinkle with basil.

(**SERVING SIZE:** about 1 cup pasta and about 1 cup Bolognese): **CALORIES** 517; **FAT** 20g (sat 4g, unsat 13g); **PROTEIN** 33g; **CARB** 56g; **FIBER** 8g; **SUGARS** 9g (added sugars 0g); **SODIUM** 705mg; **CALC** 7% DV; **POTASSIUM** 16% DV

GROUND TURKEY

Be sure to check the labels closely when purchasing ground turkey. This recipe calls for "ground turkey," which is a mix of dark and light meat—crucial for optimal flavor. If you purchase "ground turkey breast," the flavor and richness will be quite different.

GROUND TURKEY *and* BUTTERNUT RICE BOWL

Cooking the butternut squash with the rice is a smart, time-saving technique that adds a hint of sweetness to the pilaf; it contrasts nicely with the super-savory chili powder–scented turkey mixture. Bright, crisp scallions and radishes round out the texture and flavor.

HANDS-ON: 15 MIN. • TOTAL: 30 MIN. • SERVES 4

1¾ cups water, divided
1¼ teaspoons kosher salt, divided
½ teaspoon black pepper, divided
1 cup (1-inch) diced butternut squash
¾ cup uncooked long-grain white rice
3 tablespoons olive oil, divided
1 pound ground turkey

½ cup thinly sliced scallions (from 6 scallions)
1 tablespoon chili powder
½ cup thinly sliced radishes (from 4 radishes; optional)
Light sour cream (optional)

1. Bring 1⅓ cups of the water, ½ teaspoon of the salt, and ¼ teaspoon of the pepper to a boil in a small saucepan over medium-high. Add the squash and rice; return to a boil. Cover and reduce the heat to medium-low; cook until tender, about 15 minutes. Remove from the heat; let stand, covered, 2 minutes. Drizzle the rice mixture with 1½ tablespoons of the oil; fluff with a fork.

2. While the squash and rice cook, heat the remaining 1½ tablespoons oil in a large skillet over medium-high. Add the turkey to the pan; cook, stirring occasionally, until well browned and done, about 7 minutes. Stir in the scallions, chili powder, and remaining water, ¾ teaspoon salt, and ¼ teaspoon pepper; cook until fragrant and the water has almost absorbed, about 1 minute. Serve the turkey mixture over the rice mixture. Garnish with radishes and dollop with sour cream, if desired.

(**SERVING SIZE:** about ½ cup rice mixture and ½ cup turkey mixture): **CALORIES** 411; **FAT** 19g (sat 4g, unsat 14g); **PROTEIN** 25g; **CARB** 34g; **FIBER** 2g; **SUGARS** 1g (added sugars 0g); **SODIUM** 732mg; **CALC** 7% DV; **POTASSIUM** 14% DV

TURKEY SAUSAGE *and* BELL PEPPER FARFALLE

Using a little bit of the pasta water here helps to coat the pasta and prevent it from drying out. Pair this with a fresh green salad.

HANDS-ON: 15 MIN. • **TOTAL: 15 MIN.** • **SERVES 4**

10 ounces uncooked farfalle pasta
8 ounces sweet Italian turkey sausage, casings removed
3 tablespoons olive oil
2 garlic cloves, chopped
1 red bell pepper, cut into ¼-inch-thick slices
1 yellow bell pepper, cut into ¼-inch-thick slices
1 medium-sized yellow onion, cut into ¼-inch-thick slices
½ teaspoon kosher salt
¼ teaspoon black pepper
1½ ounces Parmesan cheese, shredded (about ⅓ cup)
¼ cup torn fresh basil

1. Cook the pasta according to the package directions, omitting fat and salt. Drain, reserving ¼ cup cooking water.
2. Heat a large nonstick skillet over medium-high. Add the sausage; cook, stirring to break into large pieces, until browned, about 5 minutes. Remove the sausage from the pan; set aside.
3. Add the oil, garlic, bell peppers, onion, salt, and black pepper to the pan over medium-high. Cook, stirring occasionally, until tender, about 8 minutes. Add the sausage, pasta, and reserved cooking water to the pan; toss to coat. Top with the Parmesan and basil.

(SERVING SIZE: 2 cups): **CALORIES** 527; **FAT** 20g (sat 5g, unsat 14g); **PROTEIN** 24g; **CARB** 62g; **FIBER** 4g; **SUGARS** 8g (added sugars 0g); **SODIUM** 793mg; **CALC** 17% DV; **POTASSIUM** 9% DV

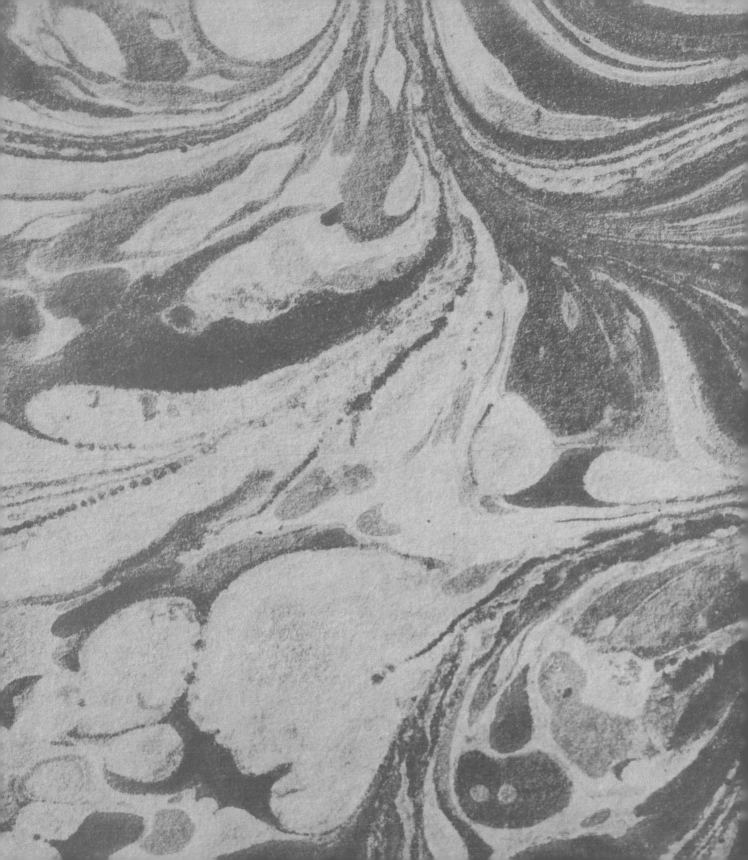

CHAPTER 7

SIDES

ASPARAGUS *with* BALSAMIC ONIONS *and* BLUE CHEESE

Roasted asparagus is taken to the next level in this pairing: sautéed sweet onions get a splash of balsamic vinegar complemented by rich, assertive blue cheese.

HANDS-ON: 13 MIN. • **TOTAL: 13 MIN.** • **SERVES 4**

1   pound trimmed asparagus
3½ teaspoons olive oil, divided
¼   teaspoon kosher salt, divided
⅛   teaspoon black pepper
1½ cups vertically sliced sweet onion

1   tablespoon balsamic vinegar
1   teaspoon fresh thyme leaves
1   ounce blue cheese, crumbled (about ¼ cup)

1. Preheat the oven to 425°F.
2. Combine the asparagus, 2 teaspoons of the olive oil, ⅛ teaspoon of the kosher salt, and the pepper on a baking sheet. Bake at 425°F for 9 minutes.
3. Heat the remaining 1½ teaspoons olive oil in a large skillet over medium. Add the onion to the pan; sauté for 6 minutes. Stir in the vinegar, thyme, and remaining ⅛ teaspoon kosher salt. Top the asparagus with the onion mixture and crumbled blue cheese.

CALORIES 104; **FAT** 6g (sat 2g, unsat 4g); **PROTEIN** 5g; **CARB** 9g; **FIBER** 3g; **SUGARS** 5g (added sugars 0g); **SODIUM** 224mg; **CALC** 8% DV; **POTASSIUM** 9% DV

STEAMED BROCCOLI *with* PEANUT SAUCE

Peanut sauce is a simple sauce with lots of flavor, making this side stand out on your plate. You can also serve it on the side if you'd prefer to dunk each bite. If you're using a crown of broccoli, trim it into florets and place it in a steamer basket over a saucepan filled about halfway with boiling water. Cover and steam 4 minutes or until the florets are crisp-tender.

HANDS-ON: 6 MIN. • **TOTAL: 6 MIN.** • **SERVES 4**

1   (10-ounce) package microwave-in-bag fresh broccoli florets
3   tablespoons creamy peanut butter
2   tablespoons water

1   tablespoon rice vinegar
1   tablespoon reduced-sodium soy sauce
1½ teaspoons toasted sesame seeds

1. Cook the broccoli according to the package instructions.
2. While the broccoli cooks, whisk together the peanut butter, 2 tablespoons water, vinegar, and soy sauce in a bowl until well combined. Drizzle the broccoli with the peanut butter mixture. Sprinkle evenly with the sesame seeds.

(SERVING SIZE: about ¾ cup broccoli and 2 tablespoons peanut sauce): **CALORIES** 100; **FAT** 7g (sat 1g, unsat 5g); **PROTEIN** 5g; **CARB** 7g; **FIBER** 3g; **SUGARS** 1g (added sugars 1g); **SODIUM** 215mg; **CALC** 4% DV; **POTASSIUM** 9% DV

PAN-ROASTED BRUSSELS SPROUTS
with BACON, GARLIC, *and* SHALLOTS ▸

Garlic, bacon, and shallots add intense flavor to the Brussels sprouts in this easy, 5-ingredient side-dish recipe. If you don't want to discard the leftover bacon drippings, carefully transfer them to a heatproof container, cool, and store in the fridge; use as a replacement for any other cooking oil or fat.

HANDS-ON: 16 MIN. • TOTAL: 16 MIN. • SERVES 6

TRIMMING BRUSSELS SPROUTS

To trim Brussels sprouts, simply cut off the stem end, and then remove any wilted leaves. You can then cut each sprout in half, or, if they're large, quarter them, just making sure the Brussels sprouts are cut into uniform pieces so that they'll cook evenly.

6 center-cut bacon slices, chopped
½ cup sliced shallots (about 1 large)
1½ pounds Brussels sprouts, trimmed and halved
6 garlic cloves, thinly sliced
¾ cup unsalted chicken stock
⅛ teaspoon table salt
⅛ teaspoon black pepper

1. Heat a large nonstick skillet over medium-high. Add the bacon, and sauté 5 minutes or until the bacon begins to brown. Remove the pan from the heat. Remove the bacon from the pan with a slotted spoon, reserving 1 tablespoon of the drippings in the pan (discard the remaining drippings).
2. Return the pan to medium-high, and stir in the bacon, shallots, and Brussels sprouts; sauté 4 minutes. Add the garlic, and sauté for 4 minutes or until the garlic begins to brown, stirring frequently. Add the chicken stock, and bring to a boil. Cook for 2 minutes or until the stock mostly evaporates and the sprouts are crisp-tender, stirring occasionally. Remove from the heat; stir in the salt and pepper.

(**SERVING SIZE:** about ⅔ cup): **CALORIES** 90; **FAT** 2g (sat 1g, unsat 1g); **PROTEIN** 7g; **CARB** 14g; **FIBER** 5g; **SUGARS** 4g (added sugars 0g); **SODIUM** 263mg; **CALC** 6% DV; **POTASSIUM** 14% DV

CAULIFLOWER POLENTA

Cauliflower lightens traditional polenta. You can also use 10 ounces of packaged prericed cauliflower and skip step 1.

HANDS-ON: 15 MIN. • TOTAL: 15 MIN. • SERVES 4

1 (10-ounce) package fresh cauliflower florets
2 cups unsalted chicken stock (such as Swanson)
1 cup water
¼ teaspoon kosher salt
½ cup quick-cooking polenta
1 tablespoon unsalted butter

1. Place the cauliflower in the bowl of a food processor; pulse until finely chopped.
2. Bring the stock, 1 cup water, and salt to a boil in a saucepan over high. Slowly add the polenta, stirring constantly with a whisk. Reduce the heat and simmer 5 minutes. Add the cauliflower; cook 5 minutes, stirring occasionally. Stir in the butter.

(**SERVING SIZE:** about 1 cup): **CALORIES** 121; **FAT** 3g (sat 2g, unsat 1g); **PROTEIN** 5g; **CARB** 18g; **FIBER** 2g; **SUGARS** 2g (added sugars 0g); **SODIUM** 207mg; **CALC** 3% DV; **POTASSIUM** 6% DV

MISO-ROASTED CAULIFLOWER

White miso paste is the mildest and most versatile of all fermented soybean pastes. It's salty, lightly sweet, and gives this dish a wonderfully savory depth.

HANDS-ON: 4 MIN. • **TOTAL: 24 MIN.** • **SERVES 4**

1½ tablespoons olive oil
1½ tablespoons white miso paste
1 grated garlic clove

6 cups cauliflower florets
Cooking spray

1. Place a jelly-roll pan in the oven. Preheat the oven to 450°F (leave the pan in the oven). (Do not remove the pan while the oven preheats.)
2. Combine the olive oil, miso, and garlic in a small bowl. Massage the mixture evenly onto the cauliflower. Carefully remove the pan from the oven; coat the pan with cooking spray. Add the cauliflower to the pan. Bake at 450°F until crisp-tender, about 20 minutes, stirring after 10 minutes.

(**SERVING SIZE:** about 1½ cups): **CALORIES** 105; **FAT** 6g (sat 1g, unsat 5g); **PROTEIN** 4g; **CARB** 11g; **FIBER** 4g; **SUGARS** 4g (added sugars 0g); **SODIUM** 254mg; **CALC** 4% DV; **POTASSIUM** 15% DV

◄ CARROT "TABBOULEH"

Fresh carrots stand in for bulgur in this no-cook, gluten-free side dish. You can use white wine vinegar in place of lemon juice. Tuck any leftover tabbouleh into a pita pocket with sliced chicken and top it with a drizzle of yogurt for a shawarma-style sandwich.

HANDS-ON: 15 MIN. • **TOTAL: 15 MIN.** • **SERVES 4**

8 ounces carrots, trimmed, peeled, and coarsely chopped (about 2 cups)
¼ teaspoon whole cumin seeds
2 tablespoons chopped walnuts
¾ cup fresh flat-leaf parsley leaves, chopped

¼ cup fresh mint leaves, chopped
¼ cup finely chopped red onion
¼ cup golden raisins, coarsely chopped
1½ tablespoons extra-virgin olive oil
1½ tablespoons fresh lemon juice
¼ teaspoon kosher salt

Place the carrots and cumin seeds in the bowl of a food processor; pulse 3 to 4 times or until coarsely chopped. Add the walnuts; pulse 3 times or until coarsely chopped. Place the carrot mixture in a bowl. Add the parsley and the remaining ingredients; stir to combine.

(**SERVING SIZE:** ½ cup): **CALORIES** 130; **FAT** 8g (sat 1g, unsat 7g); **PROTEIN** 2g; **CARB** 15g; **FIBER** 3g; **SUGARS** 9g (added sugars 0g); **SODIUM** 168mg; **CALC** 5% DV; **POTASSIUM** 10% DV

MISO PASTE

This savory, nutty paste is made from fermented soybeans; it's loaded with umami flavor and rich in probiotics. The concentrated salt content (about 400mg to 600mg per tablespoon) helps protect these good bacteria from contamination, and there's a balanced sweetness that makes the flavor much milder than most super-sour fermented products. The longer it ferments, the darker in color (often red) and the saltier and richer in flavor it gets. Another reason we love miso: It's versatile—a lovely addition to soups, marinades, grains, sauces, mayo, and dressings.

FRESH CORN SAUTÉ *with* BACON *and* CHIVES ▶

There's nothing quite like fresh-off-the-cob corn, and this recipe capitalizes on that, pairing those sweet kernels with rich, savory bacon and fresh chives. See page 43 for tips on de-kerneling corn.

HANDS-ON: 10 MIN. • TOTAL: 10 MIN. • SERVES 4

2   center-cut bacon slices
2   cups fresh corn kernels
¼   teaspoon table salt

¼   teaspoon black pepper
1   tablespoon chopped fresh chives

Chop the bacon and add to a large nonstick skillet over medium-high; cook until the bacon begins to brown. Add the corn, salt, and black pepper to the pan; sauté 4 minutes or until crisp-tender. Sprinkle with the chives.

(**SERVING SIZE:** ½ cup): **CALORIES** 75; **FAT** 2g (sat 1g, unsat 1g); **PROTEIN** 3g; **CARB** 14g; **FIBER** 2g; **SUGARS** 5g (added sugars 0g); **SODIUM** 224mg; **CALC** 0% DV; **POTASSIUM** 6% DV

GINGER-SESAME GREEN BEANS

These beans taste like takeout, but contain significantly less sodium than their order-out counterpart.

HANDS-ON: 9 MIN. • TOTAL: 9 MIN. • SERVES 4

1   tablespoon sesame oil
1   pound green beans
5   teaspoons lower-sodium soy sauce
1   tablespoon toasted sesame seeds

1   tablespoon minced fresh ginger
1   tablespoon tahini
1   tablespoon water
1   tablespoon fresh lime juice

1. Heat the sesame oil in a large skillet over medium-high. Add 1 pound green beans; cook 7 minutes or until the beans begin to brown.
2. While the beans cook, combine the soy sauce, sesame seeds, ginger, tahini, 1 tablespoon water, and lime juice in a bowl. Add the mixture to the pan. Cook 1 minute; toss to coat.

(**SERVING SIZE:** about 1 cup): **CALORIES** 105; **FAT** 7g (sat 1g, unsat 5g); **PROTEIN** 4g; **CARB** 10g; **FIBER** 4g; **SUGARS** 4g (added sugars 0g); **SODIUM** 249mg; **CALC** 5% DV; **POTASSIUM** 9% DV

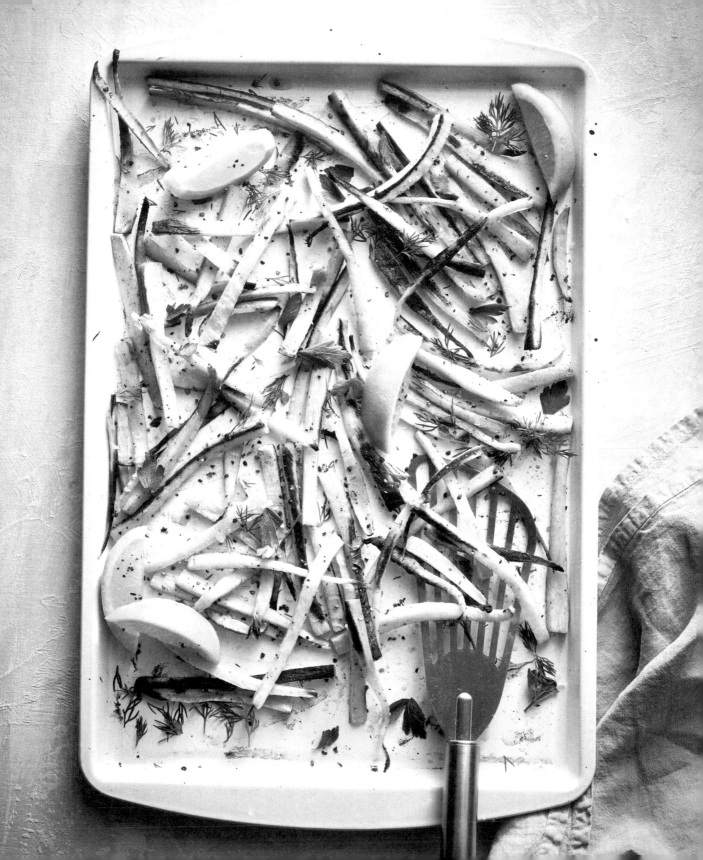

◄ ROASTED PARSNIPS *with* LEMON *and* HERBS

Parsnips have a decidedly sweet, earthy flavor that pairs well with a variety of foods. You can also toss these parsnip fries with sea salt, malt vinegar, and chopped fresh chives or rosemary, garlic, and Parmesan.

HANDS-ON: 5 MIN. • TOTAL: 15 MIN. • SERVES 4

1   pound parsnips, peeled and sliced into thin strips
2   tablespoons fresh lemon juice
1   tablespoon extra-virgin olive oil
½   teaspoon black pepper
¼   teaspoon kosher salt
¼   cup chopped fresh parsley
1   tablespoon chopped fresh dill
1   lemon, sliced into wedges

1. Place a rimmed baking sheet in the oven; preheat the oven to 500°F. (Do not remove the pan while the oven preheats.)
2. Combine the parsnips, juice, oil, pepper, and salt. Arrange in a single layer on the preheated baking sheet. Bake in the preheated oven until tender, about 10 minutes. Toss with the parsley and dill. Serve with the lemon wedges.

(**SERVING SIZE:** ¾ cup): **CALORIES** 124; **FAT** 4g (sat 1g, unsat 3g); **PROTEIN** 2g; **CARB** 23g; **FIBER** 6g; **SUGARS** 6g (added sugars 0g); **SODIUM** 134mg; **CALC** 5% DV; **POTASSIUM** 14% DV

BUYING PARSNIPS

If you're not familiar with parsnips, they look like white carrots. Opt for small to medium-sized parsnips since larger parsnips tend to have tough, woody cores. They should be blemish-free and firm. You'll find them year-round, but their peak season is from fall to spring.

SIMPLE SALAD *with* LEMON DRESSING

While radishes are available in the grocery store year-round, this salad is at its best in spring when radishes are at their crisp, peppery peak.

HANDS-ON: 5 MIN. • TOTAL: 5 MIN. • SERVES 4

1½ tablespoons fresh lemon juice
1½ tablespoons extra-virgin olive oil
¼   teaspoon black pepper
⅛   teaspoon kosher salt
6   cups mixed greens
1   cup halved cherry tomatoes
½   cup thinly sliced radishes

Whisk together the lemon juice, olive oil, pepper, and salt in a large bowl. Add the greens, tomatoes, and radishes; toss to coat.

(**SERVING SIZE:** 1½ cups): **CALORIES** 76; **FAT** 5g (sat 1g, unsat 4g); **PROTEIN** 1g; **CARB** 6g; **FIBER** 3g; **SUGARS** 2g (added sugars 0g); **SODIUM** 88mg; **CALC** 5% DV; **POTASSIUM** 4% DV

MARINATED HEIRLOOM TOMATOES
with MUSTARD *and* DILL ▶

Feel free to use different varieties of tomato for more color, flavor variation, and interest. Prepare this side just before serving so the tomatoes will hold their shape.

HANDS-ON: 3 MIN. • TOTAL: 18 MIN. • SERVES 6

1   tablespoon chopped fresh dill
2   tablespoons Dijon mustard
2   teaspoons grated lemon rind
1   teaspoon fresh lemon juice

¼   teaspoon table salt
⅛   teaspoon black pepper
2   pounds large heirloom tomatoes, cut into ¼-inch-thick slices

Combine the first 6 ingredients in a large bowl. Add the tomato slices, tossing gently to coat. Let stand 15 minutes.

CALORIES 33; **FAT** 0g (sat 0g, unsat 0g); **PROTEIN** 1g; **CARB** 7g; **FIBER** 2g; **SUGARS** 4g (added sugars 0g); **SODIUM** 225mg; **CALC** 2% DV; **POTASSIUM** 10% DV

ORANGE, RED ONION, *and* CILANTRO SALAD

This side salad is a beautifully simple combination with bright, refreshing flavor.

HANDS-ON: 7 MIN. • TOTAL: 7 MIN. • SERVES 4

1   tablespoon olive oil
1   teaspoon grated lime rind
1   tablespoon fresh lime juice
¼   teaspoon kosher salt
⅛   teaspoon ground red pepper

¼   cup very thinly vertically sliced red onion
4   medium navel oranges, peeled and sliced crosswise into rounds
¼   cup chopped fresh cilantro

Combine the first 5 ingredients in a bowl. Add the onion and oranges; toss to coat. Arrange the orange mixture on a platter; top with the cilantro.

(SERVING SIZE: about ⅔ cup): CALORIES 103; **FAT** 4g (sat 1g, unsat 3g); **PROTEIN** 1g; **CARB** 16g; **FIBER** 3g; **SUGARS** 12g (added sugars 0g); **SODIUM** 122mg; **CALC** 6% DV; **POTASSIUM** 7% DV

ARUGULA, TOMATO, *and* ALMOND SALAD

This easy salad offers a pleasing contrast in flavors and textures with crunchy almonds, peppery arugula, sweet tomatoes, and pungent balsamic vinaigrette.

HANDS-ON: 5 MIN. • TOTAL: 5 MIN. • SERVES 4

- 2 tablespoons balsamic vinegar
- 1 tablespoon olive oil
- ½ teaspoon Dijon mustard
- ¼ teaspoon black pepper
- ⅛ teaspoon kosher salt
- 6 ounces baby arugula
- 2 cups halved grape tomatoes
- 3 tablespoons sliced almonds, toasted

Combine the balsamic vinegar, oil, mustard, pepper, and salt in a medium bowl. Add the arugula, tomatoes, and almonds; toss to coat.

(SERVING SIZE: 1½ cups): **CALORIES** 87; **FAT** 6g (sat 1g, unsat 5g); **PROTEIN** 3g; **CARB** 7g; **FIBER** 2g; **SUGARS** 4g (added sugars 0g); **SODIUM** 92mg; **CALC** 9% DV; **POTASSIUM** 11% DV

◂ KALE CAESAR SALAD

This fresh take on classic Caesar salad gives you the same great taste for half the calories and double the vitamins.

HANDS-ON: 7 MIN. • TOTAL: 10 MIN. • SERVES 4

- 2 tablespoons hot water
- 2 tablespoons canola mayonnaise (such as Hellmann's)
- 1 tablespoon olive oil
- 1 tablespoon fresh lemon juice
- ½ teaspoon anchovy paste
- ¼ teaspoon black pepper
- 1 garlic clove, grated
- 2 tablespoons grated fresh Parmesan cheese
- 5 ounces baby kale
- 2 ounces baguette, cubed and toasted

Combine the first 7 ingredients in a large bowl. Stir in the Parmesan cheese. Add the kale; toss to coat. Top with the toasted cubed baguette.

(SERVING SIZE: 1¼ cups): **CALORIES** 117; **FAT** 6g (sat 1g, unsat 5g); **PROTEIN** 4g; **CARB** 13g; **FIBER** 2g; **SUGARS** 1g (added sugars 0g); **SODIUM** 243mg; **CALC** 8% DV; **POTASSIUM** 5% DV

MAKING VINAIGRETTES

Vinaigrettes are simple to prepare, but there is a method to their magic. The goal: emulsification, which means thoroughly blending a typically liquid fat like oil into a water-based liquid like vinegar with the help of an emulsifier like creamy Dijon mustard (any mustard, powdered or prepared, will work). From there, flavor as you see fit.

BULGUR

Bulgur is an ideal whole grain for the weeknight cook: Because it has been precooked and dried, it takes only about 10 minutes to make. It's made from whole wheat berries that have been cooked, dried, and then cut into smaller pieces, retaining its whole-grain properties and nutrition.

HERBED BULGUR *with* ALMONDS

This recipe works with any mix of herbs you like, so chop whatever you have on hand and add it to the mix. Similarly, use lemon or lime in place of orange rind.

HANDS-ON: 5 MIN. • TOTAL: 20 MIN. • SERVES 4

1¼ cups water
¾ cup bulgur
⅝ teaspoon kosher salt
⅓ cup chopped fresh parsley

⅓ cup chopped fresh cilantro
½ cup chopped almonds
1½ teaspoons grated orange rind
1½ teaspoons extra-virgin olive oil

Bring 1¼ cups water, bulgur, and salt to a boil in a saucepan. Cover and simmer 12 minutes. Let stand 5 minutes. Stir in the parsley and remaining ingredients.

(**SERVING SIZE:** about ⅔ cup): **CALORIES** 175; **FAT** 8g (sat 1g, unsat 7g); **PROTEIN** 6g; **CARB** 23g; **FIBER** 6g; **SUGARS** 1g (added sugars 0g); **SODIUM** 308mg; **CALC** 5% DV; **POTASSIUM** 7% DV

CILANTRO QUINOA *with* PINE NUTS ▶

A quick switch from water to stock elevates this simple whole-grain side. Substitute chopped toasted almonds for a budget-friendly alternative to the pine nuts. If you're not a cilantro fan, use chopped fresh flat-leaf parsley instead.

HANDS-ON: 3 MIN. • TOTAL: 23 MIN. • SERVES 2

½ cup plus 2 tablespoons unsalted chicken stock (such as Swanson)
½ cup uncooked quinoa, rinsed and drained
¼ cup chopped fresh cilantro

2 tablespoons pine nuts, toasted
1 teaspoon extra-virgin olive oil
⅛ teaspoon kosher salt

Bring the stock and quinoa to a boil in a small saucepan. Reduce the heat; cover and simmer 15 minutes or until the liquid is absorbed. Remove the pan from the heat; let stand 5 minutes. Stir in the cilantro, pine nuts, oil, and salt.

(**SERVING SIZE:** ½ cup): **CALORIES** 243; **FAT** 11g (sat 1g, unsat 9g); **PROTEIN** 9g; **CARB** 29g; **FIBER** 3g; **SUGARS** 3g (added sugars 0g); **SODIUM** 164mg; **CALC** 3% DV; **POTASSIUM** 9% DV

CHAPTER 8

DESSERTS

EASY ALMOND BUTTER COOKIES

These cookies are chewy, nutty, and dense. They're also easy to overbake, so look for the bottoms to be just slightly browned and the tops to give just a bit when touched.

HANDS-ON: 15 MIN. • **TOTAL: 30 MIN.** • **SERVES 30**

1   cup almond butter
¾   cup packed light brown sugar
1   large egg, lightly beaten

1   teaspoon vanilla extract
¼   teaspoon kosher salt

1. Preheat the oven to 325°F. Stir together all the ingredients in a medium bowl until combined; shape the dough into 30 (1-inch) balls. Place the balls 1 inch apart on parchment paper-lined baking sheets, and flatten gently with the tines of a fork.
2. Bake in the preheated oven until golden brown, about 15 minutes. Serve warm, or transfer to wire racks to cool.

(**SERVING SIZE:** 1 cookie): **CALORIES** 76; **FAT** 5g (sat 1g, unsat 4g); **PROTEIN** 2g; **CARB** 7g; **FIBER** 1g; **SUGARS** 6g (added sugars 5g); **SODIUM** 39mg; **CALC** 4% DV; **POTASSIUM** 2% DV

White whole-wheat flour has all the benefits of whole grains with the baking bonus of being a much lighter consistency compared to whole-wheat flour. You can find it in most large grocery stores and at Whole Foods.

CHEWY WHOLE-GRAIN HAZELNUT COOKIES

Using a food processor is a quick way to prepare the cookie dough and keeps it from getting tough or gummy.

HANDS-ON: 15 MIN. • **TOTAL: 24 MIN.** • **SERVES 8**

½ cup (about 2 ounces) white whole-wheat flour
⅓ cup packed light brown sugar
⅓ cup chopped hazelnuts, toasted
⅛ teaspoon table salt
3 tablespoons canola oil
1 tablespoon water
¼ teaspoon vanilla extract

1. Preheat the oven to 350°F. Pulse the flour, brown sugar, hazelnuts, and salt in a food processor until the hazelnuts are finely ground, 9 to 10 times.
2. Drizzle the oil, water, and vanilla over the flour mixture; pulse until the dough comes together, 10 to 12 times.
3. Scoop the mixture into 8 equal portions; roll each portion into a ball. Place the balls 2 inches apart on a parchment paper–lined baking sheet. Lightly press each ball, flattening to ½-inch thickness. Bake in the preheated oven until set and lightly brown around the edges, 9 to 11 minutes. Transfer the cookies to a wire rack to cool.

(SERVING SIZE: 1 cookie): **CALORIES** 137; **FAT** 8g (sat 1g, unsat 7g); **PROTEIN** 2g; **CARB** 14g; **FIBER** 1g; **SUGARS** 9g (added sugars 9g); **SODIUM** 39mg; **CALC** 2% DV; **POTASSIUM** 1% DV

CHEWY MOCHA-PECAN COOKIES ▸

HANDS-ON: 10 MIN. • **TOTAL: 23 MIN.** • **SERVES 16**

1 cup roughly chopped pecans, toasted
¾ cup granulated sugar, divided
2 tablespoons unsweetened cocoa
2 teaspoons instant espresso granules
¼ teaspoon table salt
1 large egg, lightly beaten
Cooking spray

1. Preheat the oven to 325°F. Pulse the pecans and ¼ cup of the sugar in a food processor just until the mixture resembles fine meal, 6 to 8 times. Transfer the pecan mixture to a medium bowl. Stir in the cocoa, espresso granules, salt, egg, and remaining ½ cup sugar.
2. Lightly coat your hands with cooking spray; shape the dough into 16 (1-inch) balls. Place the balls 2 inches apart on a large parchment paper–lined baking sheet. Flatten the cookies to ½-inch thickness with the bottom of a glass.
3. Bake in the preheated oven until the cookies are cracked and set, 13 to 15 minutes. Transfer the cookies to wire racks to cool.

(SERVING SIZE: 1 cookie): **CALORIES** 90; **FAT** 5g (sat 1g, unsat 4g); **PROTEIN** 1g; **CARB** 11g; **FIBER** 1g; **SUGARS** 10g (added sugars 9g); **SODIUM** 41mg; **CALC** 1% DV; **POTASSIUM** 1% DV

Grinding the pecans with part of the sugar makes a flour-like mixture that's the base of these cookies. Be sure you don't over-process the nut mixture—you want it to be a dry, fine, sandlike consistency. If you go too long, you'll end up with nut butter!

CHAI-SPICED PALMIERS

Don't let these impressive-looking cookies fool you—they're really easy to make. While black pepper is an atypical ingredient for a dessert, it adds some heat and spice to the chai blend.

HANDS-ON: 15 MIN. • **TOTAL: 30 MIN.** • **SERVES 16**

1½ teaspoons ground cinnamon
¼ teaspoon ground cardamom
¼ teaspoon black pepper
3 tablespoons granulated sugar, divided

½ (17.3-ounce) package frozen puff pastry sheets, thawed
1 large egg, lightly beaten

1. Preheat the oven to 375°F. Stir together the cinnamon, cardamom, pepper, and 2 tablespoons of the sugar in a small bowl.
2. Sprinkle the remaining 1 tablespoon sugar on a work surface. Lightly roll the pastry sheet on the sugared work surface to remove the fold marks. Brush the top side of the pastry with the beaten egg, and discard the leftover egg. Sprinkle the spice mixture evenly over the pastry. Starting at the short sides, gently roll each side of pastry towards the center. (Don't roll too tightly or the centers won't get done.) Cut crosswise into 16 even slices. Place the slices 2 inches apart on parchment paper–lined baking sheets. Bake in the preheated oven until golden, 15 to 18 minutes. Transfer to wire racks to cool.

(**SERVING SIZE:** 1 palmier): **CALORIES** 78; **FAT** 4g (sat 1g, unsat 3g); **PROTEIN** 2g; **CARB** 8g; **FIBER** 0g; **SUGARS** 3g (added sugars 2g); **SODIUM** 79mg; **CALC** 0% DV; **POTASSIUM** 0% DV

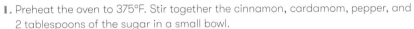

PUFF PASTRY

You'll find puff pastry in the freezer section. It's important to thaw only what you need since pastry sheets that have been thawed and then refrozen are gummy and don't puff up properly. It's easier to separate the pastry sheets when they are frozen. If you're using only one sheet, wrap the remaining sheets well to prevent drying out. To thaw, wrap the sheets you'll need in plastic wrap (or the entire package if you need it) and place in the refrigerator overnight. You can also leave well-wrapped pastry sheets on the counter for about 1 hour to thaw.

NO-BAKE ORANGE-WALNUT BITES

Fresh juice and zest lend these dense grab-and-go energy bites a lovely hint of orange flavor.

HANDS-ON: 15 MIN. • **TOTAL: 15 MIN.** • **SERVES 12**

⅔ cup crunchy reduced-fat granola without raisins (such as Back to Nature Classic Granola), divided

1 cup chopped walnuts

¾ cup chopped pitted dates

2 teaspoons orange zest plus 2 tablespoons fresh juice (from 1 medium orange)

2 tablespoons honey

¼ teaspoon table salt

1. Pulse ⅓ cup granola in a food processor until finely ground, 6 to 8 times. Measure the finely ground granola to equal ¼ cup. Set aside.
2. Process the walnuts, dates, orange zest, orange juice, honey, salt, and remaining ⅓ cup granola in a food processor until the mixture is finely ground and the dough comes together, about 1 minute. Divide the dough into 12 equal portions; roll each portion into a ball.
3. Roll each ball in the reserved ¼ cup finely ground granola until completely coated. Store the cookies in an airtight container for up to 5 days.

(**SERVING SIZE:** 1 cookie): **CALORIES** 123; **FAT** 7g (sat 1g, unsat 6g); **PROTEIN** 2g; **CARB** 16g; **FIBER** 2g; **SUGARS** 11g (added sugars 3g); **SODIUM** 63mg; **CALC** 2% DV; **POTASSIUM** 4% DV

NO-BAKE APPLE-OAT NUGGETS ▶

These little power nuggets are great for a snack as well as a dessert. They have a satisfying texture and crunch from the oats and chunky peanut butter and just the right amount of sweetness from the brown sugar and dried apples.

HANDS-ON: 20 MIN. • **TOTAL: 40 MIN.** • **SERVES 22**

1½ cups uncooked quick-cooking oats

½ cup chopped dried apple (about 2 ounces)

½ cup chunky peanut butter

½ cup packed light brown sugar

¼ teaspoon kosher salt

½ teaspoon ground cinnamon (optional)

1. Stir together the oats and apple in a medium bowl.
2. Stir together the peanut butter, brown sugar, salt, and, if desired, cinnamon in a medium-sized heavy-duty saucepan. Cook over medium, stirring constantly, just until the mixture begins to bubble around the edges and the sugar is completely melted, 2 to 3 minutes. Remove from the heat. Pour over the oats mixture; stir well to fully incorporate. Cool 3 minutes.
3. Dampen your hands, and shape the mixture into 22 (1-inch) balls. Place the dough balls on a parchment paper–lined baking sheet, and chill 20 minutes. Store in an airtight container in the refrigerator for up to 3 days.

(**SERVING SIZE:** 1 cookie): **CALORIES** 85; **FAT** 3g (sat 1g, unsat 2g); **PROTEIN** 2g; **CARB** 12g; **FIBER** 1g; **SUGARS** 7g (added sugars 5g); **SODIUM** 69mg; **CALC** 1% DV; **POTASSIUM** 2% DV

If you enjoy butterscotch, you'll love this quick and easy dessert. It gets a bit of crunch from the crackers and toasted pecans.

PEANUT BUTTER TRUFFLES

Be sure to set out your butter to let it soften—softened butter blends easier and better with the peanut butter to create the right consistency in these truffles. Adding the ingredients in stages helps keep the bars from becoming dry or gummy.

HANDS-ON: 15 MIN. • **TOTAL: 2 HOURS, 15 MIN., INCLUDING 2 HOURS CHILLING**
SERVES 16

½ cup creamy peanut butter
¼ cup unsalted butter, softened
¼ teaspoon table salt
1 cup (about 4 ounces) powdered sugar

1 cup finely ground buttery whole-wheat crackers (such as Ritz Whole Wheat Crackers)
2 ounces semisweet chocolate baking bar, chopped

1. Beat the peanut butter, butter, and salt with an electric mixer on medium speed until smooth, 2 to 3 minutes. Add the powdered sugar; beat at low speed until well combined, 1 to 2 minutes. Add the cracker crumbs, beating at low speed until just combined, about 1 minute. Divide the peanut butter mixture into 16 equal portions, and shape each portion into a ball. Place the balls on a parchment paper–lined baking sheet.
2. Microwave the chopped chocolate in a small microwavable bowl on HIGH until melted, about 45 seconds, stirring after 30 seconds. Drizzle the chocolate over the peanut butter truffles on the baking sheet. Chill until firm, about 2 hours.

(**SERVING SIZE:** 1 truffle): **CALORIES** 148; **FAT** 9g (sat 3g, unsat 4g); **PROTEIN** 2g; **CARB** 16g; **FIBER** 1g; **SUGARS** 11g (added sugars 9g); **SODIUM** 119mg; **CALC** 1% DV; **POTASSIUM** 2% DV

BUTTERSCOTCH-PECAN BARK

HANDS-ON: 10 MIN. • **TOTAL: 1 HOUR, 10 MIN., INCLUDING 1 HOUR CHILLING**
SERVES 16

Cooking spray
16 whole-wheat crackers (such as Back To Nature Harvest Crispy Wheat Crackers)
¼ cup packed dark brown sugar

¼ cup low-fat evaporated milk
1 cup butterscotch chips
¼ cup chopped pecans, toasted

1. Coat an 8-inch square baking dish with cooking spray. Arrange the crackers in the bottom of the dish, breaking them to cover the bottom of the dish completely.
2. Bring the brown sugar and milk to a boil in a small saucepan over medium-high, stirring often; cook, stirring constantly, until the sugar melts. Remove the pan from the heat, and stir in the butterscotch chips until melted and smooth. Pour the mixture over the crackers, spreading to the edges of the dish. Sprinkle the pecans over the top. Chill until firm, about 1 hour. Break or cut into 16 equal pieces.

(**SERVING SIZE:** 1 piece): **CALORIES** 126; **FAT** 6g (sat 4g, unsat 2g); **PROTEIN** 2g; **CARB** 16g; **FIBER** 1g; **SUGARS** 12g (added sugars 12g); **SODIUM** 38mg; **CALC** 3% DV; **POTASSIUM** 2% DV

MAPLE-PECAN MINIS

When a craving for pecan pie hits, these sweet, nutty tarts can be ready in a fraction of the time.

HANDS-ON: 15 MIN. • **TOTAL 15 MIN.** • **SERVES 15**

1   (1.9-ounce) package frozen mini phyllo pastry shells, thawed
¼   cup half-and-half
¼   cup pure maple syrup

2   teaspoons cornstarch
⅛   teaspoon kosher salt
½   cup chopped pecans, toasted

1. Prepare the pastry shells according to the package directions.
2. Whisk together the half-and-half, syrup, cornstarch, and salt in a small saucepan until blended. Bring to a boil over medium-high, stirring constantly. Cook, stirring constantly, until the mixture thickens, about 1 minute. Remove the pan from the heat, and stir in the pecans.
3. Divide the pecan mixture evenly among the prepared shells. Serve warm or at room temperature.

(**SERVING SIZE:** 1 mini): **CALORIES** 61; **FAT** 4g (sat 1g, unsat 3g); **PROTEIN** 0g; **CARB** 6g; **FIBER** 0g; **SUGARS** 3g (added sugars 3g); **SODIUM** 33mg; **CALC** 1% DV; **POTASSIUM** 1% DV

WHIPPED CHEESECAKE DIP

This velvety, not-too-sweet dessert dip offers the flavors of cheesecake without the heaviness. The zest provides a subtle lemon flavor. Strawberries and graham crackers are classic cheesecake pairings, but you can also serve this with pound cake bites, pretzels, or any fruit that you like.

HANDS-ON: 15 MIN. • TOTAL: 15 MIN. • SERVES 8

½ (8-ounce) package ⅓-less-fat cream cheese, softened (about ½ cup)
⅓ cup powdered sugar
¼ cup plain low-fat Greek yogurt
1 teaspoon lemon zest (from 1 lemon)
½ cup whipping cream
16 fresh strawberries (about 2 cups)
4 graham cracker sheets, each broken into 4 pieces

Beat the cream cheese, sugar, yogurt, and lemon zest with an electric mixer on medium-high speed until smooth. Add the cream, and beat until soft peaks form, about 3 minutes. Serve with the strawberries and graham cracker pieces.

(**SERVING SIZE:** ¼ cup dip, 2 berries, and 2 graham cracker pieces): **CALORIES** 146; **FAT** 9g (sat 5g, unsat 3g); **PROTEIN** 3g; **CARB** 14g; **FIBER** 1g; **SUGARS** 10g (added sugars 6g); **SODIUM** 88mg; **CALC** 5% DV; **POTASSIUM** 3% DV

CHOCOLATE PANNA COTTA

Using low-fat evaporated milk adds richness while keeping calories and saturated fat in check. Garnish with mint leaves or whipped topping, if you like.

**HANDS-ON: 10 MIN. • TOTAL: 6 HOURS, 10 MIN., INCLUDING 6 HOURS CHILLING
SERVES 4**

1½ teaspoons unflavored gelatin
3 tablespoons cold water
1 (12-ounce) can low-fat evaporated milk
2 tablespoons granulated sugar
3 ounces bittersweet chocolate baking bar, finely chopped
¼ teaspoon vanilla extract
Cooking spray

1. Combine the gelatin and cold water in a small bowl; let stand until the water is absorbed, 5 minutes.
2. Meanwhile, bring the evaporated milk and sugar to a simmer in a small saucepan over medium-high, stirring often. Add the gelatin mixture, and cook, stirring constantly, until the gelatin melts and the mixture is well blended, about 1 minute. Remove the pan from the heat, and stir in the chopped chocolate and vanilla extract until the chocolate melts and the mixture is smooth. Divide the mixture evenly among 4 (6-ounce) ramekins or custard cups lightly greased with cooking spray. Place heavy-duty plastic wrap directly on the warm custard (to prevent a film from forming), and chill until set, about 6 hours. Serve in the ramekins, or run a knife around the edges and invert onto dessert plates.

(**SERVING SIZE:** 1 ramekin): **CALORIES** 203; **FAT** 9g (sat 5g, unsat 4g); **PROTEIN** 7g; **CARB** 26g; **FIBER** 2g; **SUGARS** 22g (added sugars 14g); **SODIUM** 94mg; **CALC** 22% DV; **POTASSIUM** 8% DV

TEMPERING

Tempering is the process of slowly combining a hot liquid or mixture with a cold one, which helps prevent it from curdling. Don't skip it in this recipe!

TROPICAL RICE PUDDING

You'll find the unsweetened vanilla coconut milk in a carton in the dairy section—it's not the canned variety. Use leftovers in your coffee, with your cereal, or as a beverage.

HANDS-ON: 15 MIN. • TOTAL: 45 MIN. • SERVES 6

3   cups well-shaken refrigerated unsweetened vanilla coconut milk (such as Silk)
1   cup uncooked instant white rice
⅓   cup packed light brown sugar
¼   teaspoon kosher salt
2   large eggs
½   cup canned pineapple tidbits in 100% juice, drained
Toasted coconut (optional)

1. Bring the milk, rice, brown sugar, and salt to a boil in a medium saucepan over medium-high, stirring constantly; reduce the heat to medium-low, and simmer, stirring often, until thickened and the rice is very tender, about 6 minutes.
2. Whisk the eggs in a small bowl; stir 1 cup hot rice mixture into the eggs. Gradually add the egg mixture to the rice mixture in the saucepan, stirring constantly. Cook over low, stirring constantly, until creamy and glossy, about 3 minutes.
3. Remove the mixture from the heat. Cool until no longer hot, about 30 minutes; stir in the pineapple. Sprinkle each serving with toasted coconut, if desired, and serve warm.

(SERVING SIZE: ½ cup): CALORIES 237; FAT 4g (sat 3g, unsat 1g); PROTEIN 5g; CARB 44g; FIBER 1g; SUGARS 14g (added sugars 12g); SODIUM 131mg; CALC 27% DV; POTASSIUM 3% DV

STOVETOP SUMMER FRUIT CRISP ▶

Traditional? No. Delicious? Oh, yes. This quick-fix take hits all the highlights of a classic berry crisp—syrupy-sweet fruit, crisp topping, and cool cream—in a fraction of the time. Try your favorite summer fruits in this crisp. Blueberries, figs, plums, or peaches would work.

HANDS-ON: 12 MIN. • TOTAL: 12 MIN. • SERVES 6

2   teaspoons unsalted butter
1   pound quartered fresh strawberries
1½ cups fresh raspberries, divided
1½ cups fresh blackberries, divided
1   tablespoon packed brown sugar
½   teaspoon vanilla extract
¾   cup low-fat granola
1½ cups vanilla frozen yogurt

Melt the butter in a large skillet over medium-high. Add the strawberries, ¾ cup each of the raspberries and blackberries, sugar, and vanilla to the pan. Cook 4 minutes or until the fruit starts to soften. Stir in the remaining berries, and cook 1 minute. Divide the berry mixture among 6 bowls. Top with the granola and frozen yogurt.

(SERVING SIZE: ½ cup fruit, 2 tablespoons granola, and ¼ cup frozen yogurt): CALORIES 174; FAT 4g (sat 2g, unsat 2g); PROTEIN 3g; CARB 33g; FIBER 6g; SUGARS 19g (added sugars 4g); SODIUM 50mg; CALC 9% DV; POTASSIUM 6% DV

SPICED HONEY–GRILLED PEACHES *and* FROZEN YOGURT

Save this recipe until peaches are at peak-season perfection. Select peaches that are ripe but still firm, so that they don't fall apart or get mushy on the grill. If you can't find frozen Greek yogurt, use regular frozen yogurt.

HANDS-ON: 10 MIN. • TOTAL: 10 MIN. • SERVES 4

2   large fresh peaches, halved
Cooking spray
1⅓ cups frozen vanilla Greek yogurt
2   almond biscotti, crumbled (such as Nonni's)

2   tablespoons honey
¼   teaspoon cayenne pepper

1. Preheat the grill to medium (350°F to 400°F) or heat a grill pan over medium.
2. Lightly coat the cut sides of the peaches with cooking spray. Coat the grill grate with cooking spray. Grill the peaches, uncovered and cut sides down, 2 minutes. Turn the peaches, and grill until well marked and beginning to soften, 2 to 3 more minutes.
3. Place peach halves on 4 plates. Scoop the frozen yogurt next to each peach half; sprinkle with the crumbled biscotti.
4. Stir together the honey and cayenne pepper; drizzle over each serving.

(SERVING SIZE: ½ peach, ⅓ cup frozen yogurt, ½ cookie, and ½ tablespoon honey): **CALORIES** 184; **FAT** 2g (sat 0g, unsat 2g); **PROTEIN** 7g; **CARB** 36g; **FIBER** 1g; **SUGARS** 18g (added sugars 9g); **SODIUM** 49mg; **CALC** 1% DV; **POTASSIUM** 5% DV

KEY LIME SHERBET

Bottled Key lime juice is a convenient way to get the wonderfully tart and tangy flavor of this tiny fruit. You can find it at most grocery stores in the dry juice section. Feel free to use fresh Key limes, if you like.

HANDS-ON: 10 MIN.   •   TOTAL: 4 HOURS, 10 MIN., INCLUDING 4 HOURS FREEZING
SERVES 8

VODKA IN FROZEN DESSERTS?

While it may seem odd to have vodka in the ingredients list, it's a helpful addition to frozen desserts: Since vodka doesn't freeze, it prevents sherbets, sorbets, and ice cream from becoming hard or icy.

1   cup bottled Key lime juice (such as Nellie & Joe's)
1   cup water
¾   cup granulated sugar

2   tablespoons lime zest (from 4 limes)
⅛   teaspoon table salt
¾   cup heavy cream
2   tablespoons vodka (optional)

Whisk together the Key lime juice, water, sugar, lime zest, and salt in the frozen freezer bowl of a 1½- to 2-quart electric ice-cream maker until the sugar and salt are completely dissolved. Stir in the cream and, if desired, the vodka. Freeze according to the manufacturer's instructions. (Instructions and times may vary.) Transfer to an airtight freezer-safe container; freeze until firm, about 4 hours.

NOTE: This keeps in the freezer for up to 3 months.

(SERVING SIZE: ½ cup): **CALORIES** 150; **FAT** 8g (sat 5g, unsat 2g); **PROTEIN** 1g; **CARB** 20g; **FIBER** 0g; **SUGARS** 19g (added sugars 19g); **SODIUM** 43mg; **CALC** 2% DV; **POTASSIUM** 1% DV

LEMON-RASPBERRY PARFAITS *with* FRESH BLUEBERRIES

You can use any flavored liqueur that you like to make the boozy blueberries in this simple, refreshing dessert.

HANDS-ON: 15 MIN. • **TOTAL: 15 MIN.** • **SERVES 4**

¼ cup uncooked old-fashioned regular rolled oats
¼ cup chopped pecans
1½ teaspoons canola oil
¾ cup raspberry sorbet

¾ cup lemon sorbet
½ cup fresh blueberries
2 tablespoons (1 ounce) berry-flavored liqueur (such as crème de cassis)

1. Preheat the oven to 350°F. Stir together the oats, pecans, and oil in a small bowl until blended. Spread the mixture in an even layer on a rimmed baking sheet. Bake in the preheated oven until lightly browned, 6 to 8 minutes. Transfer to waxed paper, and let cool slightly, about 5 minutes.
2. Layer 3 tablespoons raspberry sorbet, 1 tablespoon oat mixture, and 3 tablespoons lemon sorbet in each of 4 (8-ounce) tall glasses. Top each with 1 tablespoon oat mixture. Stir together the blueberries and liqueur in a small bowl. Spoon the blueberry mixture evenly over the parfaits.

(**SERVING SIZE:** 1 parfait): **CALORIES** 211; **FAT** 7g (sat 1g, unsat 6g); **PROTEIN** 1g; **CARB** 33g; **FIBER** 2g; **SUGARS** 21g (added sugars 3g); **SODIUM** 0mg; **CALC** 1% DV; **POTASSIUM** 2% DV

◀ CHOCOLATE-ALMOND ICE POPS

If you don't have popsicle molds, use small 4-ounce disposable paper cups. Just place the filled cups in the freezer for 2 hours, and then insert wooden sticks into the centers.

HANDS-ON: 10 MIN. • **TOTAL: 6 HOURS, 10 MIN., INCLUDING 6 HOURS FREEZING SERVES 8**

2½ cups unsweetened chocolate almond milk
¾ cup granulated sugar

3 tablespoons unsweetened cocoa
½ teaspoon vanilla extract

Process all the ingredients in a blender until the mixture is well blended and the sugar is dissolved. Divide the mixture evenly among 8 (3-ounce) ice pop molds. Top with the lids of the ice pop molds, and insert the plastic ice pop sticks. Freeze until firm, about 6 hours.

(**SERVING SIZE:** 1 ice pop): **CALORIES** 93; **FAT** 1g (sat 0g, unsat 1g); **PROTEIN** 1g; **CARB** 21g; **FIBER** 1g; **SUGARS** 19g (added sugars 19g); **SODIUM** 57mg; **CALC** 7% DV; **POTASSIUM** 3% DV

CHERRY-VANILLA ICE CREAM

This creamy no-cook ice cream is sweet and slightly tart. You can use tart red cherries instead of sweet dark ones, if you like.

HANDS-ON: 10 MIN. • **TOTAL: 4 HOURS, 10 MIN., INCLUDING 4 HOURS FREEZING**
SERVES 8

4   cups frozen unsweetened pitted dark
    sweet cherries
2   cups low-fat evaporated milk
¾   cup heavy cream

6   tablespoons granulated sugar
2   teaspoons vanilla extract
⅛   teaspoon table salt

Process all the ingredients in a blender until smooth. Pour the mixture into the frozen freezer bowl of a 1½- to 2-quart ice-cream maker, and proceed according to the manufacturer's instructions. (Instructions and times will vary.) Transfer to an airtight freezer-safe container; freeze until firm, about 4 hours.

(SERVING SIZE: 1 cup): **CALORIES** 211; **FAT** 9g (sat 5g, unsat 3g); **PROTEIN** 5g; **CARB** 27g; **FIBER** 2g; **SUGARS** 25g (added sugars 9g); **SODIUM** 113mg; **CALC** 18% DV; **POTASSIUM** 6% DV

STRAWBERRY-BASIL FROZEN YOGURT ▶

Make this dessert at the start of summer when both strawberries and basil are at their tastiest. Be sure to place your ice cream freezer bowl in the freezer for at least 24 hours so it's nice and cold before you start spinning the ice cream.

HANDS-ON: 10 MIN. • **TOTAL 1 HOUR, 30 MIN., INCLUDING 1 HOUR FREEZING**
SERVES 8

2   cups vanilla low-fat yogurt
½   cup whole milk
¼   cup honey

2   tablespoons roughly chopped fresh basil
2   cups roughly chopped fresh strawberries
Fresh whole strawberries (optional)

1. Whisk together the yogurt, milk, and honey in a large bowl until thoroughly combined.
2. Pulse the basil and 2 cups of the strawberries in a food processor until finely chopped, 5 to 6 times. Stir the strawberry mixture into the yogurt mixture.
3. Pour the strawberry mixture into the frozen freezer bowl of a 1-quart electric ice-cream maker, and proceed according to the manufacturer's instructions. (Instructions and times may vary.) Transfer to an airtight freezer-safe container; freeze until firm, about 1 hour. Garnish each serving with fresh strawberries, if desired.

(SERVING SIZE: ½ cup): **CALORIES** 107; **FAT** 1g (sat 1g, unsat 0g); **PROTEIN** 4g; **CARB** 21g; **FIBER** 1g; **SUGARS** 20g (added sugars 12g); **SODIUM** 48mg; **CALC** 13% DV; **POTASSIUM** 6% DV

WATERMELON MARGARITA GRANITA

This is a perfect summer dessert. You can make a family-friendly version by using an additional ¼ cup lime juice in place of the tequila.

HANDS-ON: 10 MIN. • **TOTAL: 5 HOURS, 50 MIN., INCLUDING 5 HOURS, 30 MIN. CHILLING** • **SERVES 6**

½ cup granulated sugar

½ cup water

4 cups cubed seedless watermelon (from 1 small watermelon)

¼ cup fresh lime juice (from 3 limes)

¼ cup (2 ounces) tequila blanco

¼ teaspoon kosher salt

1. Bring the sugar and water to a boil in a small saucepan over medium-high, stirring often until the sugar dissolves. Transfer the mixture to a small bowl; cover and chill 30 minutes.
2. Place the sugar mixture, watermelon, lime juice, tequila, and salt in a blender; process until smooth. Pour the watermelon mixture into an 11- x 7-inch baking dish; cover and freeze until the mixture begins to freeze around the edges, about 3 hours. Remove from the freezer, and stir well. Cover and freeze until almost completely frozen, about 2 more hours. Remove from the freezer, and let stand at room temperature for 10 minutes. Scrape the entire mixture with a fork until fluffy.

(**SERVING SIZE:** ½ cup): **CALORIES** 119; **FAT** 0g; **PROTEIN** 1g; **CARB** 25g; **FIBER** 0g; **SUGARS** 23g (added sugars 17g); **SODIUM** 81mg; **CALC** 1% DV; **POTASSIUM** 4% DV

MAKING GRANITA

Many granitas start by making a simple syrup on the stovetop. It's important that the sugar is completely dissolved. If not, the granita will have a grainy texture.

NUTRITIONAL INFORMATION

HOW TO USE IT AND WHY

At *Cooking Light*, our team of food editors, experienced cooks, and registered dietitians builds recipes with whole foods and whole grains, and bigger portions of plants and seafood than meat. We emphasize oil-based fats more than saturated, and we promote a balanced diet low in processed foods and added sugars (those added during processing or preparation).

Not only do we focus on quality ingredients, but we also adhere to a rigorous set of nutrition guidelines that govern calories, saturated fat, sodium, and sugar based on various recipe categories. The numbers in each category are derived from the most recent set of USDA Dietary Guidelines for Americans, as shown in the following chart. As you look through our numbers, remember that the nutrition stats included with each recipe are for a single serving. When we build recipes,

we look at each dish in context of the role it plays in an average day: A one-dish meal that fills a plate with protein, starch, and vegetables will weigh more heavily in calories, saturated fat, and sodium than a recipe for roasted chicken thighs. Similarly, a bowl of ice cream may contain more than half of your daily added sugar recommendation, but balances out when the numbers are folded into a day's worth of healthy food prepared at home.

When reading the chart, remember that recommendations vary by gender and age; other factors, including lifestyle, weight, and your own health—for example, if you're pregnant or breast-feeding or if you have genetic factors such as risk for hypertension—all need consideration. Go to choosemyplate.gov for your own individualized plan.

IN OUR NUTRITIONAL ANALYSIS, WE USE THESE ABBREVIATIONS

sat	saturated fat	**carb**	carbohydrates	**g**	gram	**DV**	daily value
unsat	unsaturated fat	**calc**	calcium	**mg**	milligram		

DAILY NUTRITION GUIDE

	Women ages 25 to 50	Women over 50	Men ages 25 to 50	Men over 50
Calories	2,000	2,000*	2,700	2,500
Protein	50g	50g	63g	60g
Fat	65g*	65g*	88g*	83g*
Saturated Fat	20g*	20g*	27g*	25g*
Carbohydrates	304g	304g	410g	375g
Fiber	25g to 35g	25g to 35g	25g to 35g	25g to 35g
Added Sugars	38g	38g	38g	38g
Cholesterol	300mg*	300mg*	300mg*	300mg*
Iron	18mg	8mg	8mg	8mg
Sodium	2,300mg*	1,500mg*	2,300mg*	1,500mg*
Calcium	1,000mg	1,200mg	1,000mg	1,000mg

*Or less, for optimum health

Nutritional values used in our calculations either come from The Food Processor, Version 10.4 (ESHA Research), or are provided by food manufacturers.

METRIC EQUIVALENTS

COOKING/OVEN TEMPERATURES

	Fahrenheit	Celsius	Gas Mark
Freeze Water	32° F	0° C	
Room Temp.	68° F	20° C	
Boil Water	212° F	100° C	
Bake	325° F	160° C	3
	350° F	180° C	4
	375° F	190° C	5
	400° F	200° C	6
	425° F	220° C	7
	450° F	230° C	8
Broil			Grill

LIQUID INGREDIENTS BY VOLUME

¼ tsp	=						1	ml
½ tsp	=						2	ml
1 tsp	=						5	ml
3 tsp	=	1 Tbsp	=	½ fl oz	=		15	ml
2 Tbsp	=	⅛ cup	=	1 fl oz	=		30	ml
4 Tbsp	=	¼ cup	=	2 fl oz	=		60	ml
5⅓ Tbsp	=	⅓ cup	=	3 fl oz	=		80	ml
8 Tbsp	=	½ cup	=	4 fl oz	=		120	ml
10⅔ Tbsp	=	⅔ cup	=	5 fl oz	=		160	ml
12 Tbsp	=	¾ cup	=	6 fl oz	=		180	ml
16 Tbsp	=	1 cup	=	8 fl oz	=		240	ml
1 pt	=	2 cups	=	16 fl oz	=		480	ml
1 qt	=	4 cups	=	32 fl oz	=		960	ml
				33 fl oz	=	1000	ml	= 1 l

DRY INGREDIENTS BY WEIGHT
(To convert ounces to grams, multiply the number of ounces by 30.)

1 oz	=	⅟₁₆ lb	=	30 g
4 oz	=	¼ lb	=	120 g
8 oz	=	½ lb	=	240 g
12 oz	=	¾ lb	=	360 g
16 oz	=	1 lb	=	480 g

LENGTH
(To convert inches to centimeters, multiply inches by 2.5.)

1 in	=					2.5 cm	
12 in	=	1 ft			=	30 cm	
36 in	=	3 ft	=	1 yd	=	90 cm	
40 in	=					100 cm	= 1m

EQUIVALENTS FOR DIFFERENT TYPES OF INGREDIENTS

Standard Cup	Fine Powder (ex. flour)	Grain (ex. rice)	Granular (ex. sugar)	Liquid Solids (ex. butter)	Liquid (ex. milk)
1	140 g	150 g	190 g	200 g	240 ml
¾	105 g	113 g	143 g	150 g	180 ml
⅔	93 g	100 g	125 g	133 g	160 ml
½	70 g	75 g	95 g	100 g	120 ml
⅓	● 47 g	50 g	63 g	67 g	80 ml
¼	35 g	38 g	48 g	50 g	60 ml
⅛	18 g	19 g	24 g	25 g	30 ml

INDEX